THE FUTURE OF NEWS

THE FUTURE OF NEWS
Television-Newspapers-
Wire Services-Newsmagazines

Edited by
Philip S. Cook
Douglas Gomery
Lawrence W. Lichty

The Woodrow Wilson Center Press
Washington, D.C.

The Johns Hopkins University Press
Baltimore and London

Editorial Offices:
The Woodrow Wilson Center Press
370 L'Enfant Promenade, S.W.
Suite 704
Washington, D.C. 20024 USA

Order from:
The Johns Hopkins University Press
701 West 40th Street
Baltimore, Maryland 21211-2190
Telephone: 1-800-557- JHUP

Printed in the United States of America
⊛ Printed on acid-free paper

9 8 7 6 5 4 3 2 1

Library of Congress Cataloging-in-Publication Data

The Future of News : television-newspapers-wire services-newsmagazines
  / edited by Philip S. Cook, Douglas Gomery, Lawrence W. Lichty.
    p.   cm.
  Includes bibliographical references and index.
  ISBN 0-943875-33-1.—ISBN 0-943875-34-X (pbk.)
  1. Journalism—United States—History—20th century.   2. Electronic
news gathering—United States—History—20th century.   3. News
agencies—United States—History—20th century.   4. Cable television—
United States—History—20th century.   5. Mass media—United States—
History—20th century.   I. Cook, Philip S.   II. Gomery, Douglas.
  III. Lichty, Lawrence Wilson.
  PN48888.T4F88   1992
  071'.3'09045—dc20   91-46210
                                                               CIP

The Center is the "living memorial" of the United States of America to the nation's twenty-eighth president, Woodrow Wilson. The U.S. Congress established the Woodrow Wilson Center in 1968 as an international institute for advanced study, "symbolizing and strengthening the fruitful relationship between the world of learning and the world of public affairs." The Center opened in 1970 under its own presidentially appointed board of directors.

In all its activities the Woodrow Wilson Center is a nonprofit, nonpartisan organization, supported financially by annual appropriations from the U.S. Congress, and by the contributions of foundations, corporations, and individuals. Conclusions or opinions expressed in Center publications and programs are those of the authors and speakers and do not necessarily reflect the views of the Center staff, fellows, trustees, advisory groups, or any individuals or organizations that provide financial support to the Center.

Woodrow Wilson International Center for Scholars
Smithsonian Institution Building
1000 Jefferson Drive, S.W.
Washington, D.C. 20560
(202) 357-2429

CONTENTS

Tables   ix

Figures   xi

Acknowledgments   xiii

Introduction   xv

I   Television

1   More Is Less   3
Lawrence W. Lichty and Douglas Gomery

    Commentary   34
    Barbara Cohen

    Commentary   37
    Richard Richter

2   Blurring Distinctions: Network and Local News   45
Raymond L. Carroll

3   Super Tuesday and the Future of Local News   53
Robert M. Entman

4   Learning from Television News   69
Mark R. Levy

5   Talk-Show Journalism   73
Thomas B. Rosenstiel

II   Newspapers

6   The State of the Industry   85
Leo Bogart

    Commentary   104
    Richard Harwood

7   Unbundling the Daily Newspaper   111
William B. Blankenburg

8   News Workers and Newsmakers   121
Douglas Gomery

9   From the Heartland   127
    Jean Folkerts

10 The Daily Newsweekly   137
    James Devitt

III Wire Services

11 The Associated Press and United Press International   145
    Richard A. Schwarzlose

    Commentary   167
    Walter Mears

    Commentary   171
    Kim Willenson

12 The Supplemental News Services   177
    Nathan Kingsley

IV Newsmagazines

13 Remaking *Time, Newsweek,* and *U.S. News and World Report*   191
    Byron T. Scott and Ann Walton Sieber

    Commentary   206
    David Gergen

    Commentary   209
    Thomas Griffith

14 Foreign News: How *Newsweek* Has Changed   213
    Milan J. Kubic

V   Performance

15 How News Media Cover Disasters: The Case of Yellowstone   223
    Conrad Smith

    Epilogue   241
    Peter Braestrup

    Background Books   246
    Douglas Gomery

    About the Authors   255

    Index   261

TABLES

1.1   Distribution of Television Audiences during Prime Time   9

1.2   Ratings of Network Coverage of Some Election Year Events   20

1.3   Ratings of News and "Infotainment" Programs   27

2.1   National and International News by Production of Stories, 1986   49

3.1   Assertions Devoted to Horse Race versus Substance   56

3.2   Attention to Candidates Measured by Candidates' Assertions   59

3.3   Candidate Distribution of Substantive Assertions   60

3.4   Percentage of All Candidate-Focused Assertions on Each Station   61

6.1   Growth of Total Circulation versus Adults and Households, 1970–88   87

6.2   Top Ten Newspapers' Circulation, 1988 and 1991   91

6.3   Readers' Preferences among Newspaper Content   94

6.4   Percentage of Daily Newspapers Carrying Features at Least Once a Week   99

11.1 Newspapers' Wire Service Affiliations, 1960–90   148

11.2 Analysis of AP News Reports   159

11.3 Content of AP News Reports   161

12.1 Major Supplemental News Services and Their Clients, 1989   178

13.1 Circulation of the Big Three and All MPA Magazines, 1970–90   194

13.2 Cost per Thousand of Selected Magazines, December 1990   196

13.3 Advertising Pages of the Big Three and All MPA Magazines, 1965–90   197

FIGURES

1. 1991 Advertising Spending   7

2. Advertising Growth Spending 1985–90   7

3. Changing Anchors, 1960–91   18

4. News Events, July 1990–November 1991   19

5. Network Evening News Domestic and International Anchor Remote Broadcasts, 1985–90   25

6. Prime-Time Hours of Network News and Documentary Programming   38

7. Daily Newspaper Household Penetration 1920–87   88

8. The Hartford Courant Target Markets   115

9. General-Circulation Newspapers Published in New York City   118

10. Declining Readership at Some Black Weeklies   131

11. Growth of Spanish-Language Dailies   131

ACKNOWLEDGMENTS

We wish to acknowledge with sincere appreciation the support of the Earhart Foundation, which made this book possible. We would also like to thank the private foundations whose financial support make possible the work of the Media Studies Project, including the Lynde and Harry Bradley Foundation, the John M. Olin Foundation, the Sarah Scaife Foundation, the Greentree Foundation, the J.M. Foundation, the Horace W. Goldsmith Foundation, and the William H. Donner Foundation.

In addition, we wish to thank the staff of the Woodrow Wilson International Center for Scholars for its assistance and support. Our special appreciation goes, as well, to the members of the Media Studies Project Advisory Council: Leo Bogart, Peter Braestrup, Alan Brinkley, and William H. Chafe.

Bill Blankenburg, Dan Hallin, and Abe Peck provided an additional review of the manuscript. We are indebted to Bruce Napper and Traci Nagle of the Media Studies Project and to Joe Brinley and Carolee Belkin Walker of the Woodrow Wilson Center Press for their help throughout the course of this project.

INTRODUCTION

The American news media are struggling to meet a changing set of challenges. The costs of collecting, transmitting, and disseminating information are continuing to rise. To remain competitive, both the print and broadcast media are being forced to introduce sophisticated and expensive new equipment: computers, color presses, satellite dishes, minicams, and other innovations unheard of a generation ago.

Better-educated audiences are demanding more sophisticated news reporting and analysis. At the same time, many Americans, especially those under thirty, seem less enthralled with what the news media have to offer. Many resist the newspaper-reading habit. Some are too busy, preoccupied, or uninterested in digesting long, detailed, newspaper articles. They want their news in short, prechewed morsels. In an information-driven society where leisure time is treasured, people are absorbing information in new ways—in snippets of news via radio and television, in revamped newspapers like *USA Today* that sometimes resemble printed television, and, as always, by word of mouth. For readers who demand detailed information about specialized subjects there are magazines packaged to satisfy every need and interest.

The trend toward chain ownership of newspapers has brought greater concentrations of media power, a heightened concern for the bottom line, and a style of newspaper management that produces estrangement between publishers (and editors) and the communities they presumably serve. Is the role of the newspaper to deliver information to readers or to deliver readers to advertisers? The relentless drive to corral advertising dollars has left many communities with a single metropolitan newspaper voice challenged only by a pack of small but prosperous suburban weeklies and giveaway "shoppers."

Newspapers have developed new techniques to discover and attempt to satisfy the changing needs of readers. Focus groups, polls, and other research techniques are employed to determine the best mix of news and features. Newspapers have added new sections to convey editorial material about health, science, sports, entertainment, and something loosely labeled "lifestyles."

Newspaper ad managers and marketing specialists have expressed dismay as run-of-press advertising linage is replaced by ad inserts frequently printed by others. The daily newspaper has become less an editorial product than a delivery system for junk mail.

When polled, Americans continue to assert that they receive most of their news from television. Yet audiences for the network evening news shows have dwindled and the loyalty of TV news viewers remains suspect. Millions still watch, but they are not the same millions every night of the week and they are often distracted by other activities.

In an effort to attract a stable, loyal audience, television producers have experimented with new formats and techniques ranging from "trash TV" to simulations and reenactments of real events. The line between news and entertainment has become increasingly blurred, spawning the new term "infotainment."

Network officials bid wildly for "star" performers to boost ratings, raiding other networks and scouting local affiliate stations for new talent. Local stations tout their own news "teams" to build audience share. The conviction that particular TV personalities help to build viewer loyalty has sent salaries for "hot" TV news anchors skyrocketing.

Local stations also have invested heavily in new equipment to cover more breaking stories live. Staff correspondents have been dispatched far afield to enhance their prestige and give the local station an aura of bigtime network television. While local news shows have become longer, often incorporating film footage from the networks and other sources, the coverage has seldom matched the networks in impact and sophistication.

Ted Turner, yachtsman, entrepreneur, and iconoclast, surprised the nation by launching Cable News Network (CNN) in 1980 and ultimately making it profitable. Although increasingly ubiquitous, spreading throughout Europe, Africa, and Asia, CNN's audience is usually miniscule by network standards. By keeping costs low, Turner has demonstrated that there are profits to be made in a twenty-four-hour-a-day cable television news service.

But Turner does not offer cable television's only news-information service. The two nonprofit C-SPAN channels have brought the proceedings of the U.S. Senate and House of Representatives into more than forty million American homes, and have broadcast other meetings from the nation's capital. NBC's Consumer News and Business Channel and Financial News Network offer information from a consumer-business perspective. A wide variety of specialized news is continually available to most cable TV customers.

Lagging profits in their news as well as entertainment divisions eventually brought the three networks to the attention of Wall Street sharks who saw that their break-up values were far greater than what their stock prices indicated. The ensuing buyouts left ABC, NBC, and CBS in the hands of businessmen with no sentimental attachment to journalistic traditions of the past. In a new environment of media deregulation, profit-minded managers sliced away at expenses, firing many veteran reporters and leaving the survivors to report the news as best they could.

TV documentaries, long considered the prestige-building, prize-winning elements of network news departments, languished and were eventually displaced by "magazine" shows that featured show business personalities, the bizarre, the aberrant, and the fantastic. The networks' commitment to any form of sustained, serious journalism came into doubt, yet when there were big stories to be reported—Tiananmen Square, the Berlin Wall, the San Francisco earthquake, the Gulf War, the Soviet coup—networks still produced extraordinary television.

Caught between the immediacy of television news and the detailed interpretation and analysis found in newspapers, *Time, Newsweek*, and *U.S. News and World Report* struggled to rethink and reformulate the role of the newsweekly. Throughout the 1980s circulation failed to grow and ad pages declined while the newsmagazines changed editors, philosophies, and formats; added more color photos and graphics; reduced the length of articles; and recruited big-name columnists. The related coverage of the Gulf War in 1991 made many of these shifts more vivid. Newspapers added more interpretation, analysis, and many related stories for readers who had already seen a lot of television the night before. The newsmagazines tried to provide compact, forward-looking summaries at the end of each week knowing that few readers had the time to digest all of the details. Often nothing can communicate like a large color photo—see *Newsweek's* photos of the Oakland fire in October 1991.

Both major wire services, the Associated Press (AP) and United Press International (UPI), also are in trouble. In an effort to reduce costs while maintaining the quality of their news coverage, many papers have canceled service. Instead they have subscribed to one or more supplemental news services that offer a daily package of news and features from the desks of the finest reporters and editors in the world, often at a fraction of what the wire services charge. AP and UPI have responded by adding more analytical and interpretive material, more graphics, and faster delivery service. Always financially the weaker of the two, UPI is struggling to survive. Many predict that it will ultimately fold.

Against this background of dynamic conflict and change, journalists, wherever they work, find themselves under increasing pressure from politicians, the courts, and the public. The news media are accused of being brash, unfair, dishonest, and biased. Juries have awarded huge libel judgments to plaintiffs who claim to have been mistreated by the press. Reporters have found it increasingly difficult to guarantee the anonymity of confidential sources, and First Amendment protections are under attack on many fronts. Public opinion polls, during and after the Gulf War, showed that the general public strongly supported the military's desire to limit the access of the press.

Despite public opinion polls that show journalists to be held in low esteem, and despite low wage scales for all but the big-name talent at the top print and broadcast outlets, college students have continued to enroll in journalism and communications courses. Few anticipate employment as reporters, writers, or news broadcasters—most drift into advertising and public relations—but the chance of making it into the ranks of the celebrity journalists makes thousands persevere.

With an enormous pool of talent to choose from, the print and broadcast media have had ample reason to feel confident about the future. Instead of the "ink-stained wretches" of Ben Hecht's Chicago school of journalism—men with little formal education and often disreputable morals—nearly all entry-level reporters now have college degrees and many have had postgraduate training in law, communications, or political science. Some who aspire to work overseas have had extensive training in languages and area studies.

A glance at the newspapers or kinescopes of the fifteen-minute TV news shows of a generation ago gives substantial support for the notion that the press of today is vastly more sophisticated and informative. The breadth of reporting in specialized areas—health, science, economics, the environment—is astonishing. Correspondents are able to travel quickly by jet airliner and helicopter to distant places and file their stories instantly by satellite. The quality of writing is often better, the stories are easier to follow, and the presentation better designed, with more effective use of graphics.

With more sophisticated video equipment and communications facilities, television correspondents can report live from almost anywhere in the world and under the most adverse conditions. Often the impediment is not the technology but governments that will not allow access or the use of local facilities. The world has truly become a global village where even the most mundane event can be brought, live, to television screens in this country and around the world. Like police radio scanners, CNN's twenty-four-hour news service has become the early warning advisory of breaking news for hundreds of print and broadcast editorial offices. On big and continuing stories, such as the Gulf War, it is a visual "wire" service providing editors and writers sitting in their home newsrooms with their own view of the story.

Why, with this vast array of talent and resources, does the notion persist that the news media are unreliable—that they are biased, devious, and untruthful? A 1989 poll sponsored by the Times Mirror Company, which owns a number of newspapers, including the *Los Angeles Times* and the *Baltimore Sun*, as well as other media, found a "significant erosion of public confidence" in the ability of news organizations to be objective and impartial.

Again, reaction to the Gulf War coverage only confirms this. A skit on NBC's "Saturday Night Live" struck a responsive chord with audiences when it depicted the press as unthinking and unruly. It is possible that the public's reaction to this and other barbs at the press convinced the Bush administration that there was no public pressure to give any more information to the news media.

Some critics blame the aggressive reporting practices of the news media—the forceful intrusions into the personal lives of public figures, the harassment of news sources, the tendency to seek out conflict and controversy rather than the peaceful events of everyday life.

Others insist that journalists share a set of liberal beliefs—a hostility to authority, to business, and to conventional values—that renders them incapable of unbiased reporting.

It was against this ever-changing background that the Media Studies Project of the Woodrow Wilson International Center for Scholars in Washington, D.C., held a conference on May 12, 1989, on "The Future of News." What significant developments in technology, demographics, economics, and organizational structure occurred in the news business, both print and broadcast, in the past two decades? How have these changes affected the quantity and quality of information available to the American people? What are the prospects for the future?

To pose these questions in this manner is to suggest that the effects have been negative—that the content of news broadcasts, newspapers, newsmagazines, and wire service reports is in some way inferior to that of two decades ago. This is certainly not the intent of this book. Our purpose is to find out what happened to the news media and to assess the future implications of these changes in an objective way.

Well in advance of the conference, the Woodrow Wilson Center commissioned papers to describe and analyze major trends in the "news industry"—broadcast news, newspapers, newsmagazines, and the wire services. These papers were then sent to experts in the field for formal written comment.

Both the papers and the commentaries were discussed at the conference, which was attended by media scholars and journalists. The lively give and take stimulated ideas and suggestions of other topics that warranted investigation, some of which became the basis for additional essays. For example, we added papers on the role that local television news shows play in informing the public, on the development of supplemental news services, and on the changing quality and content of metropolitan daily newspapers in the Midwest.

As we prepared this volume for publication, the Gulf War provided news media—especially television—with one of their biggest stories ever. In the two years that have elapsed since our initial conference, many of the trends and changes that we noted have only been amplified. Authors have reviewed their papers to include as many current examples as possible.

We asked our contributors to address specific questions. Will United Press International survive as a robust rival to the Associated Press? Will one of the three networks abandon the news business? Will one of the three major newsmagazines be sold or go bankrupt? The answer to each of these questions is "probably not." More important to the public is, What will be the strains that the struggle to survive impose on fellow institutions, and how will these affect the flow of news and information?

We also asked our experts to deal with some broader concerns. Will a new tight-money atmosphere at the networks mean fewer reports from overseas or greater use of free-lance correspondents? Will the efforts of the major newspapers to build readership and advertising revenue result in more soft features at the expense of hard news reporting? Will competition between the wire services, and between the wires and the supplemental services, bring a richer menu of news to the readers of smaller daily papers or simply a homogenized editorial product prepackaged in the offices of the *New York Times, Washington Post,* or *Los Angeles Times?*

These difficult questions are certainly worth pondering. Our book offers a blend of fact, reflection, reminiscence, and analysis organized into five parts: broadcast news, newspapers, the wire services, newsmagazines, and performance. In chapter 1, Lawrence W. Lichty and Douglas Gomery provide a detailed overview of developments in television news, both over-the-air and cable. They furnish convincing evidence that network television news will continue to dominate the airwaves and the public consciousness and will spawn an assortment of small but vigorous competitors offering an enticing variety of news and information. The three networks, they conclude, will expand the amount of air time devoted to news, but this expansion will occur outside prime time and the greatest growth will be in news/

information formats (business, health, entertainment, and magazine-like programs) that appeal to special audiences.

In commenting on chapter 1, Barbara Cohen reflects on the future of network news from her vantage point as CBS Washington bureau chief, while Richard Richter deplores the demise of the network TV documentary.

In chapter 2, Raymond L. Carroll considers the changes occurring in local TV news and expresses doubt that local stations will ever be able to supplant the networks in coverage of major national and international stories. This view is shared by Robert M. Entman, who argues in chapter 3 that, judging by their performance on "Super Tuesday" during the 1988 presidential nominating campaigns, local television stations will represent no real threat to network dominance of news unless they break with traditional network news formats and learn to be more innovative.

Mark R. Levy, in chapter 4, offers some disturbing evidence that TV news is doing a poor job of informing the public—that people who say they get most of their news from television are among the least-informed members of society. And Thomas B. Rosenstiel, in chapter 5, reflects on the phenomenon of print journalists vying for celebrity status on TV public affairs shows.

In chapter 6, which opens Part II, "Newspapers," Leo Bogart, the long-time executive vice-president and general manager of the Newspaper Advertising Bureau, points out that television increasingly defines the significant world events. The problem that newspapers face is that potential readers identify big events with television and regard newspapers as the main source for local news that does not engage the reader the way that major TV stories do. Newspapers, he says, must not abandon their unique franchise as the local news medium, but they must also try to recapture the edge they seem to be losing in coverage of national and international news.

Bogart argues that newspapers must not lose the universality of their appeal. "Newspapers," he says, "have long built their audiences from a composite of both generally shared and innumerable minor interests found in any community. Editors have never assumed that every item would be read by every single reader, but rather that every reader would be able to find some items that make the whole paper worth buying." Bogart warns that the trend to publish fewer of the regular features aimed at the special interests of pet owners, stamp collectors, bridge addicts, and the like may be a mistake.

In commenting on chapter 6, veteran print journalist Richard Harwood notes that the changes described by Bogart are occurring as a generation of publishers and editors nurtured in the post–World War II years is giving way to a new and very different generation brought up in the highly competitive world of the 1970s. In chapter 7, William B. Blankenburg comments that the marketing strategies that subdivide the newspaper and its readers into segments may lead logically to the "unbundled daily paper" that is sold in a variety of combinations. Subscribers may choose to buy the Sunday edition with its many features and the Wednesday edition for its special food section, and ignore the rest of the week. A newspaper that operates in a market with two distinct population segments, such as white-collar and blue-collar, may be tempted to produce two separate products. Whether yielding to this tempation is good for society, says Blankenburg, depends on one's view of how a democracy functions and what the role of a newspaper should be.

Journalism schools remain extremely popular among young people despite the limited opportunity for lucrative careers in print and broadcast news. In chapter 8, Douglas Gomery explores the harsh realities of the news business and the difficulties facing the once powerful American Newspaper Guild in seeking to protect the interests of union members.

Journalistic quality is often measured against the performance of big eastern papers such as the *New York Times* and the *Washington Post*. But the bulk of American newspaper circulation is made up of other metropolitan dailies, small-town newspapers, and community weeklies. In chapter 9, Jean Folkerts, a historian of journalism, examines the state of metropolitan daily newspapers in the Midwest, where many independent papers have converted to chain ownership and appear to have abandoned their commitment to community service. Folkerts argues that the quality of midwestern newspapers is related not to their ownership but to their size and advertising base. The best of these papers, she says, are those that offer a strong voice in their communities.

Historical background for the segmenting of American newspapers described by Blankenburg can be found in James Devitt's discussion of the gradual development of special sections in the *New York Times* (chapter 10). The result, he says, has been the creation of a "daily newsweekly" that appropriates the format of *Time* and *Newsweek* to package information in a way that appeals both to readers and to advertisers.

Often neglected in discussions of how news is disseminated today is the vital role of the wire services—the Associated Press and United Press International—which still provide the basic news diet of most newspapers and broadcast stations. In chapter 11, which opens Part III, "Wire Services," Richard A. Schwarzlose assesses the current state of AP and UPI and says that, as participants in the competitive, changing markets that offer news to a nation of consumers, neither can expect to survive on the traditions and monopolies established decades ago by U.S. daily newspapers. The fortunes of the AP, in its present form, depend on the fortunes of its newspaper members. The beleaguered UPI, says Schwarzlose, seems destined either to go out of business or to relocate its major news reporting beyond the United States, perhaps to Central and South America, where it has traditionally been a strong gatherer and distributor of news. The commentaries of two wire service veterans, Walter Mears and Kim Willenson, describe how AP and UPI have sought to adjust to changing times and new challenges.

In chapter 12, Nathan Kingsley sketches the development of the supplemental news services that constitute growing competition for the wires while providing editors across the nation with an assortment of material from the richest and most prestigious metropolitan newspapers in the country.

The seemingly permanent niche occupied by the three weekly newsmagazines—*Time, Newsweek,* and *U.S. News and World Report*—also has been threatened, but Byron T. Scott and Ann Walton Sieber contend in chapter 13, which opens Part IV, "Newsmagazines," that the newsweeklies will survive, although perhaps in a different form. There is evidence that both the newsmagazines and their definition of news are changing in response to market pressures. They are elitist rather than general mass-media publications, and they will adapt in whatever ways are required to satisfy the particular audiences that their advertisers want to reach.

There is testimony to the adaptability of the newsweeklies in the commentaries of David Gergen and Thomas Griffith, as well as in the historical perspective of Milan J. Kubic, a veteran *Newsweek* foreign correspondent who found himself working as much for the international editions of *Newsweek* as he did for the domestic edition (chapter 14).

Readers who are persuaded that the print and broadcast media have adjusted comfortably to the challenges of modern, complex society will be sobered by Conrad Smith's analysis of the coverage of the 1988 wildfires in Yellowstone National Park in chapter 15 (Part V, "Performance"). This coverage rarely gave the public good information about the scientific context for the policy under which the fires were allowed to burn. Contrary to the sensational and often inaccurate accounts,

Yellowstone was not destroyed, fires were not allowed to burn as a matter of government policy, and the event was not an ecological disaster. The fact that the media can be so wrong in reporting a natural event gives pause about the potential consequences of their reporting on more complex and far more consequential human affairs.

In his epilogue, Peter Braestrup reflects on this and other aspects of the news industry today and in the future. With all the changes that have occurred in both the print and the broadcast media, there is a remarkable sameness about our definitions of what constitutes news. Beneath the glitter and graphics, the color and the breathless prose aimed at seizing the attention of audiences, the basic content of the news has not changed very much. The restless media "spotlight" that Walter Lippmann referred to many years ago still sweeps randomly from one event to another, occasionally stopping to explain or interpret, but preferring to leave the real analysis to historians and other scholarly researchers.

The epilogue is followed by an annotated sampling of books that have been published about the news business in recent years. These books represent only a small portion of the many studies of modern communication that reach the bookstores every year. Together they reflect a healthy trend within the news industry itself—a trend toward self-criticism and self-analysis that may, we hope, result in a better-informed American public.

I

Television

1

More Is Less

Lawrence W. Lichty and Douglas Gomery

In recent years television news programs have been changing as rapidly as the stories being covered. Predictable formats, epitomized by the authoritarian closing words of Walter Cronkite every evening ("And that's the way it is"), have given way to a cacophony of voices and images.

Although they provided an unprecedented window to the world, television stations and especially networks were beset by a declining market share and greatly increased competition. Shortly after all three networks—which also operate their own TV stations, most in the country's largest markets—were taken over by three new owners, their news divisions were required to cover dramatic developments around the globe. Fifty years earlier one newsreel had advertised itself as the "eyes and ears of the world." But in the late 1980s and early 1990s, television really did allow Americans in their living rooms—and citizens of many other countries—to watch dramatic changes of government in Czechoslovakia, Romania, and East Germany; a stirring challenge by students in China; and a very short war in the Middle East.

But the continuing story for the creators of news—the networks—has been their shrinking share of audience. At the beginning of the 1990s, only NBC, through its network entertainment operations, was making a substantial profit; CBS and ABC were at best breaking even. All three were still making substantial profits from stations they owned and operated. But they, like all media, suffered from a marked downturn in the economy, and increased competition from cable television and home video.

Still, NBC, CBS, and ABC remain the three largest generators of electronic media revenues. Even the other two largest cable/media conglomerates cannot challenge this network trio. Indeed, the biggest competition for news attention comes from the networks' own affiliated stations and from news-based alternatives to the formerly dignified—more so in retrospect—news summaries provided at the dinner hour.

Some of these new programs do not seem to provide more information. Consider the rise of "tabloid" or "trash" television. This new genre, which in format and style resembles the network evening news shows, is television's version of the *National Enquirer*, and audiences apparently love it. In a number of cities, Fox Television's "A Current Affair," a voyeur's view of the love lives of celebrities and the grizzly details of bizarre murders, or an imitator such as "Hard Copy" ranks as the most-watched program in the key early evening time period. At the same time, "Entertainment Tonight," which also spawned imitators, runs neck-and-neck in ratings with the three network evening news programs.

One response by the three networks to this new sleaze has been to include more entertainment and arts coverage in their own broadcasts—about twice as many minutes in 1990 as in 1989 or 1988. The increase came about because "there isn't anything geopolitical left" to report, according to "NBC Nightly News" executive producer Steve Friedman.[1]

Network executives often rail against the low quality and prurient appeal of these rival programs, but they never fail to find a regular place for them on the schedule of the stations the networks own.

These new programs raise profound ethical problems for the broadcasting industry. It has long been known that in local "sweeps" months (when ratings are measured for purposes of setting local advertising rates) TV broadcasters could spike the ratings by offering programs with more than the usual amount of sex and violence. Do TV viewers differentiate trash TV from straight news, as newspaper readers have long differentiated the sports section from the hard news on the front page? In a charming twist, the struggling (eventually canceled) *USA Today's* television program in October 1988 and February 1989 even provided a daily "sweeps sleaze" update, which, in the guise of reporting, gave the show's producers an opportunity to repeat excerpts of Geraldo Rivera and Phil Donahue programs featuring nudists.

Whether all this competition will drive out all serious and significant reporting or is merely offering audiences a long-wanted choice depends finally upon the audience. As Phil Donahue mused on his experience,

> It is amazing what they won't watch. They won't watch male strippers five days a week, [but] you'd better haul them out once in a while if you want to survive in the daytime arena. The audience appears to be largely interested in Madonna, not Managua. Many of our critics work for newspapers with no competition or never

see our show. By the end of the year we hope for mix of entertainment and information.[2]

The proliferation of satellites, minicams, and other new television technology has fundamentally changed news gathering, making it an around-the-clock, around-the-world operation. In the early 1960s news organizations were lucky to get film back from Vietnam in a day or so. Today, reporters cover the world—via satellite—live, in real time. As a result it is possible to program news nonstop, through the networks, Cable News Network (CNN), local stations, C-SPAN, and various other cable services.

PAST AS PROLOGUE

For many people in the news business or observers of the media, these changes represent a significant evolution. The end of the 1980s was a milepost in that epoch of change. The troubles at CBS, as chronicled by several former employees, spotlight the role of individual executives.[3] These books feature various villains—Gene Janowski, Van Gordon Sauter, Howard Stringer, Lawrence Tisch, Thomas Wyman—and present us a fascinating "inside" look at what has always been the most controversial and most chronicled broadcast news organization.

Although these personalities have had an especially important influence on specific programs and individual documentaries,[4] outside forces have had more general influence on the networks. The people who run broadcast news are driven by a need for more profit in a world of corporate raiders, greater news competition, and increasing alternative television offerings on cable, home video, and, in the future, through high-definition television. To lay the foundation for some conclusions and predictions for the 1990s, let us review recent key changes in the industry.

In March 1987 while Dan Rather worried about the budget and staff cuts at CBS News, Av Westin at ABC took a different tack. In an eighteen-page memo he wrote, "Too many resources, too much money, has undone network news, leaving it vulnerable to indiscriminate cost-cutting from above and unable editorially, creatively, and distinctively to meet the fierce competition from increasingly aggressive and inventive news operations at local stations." After comparing early "Days of Penury" at ABC with more recent "Days of Affluence," he concluded that planned reductions were not so much cuts as elements of "redesign." Westin was really calling for more thought about news and less chasing after stories. The former largess "must be replaced by editorial direction based on thoughtful journalism, insight, and creativity." He went on, "If carried out with care, 'redesign' will result in the building of a superior instrument of electronic news gathering and reporting which will ensure that network news will be around for a long time."[5]

In a *New York Times* op-ed article, Dan Rather grappled with the same issues in different language. Pondering CBS's firing of some two hundred news employees he wrote:

> Our concern, beyond the shattered lives of valued friends and colleagues is: How do we go on? How do we cover the world? Can we provide in-depth reporting and analysis with resources so severely diminished? Can we continue to do our job in the finest tradition of this great organization? In the tradition of Edward R. Murrow, Walter Cronkite, Douglas Edwards, Charles Collingwood? . . .
> I have said before that I have no intention of participating in the demise of CBS. But do the owners and officers of the new CBS see news as a trust . . . or only as a business venture?[6]

The same criticism has, of course, been made of newspapers, the wire services, and magazines as they have responded to the economic forces of the marketplace. In March 1989, James D. Squires, editor of the *Chicago Tribune*, told members of the American Society of Newspaper Editors, "The pressure of the marketing challenge forced editors to decide they'd better tear down the barriers and learn to master the whole paper or be totally at the mercy of the business side. It is in no way a compromise of editorial integrity. It is in fact the assurance of it."[7]

The "old world" of television news used to begin and end with the continuing profitability of the three networks. In the 1980s came new owners, new competitors, and new methods of operation. Several months before he was "kicked upstairs," the president of the CBS Broadcast Group, Gene Janowski, noted, "I love what I do and I'm not looking to go anywhere. But something my father told me years ago is that the trick is to be an owner."[8]

The networks, despite recent blushes, are not in great financial trouble. Under Lawrence Tisch, CBS sits on nearly $1 billion in cash, principally from the sale of its records division to Sony. Capital Cities/ABC has skillfully hedged its loss in network viewership through cable investments, in particular ESPN. NBC developed its own cable service, CNBC, in April 1989. In the end, what keeps the networks in their

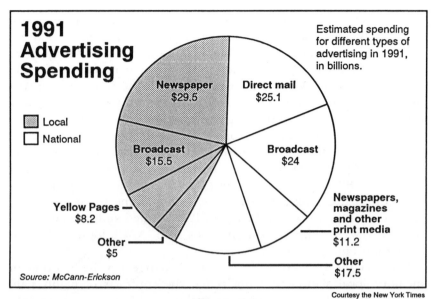

Figure 1

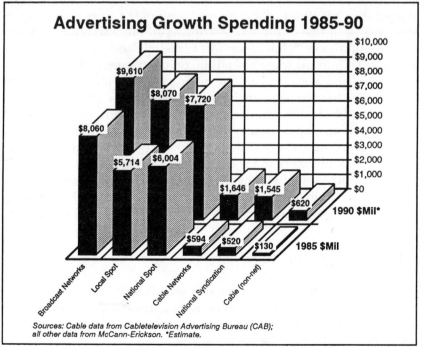

Figure 2

special niche is their singular ability to offer sizable audiences to major bulk advertisers. The complete domination of the "good old days" of the networks is over, but no one knows how far network audience shares will shrink. The most important implication of the economics of the 1980s for network operation (news or otherwise) in the 1990s is a management emphasis on "the lean and mean." Make profits now; worry about the long run later.

The networks are giants compared with their independent or cable rivals. Consider the millions involved in the "musical chairs" of news stars in 1989, when Diane Sawyer moved to ABC and Connie Chung moved to CBS. Reportedly, Sawyer earns $7.5 million under her five-year contract; Chung somewhat less. And bidding for talent is not restricted to the networks. In 1989 CBS's "owned and operated" station in New York hired Ernie Anastos from ABC's local station for more than a million dollars a year.

However, the 1990–91 recession forced change. For the first time in memory, local stations did not renew the contracts of highly paid anchors and asked reporters and anchors alike to take salary cuts. Even some network stars were asked to take substantial pay cuts. In part, this was another lesson of the competition of CNN, especially during the Gulf War. In the long run, it is not the news presenter, but the news itself that is the star. According to one executive, networks have begun to ask, "How much will he be missed if he goes? . . . how much will it hurt me when he ends up on the competition?"[9]

Owners and managers of the networks continue to pursue the reporter/anchor/star who can attract the crucial eighteen- to forty-nine-year-old viewers who bring the premium advertising rates. A small move up in the ratings for news can mean millions of extra dollars in revenue, easily enough to cover the high salaries and still generate millions more in profits. Today's "million-dollar club" of TV news stars includes Dan Rather, Tom Brokaw, Peter Jennings, Ted Koppel, Barbara Walters, Bryant Gumbel, Mike Wallace, and the top anchors in the major markets from New York to Chicago to Los Angeles.

NETWORK AUDIENCES

The future of broadcast news rests, as always, with audiences—the TV viewers across the country—and network audiences are eroding. *Newsweek* summarized the problem in apocalyptic terms in an October 1988 "Special Report: The Future of Television":

Table 1.1
DISTRIBUTION OF TELEVISION AUDIENCES DURING PRIME TIME

| | *Percentage of Audience* | | | | |
	1982	*1988*	*1989*	*1990*	*1991*
Networks	81	68	69	64	67[a]
Independents	14[b]	20	18	17	15
Super Stations	NA	6	6	5	4[c]
Basic Cable	3	11	20	16	19
Pay cable	5	7	20	5	4
Public broadcasting	5	4	4	4	4

SOURCE: Nielsen Media Research, reprinted with permission. Data are for November of each year.
[a]Including Fox affiliates would be 73 percent; Independents would be 8 percent.
[b]Includes Super Stations in 1982 only.
[c]WTBS in Atlanta (Turner Broadcasting System) moved within the Nielsen Media Research categories from Super Station to Basic Cable in 1991.
Note: Column totals exceed 100 percent because of multiple-set households.

> With many rivals gnawing at their franchise, ABC, CBS, and NBC have seen their combined share of the prime-time audience plummet from 92 to 68 percent in just 10 years. Even the networks seemingly invincible supremacy over electronic journalism is in jeopardy. Local affiliate stations have suddenly discovered that they don't need the networks anymore to cover the world. . . . According to some prophecies, the nightly network newscast— perhaps the most ritualized manifestation of our teleculture— could be a mere memory by the century's end.[10]

The TV writers' strike in the fall of 1988 further eroded network audiences. Independent stations, on average, now account for about 20 percent of all TV viewing; advertising-supported cable accounts for another 12 percent or so (table 1.1).

When the network audience share during prime time slipped to two-thirds for the thirty-week 1988 season, *USA Today* trumpeted that for "the first time the network share has dropped below 70 percent."[11] For a number of months in the past few years (in particular during the summer), however, the networks' share has occasionally dropped below 60 percent. During the 1988 political conventions, the networks scored their lowest prime-time share ever: less than 50 percent. Indeed, only about one-third of the television audience watched the convention coverage.

Did the 1991 season end the slide, or, more precisely, the rate of decline? We don't know. The three networks had averaged a 63 percent share during prime time—or 74 percent if the Fox (which behaves and advertises itself as a network, but is not a "network" under FCC rules) programs were considered. That is still a very impressive portion of viewer attention when many viewers have more than a hundred alternatives. On the one hand, in the daily press the end of the networks is near. Tom Shales, for the 1991–92 season, announced "TV's Sinking Net Worth" as "The End of an Era."[12]

Yet it seems to us that cable growth—measured in terms of new subscribers, share of viewing, and advertising generated—has slowed and soon may reach a dead calm. No other advertising medium comes close to providing network television's advertising reach and efficiency. The problems of the three networks may be numerous, but each still had revenues in excess of $2 billion.[13]

The networks' main problem is multiple competition. More than half the nation's households have cable service (many with thirty or more channels) plus home video. Still, two-thirds of the audience usually tunes to one of the three networks in prime time. Even in the half of U.S. homes that have cable, the three networks command a remarkable 50 percent share compared with 33 percent for all cable choices.

We agree with most network officials who predict that the network audience slide has begun to level off. Projections for 1995 still give the networks more than a third of all TV advertising dollars, down slightly from today's 37 percent. During the same period advertising dollars for cable are expected to grow from about 5 percent to 7 percent, but the networks will still be the big players on the television block.

Playing of rented or purchased videotapes at home has cut into the network TV audience, particularly for the next generation of adult viewers, today's teenagers and children, but to date at least, most households use home taping as "time shifting," to view a favored program at a different time. Thus, although home video recording certainly has had an effect, it may not be so big a threat to broadcast television as was first thought.

At the end of the 1980s, the go-go world of media takeovers had slowed for several reasons, including the difficulty of determining real value in the face of increased competition among cable companies, networks, and independents, and the threat of government reregulation. The market for the nation's 650 network-affiliate stations appears to have peaked. With single-digit growth expected for advertising and the competing attraction of new television technologies, the over-the-air television business is simply not as good as it once was.

These numbers will remain the order of the day even as the number of television households continues to increase. (By 1995 we should be nearing 100 million television households.) Weep not for the networks; they will survive because they continue to offer the advertiser the best value and reach for the money. There simply is no viable alternative on the horizon.

NEWS COMPETITION

With regard to news competition, our conclusions may be summarized as follows:

- There will always be several national newscasts.
- There will be one newscast on each of the three "traditional" national networks (ABC, CBS, NBC).
- Total news time (morning, evening, late night, weekends, specials) will expand on these three networks.
- It will be a long time indeed before there is less time devoted to news than there is now.
- Expansion will take place outside prime time.
- The greatest growth will be in news/information and magazine formats, especially those providing specific categories of information or appealing to special audiences, such as business, entertainment, and health programs.
- All news-gathering organizations, especially the networks, will seek more cooperative deals, alliances, and exchanges among themselves in order to reduce costs further.
- Networks will continue to seek ways to earn additional income from their news gathering and other current activities—providing news to local stations and worldwide, selling footage and videotapes of coverage, and producing special and historical programs.

"Local" news will follow a different path. The relationship between local newscasts and network news has always been complementary. It is now possible for local stations to use their own or rented satellite uplinks and to send reporters and anchors to cover important stories. Hundreds covered Mikhail Gorbachev's visit to Washington in December 1987, several presidential primaries, and both political conventions in 1988. Despite all the talk about the supremacy of CNN, coverage of the Gulf War reminded many viewers of the primacy of the networks in providing international news. Furthermore, dozens of

Television trucks stand by in New Madrid, Missouri, where earthquake could occur. (AP/ Wide World Photos)

local stations sent their own reporters and camera crews to Saudi Arabia. Virtually all this effort was for promotional reasons: Local stations covered these stories primarily to build the credibility of anchors and reporters. Some of this reporting may be excellent and useful, but it provides no real competition for the networks on a day-to-day basis.

Circumstantial evidence clearly supports the notion that network news audiences and local news audiences are closely linked. Statistical analysis shows the most important determinants of local news ratings for individual stations are, first, the rating of the network news program that follows it, and second, the rating of the preceding program.[14]

Analysis of early evening news programs on fifty-seven stations in major, medium-size, and small markets by Raymond L. Carroll shows that the early evening newscast on these stations devoted an average of less than three minutes (15 percent) to national and world news, compared with more than fourteen minutes (82 percent) to local and state items.[15] Satellite feeds from the networks to local stations, broadcast before the network evening news is on the air, are really important only for the occasional, big, breaking stories, especially sensational crimes and disasters.

The trend to longer, one- and two-hour, early evening newscasts by network affiliates is one (small) factor in the decline of network news audiences. The effect has been greatest in the West and at the largest market stations. The majority of stations throughout the country still offer only thirty minutes of local news in the early evening.

The local late-night newscasts are heavily dependent on edited network news stories narrated by the local anchors. To meet the competition of other syndicated news services, the networks have increased their own "feeds" of news material using stories not needed for the evening newscast, material from other news programs (such as the early morning), and material provided by affiliate stations.

A vivid, if self-serving illustration of the interrelationship between station and network is provided by the frequent use by late-night local newscasts of "news stories" directly related to preceding entertainment programs. Especially during sweeps, the networks give affiliates a few extra seconds before the end of entertainment programs that precede the late local news for promotion of upcoming news items. The networks also suggest local stories that tie in to the preceding network dramas. NBC, for example, prodded affiliates to inject "news" stories on "how the rich and famous in your area live" to follow an NBC movie about a Hollywood star who was killed. NBC also suggested that a story on "colorful and flamboyant lawyers in your area" follow a "Perry Mason" TV movie. Memos to stations prepared by a "Sweeps Task Force," according to one network executive, sought to exploit the "great impact on both the lead-in show and your late news, if you find a common thread of promotion."[16]

Since the early 1980s, cable has clearly been cutting into the ratings for local news. Research by James Webster shows that between 1982 and 1987 local news audiences declined about 6 percent in larger markets in homes with basic cable and nearly 20 percent in homes with pay cable as well. The loss of audience was even greater in smaller markets.[17]

Newscast competition is likely to be keener among stations in the same market than between affiliates and networks. This competition is

Cable News Network newsroom during the Gulf War (Cable News Network)

evident in the growing use by local stations of video footage created by amateurs. For example, Seattle TV stations aired the first footage ever of the FBI apprehending a fugitive on its "Most Wanted List." (The person who tipped off the FBI also alerted a friend who appeared on the scene with his personal camcorder.) The camcorder has become a staple of Fox Television's "A Current Affair," which has aired footage ranging from tapes of "preppy" murderer Robert Chambers, out on bail and partying, to a child's recording of his toys being bounced around in a California earthquake.

TV news organizations, under budget and competitive constraints, now recognize the nation's 2 million camcorder owners as a pool of 2 million potential stringers. Some actively solicit footage. No one rejects unique coverage, whatever the quality, of a disaster or crime in progress, and most organizations pay little more than a token fee ($100).

CNN has been the most aggressive. Since January 1987 CNN has been promoting its "News Hound" service, encouraging viewers to call a toll-free number if they have a scoop. CNN has used about four submissions per month, including scenes of a train wreck in Sacko, Montana, and a tornado in Hilton Head, South Carolina. An amateur with a camera was on the scene when the Aloha Air Boeing 737 made its miraculous landing in Maui, Hawaii, after its fuselage had ripped open. While professional news media were flying in to cover the aftermath, CNN airlifted the VHS cassette to the island of Hawaii, where it was converted to three-quarter-inch tape and sent by satellite to CNN headquarters in Atlanta.[18]

The most explosive recent examples include a March 1991 tape of Los Angeles police officers beating a suspect—a tape shot from a balcony overlooking the scene. In Washington, D.C., robbers even videotaped their own crimes—the tapes were shown at the trial and many times on national and local newscasts. Anyone who has vacationed recently has a good idea of the millions of portable video cameras available to catch almost any dramatic event.[19]

At the local level the CBS-owned and -operated station in Philadelphia, WCAU, has had "Channel 10 Newswatchers" since June 1988. One "Newswatcher" classic was submitted by two college students who witnessed a tractor-trailer accident that closed Interstate 95, the main East Coast artery. The accident was the lead story of the day, and WCAU had an exclusive. Frank N. Magid Associates, the broadcast news consultant firm, has urged its local station clients around the nation to set up similar operations.

Put simply, local news is important to stations because it is profitable and it is virtually the only programming that originates with the local stations. Thus local news makes money, distinguishes these stations from the cable networks, and helps build an image in the local market. The ratings and shares for local television news remain impressive; in New York City, the local CBS, NBC, and ABC stations, all owned and operated by the networks, generate $100 million in revenue annually.

The topic of revenue brings us back to the need to recruit and pay "talent." Consider the results of talent raids in St. Louis in recent years. In 1986 the third-ranking CBS affiliate KMOV challenged the second-place ABC affiliate by hiring a new anchor, a new consumer reporter, and a new weekend anchor. Soon KMOV was challenging the top-ranked station. According to Arbitron, KMOV's 5 P.M. news broadcast rose from a 9 rating in May 1986 to a 15 early in 1989.[20] The 10 P.M. news (late night in the central time zone) went from a 13 rating to a 17. In St. Louis, where anchors typically earn $200,000 to $250,000 a year, those rating increases were worth several million dollars in ad revenue.

Members of Congress certainly understand the new environment of local news and, in recent years, have become even more sophisticated in their use of television, creating "interviews" that air on local stations in their districts.

Congress has long maintained studios on Capitol Hill, but until recently they were rarely used for breaking news stories. Instead, shows were taped days in advance and carefully scripted, to be broadcast on Sunday morning public affairs shows, not the nightly news.

Now, however, the Senate and House recording studios have satellite links to beam live shows to local stations. Increasingly, the studios are taking a backseat to the productions of the National Republican Campaign Committee, the Democratic Congressional Campaign Committee, the Senate Republican Conference, and the Senate Democratic Policy Committee.

The Senate Republican Conference set the pace in 1985 when it installed a microwave tower atop the Hart Senate Office Building. The Democrat's flagship facility, which had opened a year earlier, did not establish a satellite link until 1987. It is located in the Democratic Congressional Campaign Committee's $3 million Harriman Communications Center in the basement of Democratic Party Headquarters on South Capitol Street.

Every Wednesday afternoon when Congress is in session, the National Republican Campaign Committee positions a camera crew on the lawn outside the Capitol and invites Republican members of Congress to stop by and make "news" for local stations back home. One by one, members appear before the camera, and "field" questions posed by their own press secretaries. Later the same day (in time for the evening news) the National Republican Campaign Committee beams the appropriate portions of the tape to the local stations that have been alerted for the satellite feed.[21] Viewers are not told that these are not typical interviews in which an objective reporter asks questions. Local stations pay nothing for these submissions, and many news directors not only use them but request them.

THE CHANGING NETWORK NEWSCAST

Network owners have begun to bring in new managers to redesign their nightly news. Some of these managers have come from outside

When the air attack began on January 16, 1991, Bernard Shaw, John Holliman, and Peter Arnett reported live via a four wire telephone hookup. Later, Iraq allowed CNN to import a flyaway, or a portable TV satellite uplink. Some critics argued that the reporting from Baghdad was propaganda for America's enemy. But live coverage also allowed the U.S. administration and military access to a world audience and much of the coverage showed U.S. technology and sophisticated weapons. (Cable News Network)

the television field, as is the case with NBC News, headed since July 1988 by a veteran print journalist, Michael Gartner. Controversy has swirled around him ever since. Upon the appointment of new presidents for the CBS Broadcast Group and CBS News in July 1988, Lawrence Tisch was quoted as saying, "If we can't win the war with this bunch, then it's my fault."[22] He seems to have lost the initial battle, for his new chief of news operations lasted only two years.

The war was being fought under new rules of engagement. The deregulation of American broadcasting, begun under President Carter and accelerated in the Reagan years, enabled the networks in general, and the news departments in particular, to operate simply as profit-making sectors of major economic institutions. NBC News (and the other networks) made deep staff cuts while General Electric,

What Changes Network News Ratings?

I. The Anchors

Audience ratings of network evening news programs have always been closely associated with their anchors. Chet Huntley in New York and David Brinkley in Washington were teamed for the "The Huntley-Brinkley Report," which debuted on October 29, 1956, after they did well reporting the political conventions. Walter Cronkite, who was a United Press reporter in World War II, Washington correspondent for CBS, and morning show personality was best known for his live coverage of politics and special events. Often mentioned as a replacement for Douglas Edwards, Cronkite's star rose even higher after his well-prepared, careful and steady presence during the 1952 and especially 1960 conventions. He became the CBS anchor in (a) April 1962. On (b) September 2, 1963, the *CBS Evening News with Walter Cronkite* was expanded from fifteen to thirty minutes. One week later NBC, which had planned the move earlier, did the same for Huntley-Brinkley. Both also changed from black and white to color shortly thereafter. On (c) February 1, 1965, a young Canadian, Peter Jennings, took the chair at ABC that over the years was more like a revolving door. The ABC program went to (d) 30 minutes and color in January 1967.

Jennings was replaced in several combinations by (e) Bob Young in January 1968, (f) Frank Reynolds and Howard K. Smith, (g) Smith with Harry Reasoner, (h) Reasoner and Barbara Walters, and (i) Reynolds in Washington, Max Robinson in Chicago (or roaming the United States), and Jennings, again, from London (or with big stories usually in the Mideast or Europe).

NBC had tried (j) three rotating anchors—Brinkley with Frank McGee and John Chancellor—after Huntley retired at the end of July 1970. But (k) a year later

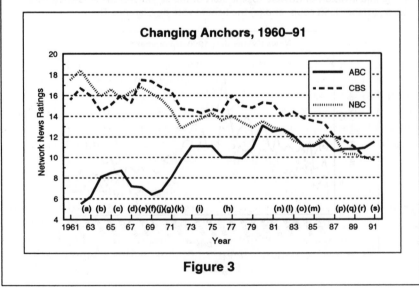

Figure 3

Chancellor was the sole anchor. Then came (l) Tom Brokaw and Roger Mudd—an expatriate from CBS—and finally (m) Brokaw alone.

In the most heralded change (n) Dan Rather, controversial former White House correspondent and *60 Minutes* reporter, replaced Cronkite in March 1981—and for more than four years remained in first place.

By September 1983 (o) Jennings was again the sole ABC anchor, and gaining. ABC's rise in the ratings for its evening news over the years was clearly correlated with the growth of prime-time audiences but that was not the case in more recent years when NBC was number one. Each program's national ratings are also very closely tied to the programs that precede and follow—local news and popular access programs such as "Wheel of Fortune." Critics still argue over whether an on-air argument (p) between Rather and candidate George Bush helped or hurt either. After falling behind, CBS tried having (q) Rather stand to lecture the news, then he (r) sat again, and (s) the visual style was revised once again.

Former CBS, NBC, and *World Monitor* anchor John Hart once said that the major theory of TV news was, "Let's try." Let's try a new anchor, let's try a set, let's try new color for the background or the visuals, let's try. . . . These are only a few of the more major changes.

II. The Events

The season—hours of daylight and temperature—is the most important factor influencing how many people watch the early evening news programs. However, there is increased tuning in for some big stories. Ratings were up 10–20 percent when the shuttle exploded in January 1986, in 1989 while students in China rioted and after the earthquake in San Francisco. The chart shows the impact of (a) the Iraq invasion of Kuwait, (b) the start of the air war, (c) the massive ground attack, (d) the USSR coup, and (e) the Senate vote on Clarence Thomas.

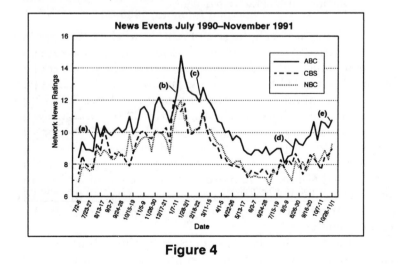

Figure 4

unhindered by federal regulators, diversified NBC by moving into the cable television business. The networks were no longer "single-product" companies delivering their wares via the "public" airwaves. They had become part of big business, aiming at profits and caring little about "public interest" obligations fostered by earlier administrations in Washington. As always, the networks were locked in an all-out struggle for higher ratings.

Table 1.2

RATINGS OF NETWORK COVERAGE OF SOME
ELECTION YEAR EVENTS, 1988

	ABC	*CBS*	*NBC*
Super Tuesday	7.2	5.7	*8.5*
(February 8, 1988)			
Democratic Convention	6.9	6.5	*7.4*
(July 18–21, 1988)			
GOP Convention	*6.7*	5.7	6.3
(August 15–18, 1988)			
Second Bush-Dukakis debate	9.2	9.6	*12.5*
(October 13, 1988)			
Election night	11.5	10.0	*11.7*
(November 8, 1988)			
Election night	*12.2*	8.0	10.4
(November 9, 1990)			

SOURCE: A. C. Nielsen/Nielsen Media Research reported in various trade publications and newspapers. On Super Tuesday 1988, ABC reported from 9 to 11 P.M., CBS from 8 to 9 P.M., and NBC from 10 to 11 P.M., eastern time.

Most striking has been the rise of ABC News since the appointment of Roone Arledge as president in 1977. ABC's news audience has expanded along with ABC's entertainment audience. More recently, ABC has been aided by the growing stature of anchorman Peter Jennings, by the addition and retention of a number of veteran correspondents (while others were being fired at CBS), and by the growth of other news programs, in particular "Nightline," "Good Morning America," and "This Week with David Brinkley." Arledge is often praised by "insiders" for his ability to recognize and build "talent" like Jennings, Ted Koppel, and, more recently, the morning news anchors, Paula Zahn (who left for CBS) and Forrest Sawyer. But "Primetime Live," featuring Diane Sawyer and Sam Donaldson, took much longer to find its audience.

From the time the special chemistry of Chet Huntley and David Brinkley was discovered at the 1956 political conventions and Walter

Cronkite began his rise to evening news anchorman at the 1960 political conventions, the networks have considered the quadrennial elections as the "Super Bowl" for news ratings. The primaries are the seasons, the conventions the playoffs, and election night is the championship. Probably because of higher prime-time network ratings, NBC won top ratings for four of five important election events in 1988 when the three networks were on the air at the same time (but lost to ABC on election night 1990).

For all the problems of the three network evening news shows, their share of audience (the percentage of homes with the set on watching a specific program) has remained about the same for five years—about 60 percent of all viewing during the hour in which they are broadcast. Much competition among them is waged with dueling anchors. Dan Rather stayed steadily in place after replacing Walter Cronkite. For several years Peter Jennings seemed poised to move into first place. Even NBC's Tom Brokaw said that Jennings "has the better élan" and is a "better performer" than himself or Rather.[23] "World News Tonight," the ABC evening newscast, was briefly in first place in the spring of 1988 and again in the spring of 1989. By early 1990 Jennings began to be ahead most weeks, with NBC most frequently third. During the Gulf War the audiences of all three evening news programs increased, and special coverage was often the highest rated of all programming during the week. The Gulf coverage seemed to solidify ABC's hold on first—critics and viewers often noted Jennings's greater foreign experience and ABC's broader range of news stars. More than ever before it is a very close race tallied weekly in most major newspapers and all trade publications. Often less than a single, sometimes only a tenth, of a rating point separates the triad.

SPECIAL PROMOTIONS

Note the appeals of these CBS news promotions:

- Rather: "You know your mother always told ya—stand up, look 'em in the eye, and tell them what you know. That's what we do on the 'CBS Evening News.'"
- Rather: "A good evening news broadcast includes the following: what you need to know, what you want to know, perspective, context, and maybe a new way of looking at a story you already know about."
- Announcer (over pictures of Dan Rather reporting from Mississippi, Georgia, Vietnam, Cuba, Mexico City, and Moscow): "Dan Rather, he's been there, he'll be there."

- Announcer (over a picture of Dan Rather in Vietnam, 1966): "Before Dan Rather went to the front desk he went to the front lines."

Although these promotions illustrate the image that CBS seeks to project for Walter Cronkite's successor, Rather has become the most controversial of TV news anchors as a result of a series of incidents—including a six-minute sulk away from the anchor desk in September 1987 when CBS tennis coverage ran over its projected time and the interview-turned-shouting match with candidate George Bush in January 1988. *TV Guide* even built a recent article around the observations of a few "therapists" who were asked to comment on Dan Rather.[24]

According to several surveys, Rather is the most popular with the general public.[25] He wrote in his first autobiography, "I am not, never have been, a natural smiler."[26] But particularly during the 1988 presidential campaign he tried, strained even, to be homey and personal. Can anyone imagine Walter Cronkite's making any of the following comments Rather made?

- "An Iceland chill back in the air . . . close but no cigar . . . " (on the summit in October 1986).
- "One of the candidates saw the light at the end of the tunnel, and the light was out" (referring to Pat Robertson).
- "You talk about your blowouts . . . the big train, George Bush, keeps rolling along."
- "What's at stake has always been the sizzle" (concluding a "48 Hours" segment about auto racing).

One week, Rather ended the broadcast with "Courage"; later he tried "That's some of the world today"—as if he was still searching for a persona to replace Cronkite with his familiar closing. These are minor points but from just such trivialities network news programs rise and fall.

Most journalists and TV critics would like newscast content, rather than presentation, to be the most important part of television reporting. Executives and producers are undecided on the relative weight of each, but all agree on the value of anchors, star reporters, sets and visuals, story order, and the rest. It is an evolving business and with the large audiences for TV news (at least relative to other news media) and the high salaries have come the public attention that most serious journalists disdain.

One of the first acts of David Burke, who moved to CBS News from ABC in the summer of 1988 and was let go two years later, was to read the riot act to employees about leaking stories and talking to the press. Tom Brokaw also has suggested that the news organizations should be allowed to do their business in "private." Howard Stringer, who moved up from CBS News president to head of the CBS/Broadcast Group, has given a number of speeches arguing that the network's salvation is "good programming and ratings which generally increase sales." He proposes "nurturing the creative process" and working more closely with the Hollywood producers who provide the bulk of prime-time programming. Presumably, a stronger network means a larger budget for the news division and more money to the affiliates. In 1991, Stringer argued that another solution was to "find ways to get the costs down."[27] The network's continued economic problems reemphasized the dependence of TV news on the entertainment part of the business.

Within the news division at CBS another evolving strategy has been to project a single "news presence" across all programs. Note these examples:

- For several years an increasing number of reporters, especially those from Washington, have gone to New York to present their stories and sit across from Rather to chat or exchange small talk.
- "60 Minutes" reporters were used as special correspondents on the evening news as an experiment for several weeks.
- Charles Kuralt assisted Rather in reporting from Moscow and Japan.
- When President Bush traveled to Japan for Emperor Hirohito's funeral, CBS used a staff of more than one hundred and had segments related to Japan and the trip, many with Rather's presence, on all the news and magazine documentary programs.
- During the Gulf crisis a special war room set was built, Rather traveled to the Middle East several times, appeared on many special reports, and usually was the primary interviewer of the network's expert consultants.

Will President Robert Wright of GE allow NBC, the top-rated network overall, to remain clearly in third place in evening news and other prime-time information formats?[28] Will CBS quietly let ABC-Jennings-Koppel inherit the mantle of first place in news? As though goading the others, ABC, using the cumulative ratings of its news programming, has advertised that "more people get their news from ABC than any other source."

Over the years the single most striking feature of the network evening news programs has been their sameness. In a sample of network evening news programs during 1988 we found that all three had the same lead story more than one-third of the time, and the initial stories were different on all three only one-fifth of the time.

Anchors Away

Since the mid-1950s, when anchors became the focal points of network news organizations, opportunities have arisen to showcase those superstars in remote locations. The presence of Huntley and Brinkley at the party political conventions in the fifties and Walter Cronkite at the space launches in Florida in the sixties signaled a trend that would accelerate over the next three decades.

Since the mid-1980s, anchors have increasingly left their desks in New York to roam the globe, armed with the technology and the budget to intersect with breaking news. By placing anchors in closer proximity to the flow of news, the networks have strived to gain maximum exposure from their high-priced talent and differentiate themselves from their hard-driving cable and local competition.

A study of network news over a six year period shows that the number of times when anchors have left their studios in New York and Washington doubled between 1985 and 1990. In 1988, the record number of presidential primaries provided a strong incentive for doing remote broadcasts. In 1989 and 1990, turmoil from China to Eastern Europe to the Persian Gulf sent anchors scurrying around the world.

By the end of the eighties, at least one of the three networks was broadcasting outside New York and Washington an average of twice a week. All three networks were four times more likely to be broadcasting from the same remote location in the late 1980s than in the early 1980s.

Also, the number of remote broadcasts lasting five sequential days more than tripled between 1985 and 1990. The networks, having made a heavy investment in "the" story, obviously had a strong incentive to recoup their investment by lingering on the scene perhaps longer than news judgments warranted.

Dispatching anchors to distant places remains one of the few heavy-firepower weapons in a news producer's shrinking arsenal. The rapidity with which anchors can charge to the middle of a big event is often equated with superiority in television news coverage. According to this logic, to be at the anchor desk in New York is to be hopelessly distanced from the action. The presence of a Brokaw, Jennings, Koppel, or Rather legitimizes the story.

The flurry of remote activity has been more than cosmetic. Research shows that stories reported by the anchor from a remote location area are usually longer and given greater prominence than the same story anchored from New York. For example, while CBS was spending thirteen minutes one day in January 1989 finishing its week-long coverage of the funeral of Emperor Hirohito from Tokyo, NBC in New York was squeezing the story into less than three minutes as the last item of its newscast.

Often, the decision on where the news will be anchored affects decisions on what to include in the story. News may conform to the resources allocated to it rather than vice versa. Thus, the risk increases that remote anchor stories will be overplayed, leaving the networks geographically isolated, overcommitted to one story, and open to manipulation by remote sources. ABC News President Roone Arledge admitted so: "There's always a tendency, when you send an anchor, to skew a story."

Network Evening News Domestic and International Anchor Remote Broadcasts, 1985–90

	ABC World News		CBS Evening		NBC Nightly	
	Domestic	International	Domestic	International	Domestic	International
1985	2	17	9	12	2	9
1986	8	15	16	2	10	4
1987	8	7	2	0	7	10
1988	23	10	24	8	22	14
1989	3	32	7	26	10	28
1990	7	24	17	45	4	30

Number of broadcasts (of 260 each year) that the program was anchored from U.S. or foreign cities other than New York or Washington.

Source: Computed by Joe Foote, from Vanderbilt Television News Archive Index and Abstracts.

Figure 5

Because local stations and CNN already cover most major national and international stories before the network evening news is broadcast, critics question whether sending anchors away is simply a ploy to differentiate the network evening news.

Still, despite its drawbacks, the traveling anchor strategy will remain a distinguishing characteristic of network news and figure prominently in its future. It is ironic that the technology that has given anchors the ability to draw the whole world to their New York doorstep electronically has compelled them to retreat to an earlier age where personal observation was the only available path to reliable information.

Joe S. Foote
Southern Illinois University at Carbondale

A clear recent trend is for each program to try for distinctive, longer-than-average features; both ABC and NBC have regular end-of-the-week features—"Person of the Week" and "Assignment America," respectively. After the election in November 1988 ABC's newscast began offering a regular "in-depth" segment labeled "The American Agenda." NBC has had such features since the 1970s.

In September 1990, "NBC Nightly News" began offering a feature report each night under the rubric "Daily Difference." These were suspended during much of the Gulf War, but began again in March 1991. CBS had been less routine in this regard; except for stories divided into several parts or major excursions involving Rather, such features are confined to weekend shows such as "Inside Sunday." In April 1991 CBS instituted "Eye [the CBS logo] on America." Rather explained: "We try to bring you interesting stories each night about important issues facing our country." We wonder what this definition says about the other stories in the newscasts. But the trend is obvious, as the networks cut budgets, fire personnel, and close foreign and local bureaus. The emphasis will remain, according to an NBC spokesperson, "on analysis and interpretation of news."[29]

TABLOID TELEVISION

"Well, I guess there's . . . good trash and there's bad trash."
—Fred Silverman to Morley Safer, "CBS Reports: Don't Touch That Dial!" December 23, 1982.

In 1989 the "CBS Evening News" covered, with a hidden camera from a local station, the confrontation of a U.S. Representative from Ohio by the mother of a thirteen-year-old girl with whom he had allegedly had an affair. Other stories also dealt with one baseball player's travels with his mistress and another's illegitimate children. Do such stories on the evening news reflect the changing taste of the American public or are they induced by the growing pressure of so-called trash news programs?

Nothing has received so much attention in the past few years as "Trash TV."[30] Indeed, the tabloid programs themselves—especially "Entertainment Tonight," "A Current Affair," and "Hard Copy"—have often used the subject of trash TV itself as an excuse to show various examples of the medium's excesses and bad taste. On March 20, 1989, Mary Hart concluded a story on TV reporting (with examples as much as six years old) by saying that television is so ratings-driven that "ethics are sometimes sacrificed." The same program featured this "information": "The trend in Hollywood is bigger when it comes to breasts. . . . Hollywood has decided it's what's up front that counts and the more the better."[31]

Exactly two years later, "Entertainment Tonight" informed us that: "the bigger is better days have gone bust, so to speak." Anchor Mary Hart said that perhaps the savviest take on this fashion whim comes from Jessica Hahn—who became famous in the fall of TV evangelist Jim Bakker, then posed in *Playboy* and had her own syndicated TV show. In an interview Hahn said: "Trends come and go. . . . You do what you have to do for yourself."[32]

Table 1.3
RATINGS OF NEWS AND "INFOTAINMENT" PROGRAMS

	1989		1991	
	Network	*Syndicated*	*Network*	*Syndicated*
"60 Minutes"	21.3		20.7	
"Unsolved Mysteries"	17.9		16.4	
"20/20"	14.2		13.6	
"World News Tonight"	10.1		11.6	
"America's Most Wanted"		10.0		6.3
"CBS Evening News"	9.9		9.7	
"48 Hours"	9.3		8.9	
"Oprah Winfrey"		9.1		8.9
"NBC Nightly News"	8.9		9.8	
"Entertainment Tonight"		7.0		9.8
"A Current Affair"		6.7		8.2
"Donahue"		6.3		6.9
"Geraldo"		6.1		3.7
"Cops"[a]		5.1		5.1/5.3

SOURCE: Season average, from Nielsen Media Research.

[a]"Cops" played twice weekly in 1991.

Is there a Gresham's law in television; that is, will the bad drive out the good? The rising popularity of so-called infotainment programming is clear.

Is such programming really a threat to network television news? Should we broaden the discussion, as suggested by John J. O'Connor of the *New York Times*, and ask the key question, "What kind of people do we want to be?"

CABLE TELEVISION

Almost every major cable network boasts some news or information during the day. Programmers as varied as C-SPAN, the Discovery Channel, the Arts and Entertainment Cable Network, the CNBC, ESPN, Black Entertainment Television, Movietime, Showtime, HBO, MTV, VH-1, the Weather Channel, the Travel Channel, and localized "News 12 Long Island" offer some information programming. Surveys indicate that once cable has been in a household for a while, these information/news services become important to the typical subscriber.[33]

There have been innovations in news reporting on cable television, particularly with the rise of CNN, both its regular and headline services; the financial and weather channels; and the two C-SPAN channels, which telecast the proceedings of the United States Senate, the House of Representatives, and other governmental and nongovernmental activities, both in the United States and abroad. Cable news networks, which now reach more than half the nation's households, offer television watchers significant viewing alternatives, thus forcing news offerings to compete even more strongly for audiences.

CNN achieved recognition at the two political conventions in 1984. Executives at the three major network news organizations (and many other news-gathering offices) now stay tuned to CNN Headline News service all the time. CNN may not be an equal competitor, but it is certainly a growing—and profitable—force. CNN runs a lean operation, based on nonunion (save in New York, Washington, and Los Angeles) young workers. To quote executive vice-president Ed Turner (no relation to Ted), "We don't have the fat that accumulates with any organization that is 20 or 30 years old like our friends at the other networks." CNN has more than one thousand employees and bureaus in cities around the world, including Madrid, Brussels, Geneva, Athens, Manila, Seoul, and Santiago. In 1991 it added offices in India, Brazil, and Jordan.

While the Gulf coverage momentarily boosted CNN's popularity in the United States, the lasting effects are not yet measurable. CNN was already well established; its position is now assured. Most important, during the war CNN was introduced to many new viewers worldwide; often stations carried CNN in lieu of their own programming during the most dramatic incidents.

CNN's highest ratings have been tied to disasters and major breaking stories. The highest rating CNN had received before the Gulf War was a 7.4 for its October 16, 1987, coverage of infant Jessica

Shoe, *by Jeff NacNelly (Reprinted with permission of Tribune Media Services)*

McClure's entrapment in a well in Midland, Texas. Next highest was a 7.0 rating for the August 2, 1985, Delta airlines crash in Dallas and the April 14, 1984, bombing of Libya by the U.S. Air Force. At the beginning of the Gulf air war, January 16, 1991, CNN was being watched in nearly a fifth of all cable homes, but this sum, however impressive, still did not equal the ratings for any of the three networks. The networks still had a much larger potential audience (only 61 percent of all households received cable). Nonetheless, with three reporters in Baghdad telephoning the only reports of the first night of bombing to the outside world, and with its later, controversial, live coverage by Peter Arnett from Baghdad via satellite, CNN clearly received a significant boost. But many critics did note that after this dramatic beginning, CNN's halo seemed to dim. Several studies did indicate, however, that a growing share of viewers thought CNN had provided the "best coverage." Clearly, the Gulf War marked a beginning; CNN is poised to be the television news organization of the future.

CNN was evolving in other ways as well. According to Paul Amos, executive vice-president in charge of news programming, "As we mature, we are beginning to look at ourselves more as a program-driven network than [as] a generic news network."[34] By May 1988, almost 40 percent of CNN's weekday schedule consisted of five and a half hours of talk programming and four hours of show business, financial, and sports news programs, plus repeats of programs.

For a year leading up to the 1988 presidential election, CNN presented a nightly thirty-minute program of campaign news. The program did not have a large audience—in the East and Midwest it competed with the network evening news in most markets—but it helped establish the network image. It was also a feast for political news junkies. Live coverage of a number of events, including congressional hearings, have similarly shaped the public's view of CNN. Some recent research indicates that people often think of CNN on a par with the older networks when a big story breaks.

To counter CNBC, CNN Headline News began early in 1989 to put a business ticker at the bottom of the frame, and inserted more business news into its features. With CNN Headline News promoting the regular headlines on the hour and the business news as well, CNN aims to functions more like a magazine. To quote Ed Turner again, "Any good magazine offers room for many different departments. But the glue that holds it all together is the news of the day."[35]

In covering the news for cable TV, CNN dominates but it is not alone. C-SPAN has become more than simply a television record of the activities of the United States Congress, especially during 1990–91 with live coverage of state and defense department briefings and a plethora of other special wartime coverage. Indeed, of the more than 17,000 hours of programming on C-SPAN each year, Congress now accounts for only 2,000 hours. C-SPAN's viewership has broadened in recent years. The highest percentage of viewers among the 42 million subscribers comes from people between the ages of twenty-five and fifty-four. The 1988 election pushed up viewership; indeed, between 1984 and 1988 C-SPAN's audience grew 184 percent. In 1989, C-SPAN stepped up its promotion with advertising campaigns in major national publications, and it has wooed cable operators with behind-the-scenes tours of Washington.

A unique local cable news program is "News 12 Long Island," a unit of Rainbow Programming Enterprises, which is a subsidiary of Cablevision and NBC Cable. Launched on December 15, 1986, "News 12" took a local access channel and brought news to an area that had been inadequately served by the New York stations. In the first year, "News 12"'s goal was simply to persuade people to tune in. In 1988 the goal was to gather advertisers. "News 12" serves more than a half-million subscribers on Long Island. The same concept may be tried in Connecticut, New Jersey, and Westchester County.

"News 12" programming mimics all-news radio on television. From 6 A.M. to 9 A.M., viewers get a glimpse of the news headlines, sports, weather, and traffic conditions. Cameras positioned along major highways into New York City provide traffic news. Every fifteen minutes, the segments are repeated. From 9 A.M. until 5 P.M., "News 12" offers a series of breaking news reports, features, interviews, and weather information. From 5 P.M. to 10 P.M., "News 12" summarizes the day's events on Long Island, as well as presenting world news from the CONUS World Network and Worldwide Television News. The staff, including technicians, tops one hundred. Although "News 12" is clearly the most ambitious local news service, hundreds of individual cable systems also provide area news, albeit less comprehensively.

A number of other regional all-news cable programs have been proposed. By October of 1991, however, only those in Orange County, California, and Washington, D.C., are actually operating. A European all-news satellite service operated from London but was available only on a limited basis and seemed in grave financial trouble.

The smallest changes often indicate the bigger trends. In 1991 first CNN, then NBC and CBS each began to display its network logo—the stylized CNN, a peacock, and an eye—at regular intervals in the bottom right hand of the corner of the screen. Station call letters had been used before to remind cable viewers what station they were watching—because one station was often found on different cable "channels" on different systems. Such devices are the equivalent of radio stations' constantly repeated call letters and slogans. This practice may remind us how interchangeable the news formats and personnel are, but it says more about the audience. With remote tuners, viewers can zip from channel to channel.

THE SURVIVAL OF NEWS PROGRAMMING

To conclude, let us return to the changing economics of network news. The enormous investment in news by the three networks, estimated to be $750 million per year, assures the continued dominance of network news, but a growing variety of continual news will probably be offered by a multitude of sources. CNN, C-SPAN, and CNBC/FNN, to name but three, will tender information around the clock. Television news will never approach the narrow casting formulas of today's radio industry, but the cable subscriber will be able to watch more news than anyone thought possible during the heyday of the three television networks two decades ago.

This proliferation, however, will continue to have its downside. Some form of news as entertainment, in a changing format, will always be with us. Talk shows may go out of fashion, and tabloid TV will certainly not maintain the ratings it enjoyed in the late 1980s.

Exactly how evolving technology will affect the television news business remains unpredictable. As recently as 1974, when the Vietnam

War was winding down, film still had to be flown out, and satellite time had to be booked in advance.

During the Gulf War, however, live coverage from all over the globe served the world twenty-four hours a day. It is safe to predict that, as the technology improves, the effects of television news will be felt in ways we cannot yet anticipate. Television news will continue to change, if only because its role in society and in the economy will continue to be redefined.

NOTES

1. J. Max Robins, "Nets' Newscasts Increase Coverage of Entertainment," *Variety*, July 18, 1990. The analysis was by the Tyndall Report.
2. Phil Donahue on "Sunday Today," NBC television, May 26, 1991.
3. See Peter J. Boyer, *Who Killed CBS?: The Undoing of America's Number One News Network* (New York: Random House, 1988); Ed Joyce, *Prime Times, Bad Times* (New York: Doubleday, 1988); and Bill Leonard, *In the Storm of the Eye: A Lifetime at CBS* (New York: G. P. Putnam's Sons, 1987). Also see Ken Auletta, *Three Blind Mice: How the TV Networks Lost Their Way* (New York, Random House, 1991), and Edwin Diamond, *The Media Show: The Changing Face of the News, 1985–1990* (Cambridge, Mass.: MIT Press, 1991).
4. See Burton Benjamin, *Fair Play: CBS, General Westmoreland, and How a Television Documentary Went Wrong* (New York: Harper and Row, 1988).
5. Avram Westin, "'Days of Penury, Days of Affluence,'" *Variety*, March 4, 1987.
6. Dan Rather, "From Murrow to Mediocrity?" *New York Times*, March 10, 1987.
7. Alex S. Jones, "Issue for an Editors' Meeting: News vs. Profits," *New York Times*, April 12, 1989.
8. Quoted in *Electronic Media* (January 2, 1989): 59.
9. J. Max Robins, "Pricey Talent Cut Lose in News Pay Plunge," *Variety*, June 24, 1991.
10. Harry F. Waters, "The Future of Television," *Newsweek* (October 17, 1988): 85.
11. Brian Donlon, "Nearly One-third Tune Out TV Big 3," *USA Today*, April 19, 1989.
12. Tom Shales, "TV's Sinking Net Worth," *Washington Post*, June 7, 1991. Also see Charles Paul Freund, "Save the Networks! They May Be a Wasteland, but They're the Wasteland We Share," *Washington Post*, July 28, 1991.
13. "Wall Street Week with Louis Rukeyser," PBS, May 24, 1991.
14. James G. Webster and Gregory D. Newton, "Structural Determinants of the Television News Audience," *Journal of Broadcasting and Electronic Media* 32 (Fall 1988): 386.
15. Raymond L. Carroll, "Market Size and TV News Values," *Journalism Quarterly* 66 (Spring 1989): 51.
16. J. Max Robins, "Sweeps Stunt Pushes Ties That Bind," *Variety*, April 25, 1991.
17. James G. Webster, "Cable Television's Impact on Audience for Local News," *Journalism Quarterly* 61 (Summer 1984): 420.
18. See Hilary Dunst, "Eyewitness Video: Smart, Plucky Amateurs Are Changing the Face of TV News," *Video* (April 1989): 48–50.
19. For a summary see Howard Rosenberg, "Minicam Witness News—Welcome to the Revolution," *Los Angeles Times*, March 8, 1991; and "Video Vigilantes," *Newsweek* (July 22, 1991): 42–47.
20. "Rating" is the percentage of households out of the total market population tuned to a station or program. See James G. Webster and Lawrence W. Lichty, *Ratings Analysis: Theory and Practice* (Hillsdale, N.J.: Lawrence Erlbaum Associates, 1991).

21. For more on the use of television from Capitol Hill see Carol Matlack, "Live from Capitol Hill," *National Journal* (February 18, 1989): 390–4.
22. Cited in *Electronic Media* (January 2, 1989): 59.
23. "Later" with Bob Costas, April 25, 1989.
24. Roderick Townley, "Rather Strange: Behind Dan's Odd Behavior," *TV Guide* (February 25, 1989): 4.
25. Michael Robinson, "Dan Rather Wins the Battle of the Network News Stars," *Public Opinion* (December/January 1986): 41.
26. Dan Rather with Mickey Herskowitz, *The Camera Never Blinks: Adventures of a TV Journalist* (New York: William Morrow, 1977), 274. Rather is also very frank about the problems of the "Celebrity Syndrome." Also see Dan Rather with Peter Wyden, *I Remember* (New York: Little, Brown, 1991).
27. Bill Carter, "TV Networks, in a Crisis, Talk of Sweeping Changes," *New York Times*, July 29, 1991.
28. See, for example, Jennet Conant, "Michael Gartner: What's behind the Bow Tie?" *Manhattan, Inc.* (March 1989): 51–59; Elizabeth Jensen, "An Ill Will Festers within NBC News," *Chicago Tribune*, April 4, 1989; Kenneth R. Clark, "NBC News Boss Angered by Rumors," *Chicago Tribune*, April 25, 1989.
29. Geraldine Fabrikant, "NBC Is Closing News Bureau in New York," *New York Times*, July 12, 1991. Another example should be provided in the summer of 1992 when NBC and PBS cooperate for live reporting of the political conventions—the former to provide more of a summary and interpretation with the latter providing continuous coverage.
30. See, for example, "Trash TV," *Newsweek* (November 14, 1988): 72; "News Directors Bash Trash TV," *Variety* (November 23, 1988): 1; "Sleazy TV—The Lowest of the Lows," *USA Today*, December 1, 1988.
31. John Tesh, "Entertainment Tonight," November 29, 1988.
32. "Entertainment Tonight," November 19, 1990.
33. Ronald Hawkins, "The Changing Face of Cable News," *Cable Television Business* (March 15, 1989): 26.
34. Quoted in Elizabeth Jensen, "CNN Finds That News Is No Longer Its Only Thing," *Chicago Tribune*, December 29, 1988.
35. Quoted in Diane Mermigas, "Q & A: Cable's Top News Boss," *Electronic Media* (January 30, 1989): 26.

Commentary

Barbara Cohen

It has become fashionable to predict the demise of network news in general and the evening news broadcasts in particular. Although it is true that the three network news divisions are under enormous pressure to rethink what they do and how they do it, I believe that there will continue to be a role for them and that their role will include evening newscasts, even if those newscasts look very different five years from now.

Before cable and VCRs and independent stations and the expansion of local news programming, the evening news shows had a monopoly, split three ways, on the audience. Now they are competing for a shrinking audience that is no longer content to wait until 7 P.M. each night to find out what happened in the world. Still, as the recent Persian Gulf war showed, there is a distinct role for network news that can attract and hold an audience.

The Persian Gulf war has been described as the story that proved that CNN had come of age. Indeed, the cable network saw ten years of hard work and skillful targeting of audience come to fruition. Audiences soared and critical acclaim rolled in. On CNN, you didn't have to wait for the story. On CNN, you could see the day's events in their entirety without reporter intervention. And on CNN, which had invested considerable time and energy in building its links with foreign governments, you could benefit from such significant journalistic coups as its being the only network able to stay on the air when the bombing began in Baghdad.

The success of CNN, together with the 1990 economic downturn, which had a devastating impact on network revenues and prompted cuts in the budgets of all three networks' news divisions, poured gasoline on the already blazing fire of predictions that one or two networks would get out of the news business altogether.

But two important factors were overlooked in those predictions. First, if CNN's audience grew, so did the audience for network coverage of the war. Evening news broadcasts experienced big jumps in ratings, and on CBS prime-time specials on the war consistently beat the entertainment competition.

Second, when the war was over CNN's audience dropped back to its pre-war level. Network news audiences declined also, but not by as much. This meant that CNN was still reaching only a half-million homes in a half-hour, while each of the three network broadcasts reached 8 to 9 million. CNN played an important role, but it did not supplant the networks. Viewers who watched the war coverage on CNN during the day still watched a network broadcast at night. The familiar correspondents, the access to worldwide news gathering, and the role of the evening news summaries in putting the day's events in context all continued to appeal to the audience.

There is no question, however, that network producers must respond to the changing climate for their business. The networks are no longer the only game in town, and it cannot be assumed that the audience watching an evening news show is seeing the pictures or hearing the story for the first time. Increasingly, evening news broadcasts showcase not only the news of the day but also the stories that analyze, put in context, study trends, or break news that cannot be found anywhere else. Just as newspapers had to change when television came along, network news shows have to change to offer something more than cable or local news.

One evening news executive producer predicts that in five years only two of the three broadcasts will survive. I find it hard to imagine the circumstances under which a network's owners would decide to be the first to get out of the news business. It is more likely that one or more evening newscasts will evolve into a different kind of broadcast—perhaps an hour that permits longer pieces, more analysis, and more interviews, perhaps in a different time slot to wrap up the news at the end of the day and compete with entertainment programs, perhaps as an interactive broadcast that mixes news from a national anchor with local news.

Financial pressures on news divisions are real, and the news divisions have responded. The networks no longer practice "protective coverage"—sending a camera to every public appearance of every important official. News managers are forced to make better news judgments and to put a premium on planning. These are all healthy developments. More coverage is pooled, but that is not a setback to good journalism. No longer do four cameras line up getting exactly the same shot of an event. One crew can do that work, and the other crews are free to work on exclusive, enterprise stories for their own networks.

Networks' relations with affiliates are complementary, not competitive. Certainly the network newscast benefits when the affiliate news serves as an effective lead-in program. The affiliates also benefit from their relationship with the network, when it comes to news. Each network has expanded the feeds of material it provides to affiliate stations. Conversely, stations serve as an essential source of material when news of national importance breaks in their areas.

Even as the traditional forms of presenting news on the networks are questioned, new forms are emerging and proving profitable. Documentaries may have vanished from the schedule, but prime-time news shows are proliferating and, given enough time, as "60 Minutes" and "20/20" have been, competing effectively with the entertainment programming. Newer broadcasts, such as CBS's "48 Hours," are building their audiences while costing less than entertainment programming. And, "48 Hours"'s innovative video vérité style has been adapted in some instances for pieces on the "Evening News," enlivening the traditional format.

Commentary

Richard Richter

For a network news department to keep its viewers fully informed, the documentary is essential because it alone of all forms of the television medium provides intelligent, deep examination of complex and important issues. Tragically, the serious documentary on CBS and NBC is dead, and appeared moribund at ABC until recently, when there were some flickering signs of life. What follows is my view of the flowering—and decline—of documentaries at ABC News, where I was senior producer of documentary programs for ten years. (I am now executive producer of news and public affairs at WETA, the public television station in Washington, D.C.)

The scene: a screening room at ABC News headquarters in midtown Manhattan. The time: June 1978. The players: Leonard Goldenson, chairman of the board; Fred Pierce, president of the television network; Alfred Schneider, vice-president of standards and practices; William Sheehan, senior vice-president, ABC News; Pamela Hill, vice-president and executive producer of documentaries; me, Richard Richter, senior producer of documentaries; and Helen Whitney, documentary producer.

For more than forty minutes, the group sat quietly and watched the final cut of Whitney's documentary, "Youth Terror—The View From Behind the Gun," a raw look at the streets of New York and the young people who strutted, swaggered, and slashed themselves, and anyone in their way, to death. The look was indeed behind the gun, trying to explore the reasons for the behavior.

It was the film's climax, however, that brought the extraordinary assemblage of executives together to pass judgment on the film's suitability for broadcast. A young black man sat in a Brooklyn playground and let his pent-up frustration and anger pour out in a soul-searing diatribe about the world in which he lived. It was a marvelous speech that illuminated all that had gone before—the cap to an extraordinary broadcast. But the speech was replete with the language of the street. "Mother fucker" was repeated over and over. We, the documentary unit, felt the language had to be retained—to bleep or eliminate the

Prime-Time Hours of Network News Documentary Programming

Documentaries. The 1961–62 season had an unusual number of documentaries for several reasons. Meetings between the heads of ABC, CBS, and NBC, convened by Federal Communications Commission Chairman John C. Doerfer in early 1960, exacted an agreement to broadcast more cultural and public affairs programming as penance for the quiz program scandal of 1959. This coordinated impetus was reinforced by 1961 FCC Chairman Newton Minow, most famous for his criticism of television as a "vast wasteland."

Magazine Programs. These began to supplant the traditional documentary, particularly after CBS's "60 Minutes" became an established ratings success. During the 1980–81 season, for example, "60 Minutes" and ABC's "20/20" were joined by "NBC Magazine" weekly. Each network broadcast at least one, and sometimes two, weekly magazine programs during most seasons that followed.

Instant Specials. These came to prominence in the late 1950s. During the 1958–59 season, they covered President Dwight Eisenhower's European trip and the visit of Soviet Premier Nikita Krushchev to the United States. Instant specials continued to report on presidential travels in the following season, with trips by Eisenhower to India and Europe, South America, and the Far East. The presidential election campaign was the subject of much instant special coverage, as was the U-2 spy plane incident in 1960. There was heavy coverage of the overseas trips of President Richard Nixon during the 1968–69 season. During the 1971–72 season, the majority of the instant specials were reports on Nixon's historic visits to China and the Soviet Union. During the following 1972–73 season, most instant specials dealt with the Watergate scandal and Richard Nixon's resignation from the presidency. In the 1975–76 season, most instant specials were reports on the presidential election campaign.

Raymond L. Carroll

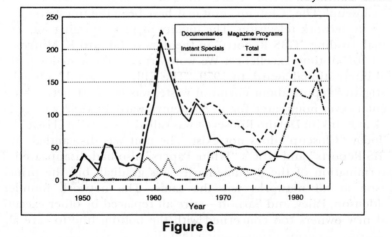

Figure 6

words would rob the speech of its power and damage the integrity of the entire documentary.

When the lights came on, no one said a word for a minute or so. Then Goldenson said simply, "I don't see how we can cut the language." That did it, the chairman had spoken, and although everyone in the room knew there would be a firestorm of protests from local stations, the offending language was left in. Nineteen stations refused to carry the broadcast. Many stations asked whether they could bleep the offending words. They were told no. Never before had such language been heard on network television.

Most critics said the program—the first documentary produced by the newly reorganized "Closeup" unit at ABC News—was brilliant. *Time* said it might be the finest documentary ever seen on network television. That was 1978, and I had just come from the hard-news side of the news department to complement the filmmaking skills of Pamela Hill.

Our second broadcast, "Terror in the Promised Land," created waves of protest too. It took a look at PLO terrorists, examining them as human beings to try to explain why they acted as they did. The simple fact that a show on this subject was being done at all disturbed many American Jewish organizations. ABC's corporate headquarters was picketed in an attempt to prevent the program from being shown. No sponsors would be identified with the broadcast, but network management held firm and the broadcast went out as scheduled. The Overseas Press Club subsequently honored the film as the year's outstanding program on foreign affairs.

This was the exhilarating beginning of my largely wonderful decade at "Closeup." The "Closeup" unit may have been the finest ever assembled in network television. The quality of programming was exceptional, rivaling "CBS Reports" in the days of Edward R. Murrow and later for all-time excellence. We won virtually every major national and international award. In 1979, "The Killing Ground," a tough, investigative report about chemical waste, was the first network documentary ever nominated for an Academy Award. In 1982, a three-hour look at Franklin Delano Roosevelt was called "an instant classic."

Today "Closeup" does not exist. The unit was dismantled, just as "CBS Reports" and NBC's "White Papers" also had disappeared. The extermination of the documentaries was gradual, but the principal reason at all networks was the same. The network founders— Goldenson, Paley, and Sarnoff—were all replaced by other executives and new owners too concerned with the bottom line to care about nurturing superior programming that did not make money. Once all three networks had been taken over in the merger mania that has gripped the nation, serious network documentaries were essentially dead.

The big blow for "Closeup" came in 1984, ironically after a successful 1983 season with a range of subjects that included South Africa, the massacre in the Beirut refugee camps, water pollution, foreign debt, the cocaine cartel, McCarthyism, art theft, and a two-hour assessment of the presidency of John F. Kennedy twenty years after his death.

At that time, Capital Cities was in the process of taking over ABC. The "Closeup" unit looked to the new owners hopefully, because they were known to be personally committed to the serious issues we dealt with. And, more important, they had gone to unusual lengths to carry documentaries on Capital Cities stations. But the promise was not fulfilled. Their arrival resulted in budget slashing, personnel reductions—the ultimate destruction of our unit.

As air time was taken away, it was not particularly comforting to read old reviews and crow about past triumphs. In a desperate effort to attract more attention, we resorted to blockbuster programming, turning first in 1984 to three hours that took over all of prime time for an evening. That year the subject was education, "To Save Our Schools, To Save Our Children." It was a professional and critical success, and the script was expanded into a book. But the program did not make money. The fact that it was probably the best television examination of America's faulty education system to that date—and the fact that it rang the alarm in prime time trying to raise the consciousness of a nation destined to deteriorate because of bad education—did not weigh heavily with network executives.

Of course, the big problem with documentaries for networks has always been that they are thought to be incapable of attracting audiences and ratings high enough to justify charging more for commercial spots. Yes, "Cosby" will normally outdraw a serious documentary. But certain serious shows on certain subjects, if well promoted and given a good slot in the programming schedule, will draw audiences sufficient to satisfy an intelligent network manager. "JFK" did well, and so did "FDR" and "Youth Terror." In December 1979, "Homosexuals" rated phenomenally well, drawing 35 percent of the audience at a time when television did not feel comfortable with the subject. In fact, ABC was so uneasy about the broadcast that one executive wondered whether the documentary might win converts to homosexuality. He was so timid that he decreed that the broadcast should not be offered to sponsors, and thus prevented the 35 percent audience share from being included in the overall network ratings for the week (because a no-commercial program does not count, according to Nielsen and Arbitron).

But network documentaries always were scheduled for broadcast on dates with low viewer potential. It was a given that none could be shown during network sweeps when commercial rates would be established on the basis of overall ratings.

In addition, no regular dates—say, the first Tuesday of every month—were possible. Hence, viewers needed to consult listings every day to discover when a serious program might be scheduled. Saturday nights and the week between Christmas and New Year's Day, when viewing is low, were always favorite dumping grounds for documentaries. How could anyone have expected the ratings to have been higher?

Clearly, support from network executives was inadequate, and sometimes it seemed as though they engaged in outright sabotage. The most bizarre case occurred when the president of ABC News, dissatisfied with his own interview in a documentary on the role of television in the selection of a presidential candidate, actually denounced the program as "shallow" in an interview with a critic before the show aired. In addition, competition between individual units at ABC News was so keen that cross-promotion of documentaries was done reluctantly, and daily broadcasts almost never pursued the solid news-breaking information that was revealed in a documentary. The shocking conditions at nuclear weapons plants uncovered by producers Steve Singer and John Fielding in "The Bomb Factories" in 1987 were not touched by the rest of ABC News until the *New York Times* printed much of the same material a full year later. The *Times* thought enough of their reporters' stories to nominate them for a Pulitzer prize.

Although the *Times* has endlessly decried the sorry state of network television, calling for more serious programming, one of its former television critics, John Corry, was occasionally inattentive to significant documentaries. In 1983, producer Chris Isham and correspondent Marshall Frady put together a "Closeup" program on a subject never before dealt with on television: black labor unions in South Africa. The drama of the broadcast was heightened by the fact that certain low-level South African government officials, frustrated about coverage of a union meeting, sabotaged the film, exposing it to the light, but fortunately, just enough light seeped in to create a flaring around the edges of the film, adding extra eerie drama to the meeting. The hour was the first about South Africa by an American network in many years, but somehow the *Times* and Corry neglected to review it. He also managed to ignore a three-hour broadcast, "Growing Old in

America," in 1985, when most of America was relatively oblivious to the fact that the population explosion among the elderly was a staggering national problem not being adequately dealt with. It was a subject that no one else in network television news was dealing with at all. Currently, the *Times* critics do seem more attentive.

The record of the *Washington Post*, the other general-circulation newspaper that reaches large numbers of decision makers, also bears examination. Television critic Tom Shales is a brilliant writer, and his reviews generally command good placement and considerable space. But his pieces often spin off in such a way as to obscure the subject he is supposed to be writing about. In addition, he frequently declares himself uninformed about certain subjects and hands off reviewing assignments to others. The result is a short review by someone who may be well intentioned, but who is not a skilled critic. In such cases, the newspaper has not lived up to its responsibility to inform its readers.

The networks have responded recently to their responsibility to viewers by throwing some other programs into the breach, but they are mostly insubstantial substitutes, such as embarrassing bits of fluff about weight problems or advertising on NBC. ABC has aired a few solid documentaries recently: Ted Koppel's broadcast about Romania and Peter Jennings's intelligent examination of Cambodia. ABC's idea obviously is to take advantage of the audience-drawing power of the two dominant anchors on network television. The question now is whether the documentaries will continue and multiply. CBS's "48 Hours" is a slick, well-produced weekly newcomer lacking in ideas and thoughtfulness.

Could anything have been expected of ABC's highly promoted "Primetime Live," starring Sam Donaldson and Diane Sawyer? Sam is an excellent journalist when he wants to be, but the teaming of him with Sawyer, the network's new glamour queen, was born of ABC's desperation to find a place for him after his twelve rowdy years at the White House. No one ever articulated cogently what the show would attempt to be except a star vehicle, so its awkward vacuity should be no surprise.

After more than a dozen attempts at magazine documentaries with titles such as "First Tuesday," "Chronolog," "Weekend," and "Almanac," in the 1990–91 season NBC failed again with two half-hour entries, "Real Life with Jane Pauley" and "Exposé," the latter hosted by Tom Brokaw but based mostly on the investigative reporting of Brian Ross and Ira Silverman.

The "60 Minutes" series should be excluded from this discussion because it has been consistently excellent for more than a decade. It is a series of well-crafted stories excellently produced and well presented by star reporters. It is also the unique creation of Don Hewitt, one of the medium's most intuitive producers. ABC's "20/20," the only successful imitation of "60 Minutes," is often shallow and embarrassingly amateurish.

Koppel on ABC's "Nightline" is unique, the quintessential intelligent interviewer. His broadcast would be nothing without him, and it supersedes the old special events unit productions that often used to pop up in late night on big news days. But even his excellent marathon on "D.C.—A Divided City" did not take the place of a good documentary, because it made no attempt to dissect the city systematically and lay out the reasons for its chaotic condition.

Public television has increasingly moved into the documentary vacuum left by the networks. There have been some wonderful hours and excellent series, and better work may yet be done as the Public Broadcasting System becomes more coherent. But there is too little indication at this time that the networks will support a meaningful revival of the documentary, which has been the vehicle for their finest hours. The days of "CBS Reports" and "ABC Closeup" are over.

2

Blurring Distinctions: Network and Local News

Raymond L. Carroll

Until the 1980s, television reports on national and international events were virtually the exclusive domain of the network evening news programs. Now, locally produced news broadcasts routinely inform viewers of momentous events before the network programs go on the air. As a result, the distinction between the network evening news and local newscasts is being blurred. A proliferation of satellite news services has given stations the ability to report news of their states and regions while reducing their reliance on the networks as sources of national and international news.

THE EXPANSION OF LOCAL NEWS

Most network affiliates in the largest (the top thirty) markets program ninety or more minutes of news during the early time period in addition to a network news program.[1] And overall, 42 percent of network affiliates now broadcast at least one hour of local news during the early period (4:00 to 7:30 P.M.).[2] Moreover, more than 500 network affiliates now broadcast half- or full-hour news programs beginning at 6 A.M. on weekdays.[3]

The extent of news programming seems to hinge on market size and the commensurate financial resources and competition. Still, regardless of market size, it may be possible to expand news programming at most stations with only a relatively modest increase in operating costs. In comparison to the expense of acquiring other programming, a station might be able to add another half-hour or more of local news by recycling or updating much of the material gathered for use in the original program. But any such expansion does increase demand for fresh news content, a need met by satellite-distributed news services.[4]

THE SATELLITE REVOLUTION

The blurring of local and network news began with the inauguration of Group W's Newsfeed service in January 1981. Newsfeed, with over one hundred affiliates, was joined in 1985 by CONUS, which serves more than one hundred domestic stations and fifty overseas affiliates. Both act as cooperatives for transmittal of reports contributed by participating stations. Each feeds reports from Washington, D.C., on news of interest in the stations' coverage area.

Other major satellite news services include CNN and CNN Headline News, used by 185 stations. The Local Program Network provides about fifty stations with reports on breaking news, features, magazine material, and access to newsmakers who can be interviewed by local reporters or anchors. Potomac News provides interview and feature packages to some eighty stations from Washington, D.C. The News and Information Weekly Service (NIWS) delivers reports to over 125 stations twice a week.[5]

The Florida News Network provides member stations with reports from the largest markets in the state.[6] In Florida and in other states, satellite cooperatives enable stations to provide coverage of other cities, including the state capital, that would otherwise be beyond their budgets.[7]

A majority of network affiliates receive regularly scheduled feeds from a variety of sources and can choose from among several reports for the version best suited to their needs. Increasing amounts of equipment and personnel time have been allocated to recording these satellite feeds. And some stations have developed contacts in their markets to localize feature stories, such as medical news.[8]

In response to these ventures, ABC, CBS, and NBC have expanded their own satellite news services to stations. ABC and CBS provide regional news services and, along with NBC, feed reports to affiliates even before they themselves have had the opportunity to air them. The alternative to providing this valuable service to stations is to risk losing affiliates, which could turn to other sources of supplemental news content.[9]

Through their satellite services, the networks have strengthened their ability to cover breaking news across the country. The affiliates benefit from better news coverage in their regions and from network subsidies to help them purchase satellite news-gathering (SNG) trucks.[10]

The SNG system makes it possible for the approximately 160 stations in the United States that have SNG trucks[11] to beam stories back to their stations and to make these available live to other stations across the country from remote sites. The best journalistic use of SNG vehicles has been to cover breaking on-the-spot news like hurricanes or plane crashes.[12] In many cases, though, it is too expensive and impractical to dispatch the vehicles on short notice to cover breaking regional or national stories; by the time the vehicle could arrive at the scene of a story, the action would be over.[13]

As a result, much of what is gathered by SNG equipment is "soft" news rather than news of the caliber that would be obtained from a network feed.

Coverage of international or national news that is originated by a station has the important characteristic of local interest. For example, after the earthquake in Mexico in 1985, stations from Texas and California, where interest was great, provided their own reports from Mexico City. And the many stations that originated reports from the 1988 national political conventions had at least one thing in common: all had delegates from their service areas.

In his analysis of station coverage of the 1988 Democratic and Republican national conventions, E. Albert Moffett concluded that stations' decisions to cover such activities are based on four considerations:

1. Presence of a station's own news-gathering team at an event increases the prestige of the station.
2. The event offers opportunities for originating stories that feature local or state participants.
3. The event is of a magnitude that can produce "lead-worthy" reports for several days, amortizing costs over sufficient revenue-producing time.
4. Coverage is within the reasonable reach of a station's news operating budget, and personnel are available.[14]

THE RELATIONSHIP BETWEEN LOCAL AND NETWORK NEWS AUDIENCES

The symbiotic relationship between station and network news audience ratings is weighted more toward local than network news programs. In some cases, the networks have even pressured stations to program local news in order to provide an audience for the network news program that follows it or risk loss of affiliation.

TV industry analysts believe that the smaller audiences gathered by major market affiliates have hurt the ratings competitiveness of the

"NBC Nightly News." Conversely, analysts credit the high lead-in ratings provided by affiliates in the top markets for ABC's "World News Tonight" and high prime-time ratings with helping that program achieve top ratings in competition with CBS and NBC.[15] Similarly, research conducted by James G. Webster and Gregory D. Newton showed that network program audiences appeared to be more dependent on the success or failure of local news than local programs were on network news ratings.[16]

SCHEDULING

The network news programs are also vulnerable to local programming moves stimulated by local profit-making opportunities. Regardless of past programming practices, the time period for network news is no longer sacrosanct.

A number of stations have altered the traditional schedule for network news in order to counterprogram with game shows. One strategy is to move the news back a half-hour (from 7:00 to 6:30 P.M.) to create a "double access" period of sixty minutes between 7 and 8 P.M. eastern time, during which syndicated programs can be scheduled against other stations' news.[17]

This practice permits a station to schedule two half-hours of profitable programming and avoid face-to-face competition on news. CBS Vice-President for Marketing David Poltrack has pointed to the damage to network news ratings by syndicated programs offered during the same periods, citing the adult appeal of programs like "Wheel of Fortune" and "Jeopardy."[18] By implication, lowered network news ratings could be justification for stations to rely on local news programs and cancel network news.

THE RELATIONSHIP BETWEEN MARKET SIZE AND NEWS PROGRAM EMPHASIS

An analysis of weekday local news broadcasts in the early evening period from August through November 1986 has shown that television stations in the top thirty markets (those with the greatest resources and the ability to subscribe to satellite services) devoted more time to national and to international news than stations in medium-size and small markets (markets ranking 31st to 70th and 71st to 214th, respectively).[19] Further analysis of those data supports this pattern, particularly for stations in the largest television markets.

In the largest markets, more than 17 percent of the local evening news program "news hole" (total program time devoted to news content) was given over to national and international news; the figure was similar—15.5 percent—for medium-size markets. In small markets, however, only 6.1 percent of the news hole was devoted to national and international news (see table 2.1).

Table 2.1
NATIONAL AND INTERNATIONAL NEWS BY PRODUCTION
OF STORIES, 1986
Percentage of News by Market Size

	Large		Medium		Small	
	Nat'l	*Int'l*	*Nat'l*	*Int'l*	*Nat'l*	*Int'l*
Anchor reporting	2.7	1.9	3.3	*	2.4	*
Live interview and on-the-scene reporting	1.3	*	*	0	0	0
"Localized" videotape reporting	4.9	2.7	2.7	2.5	*	*
Correspondent on-the-scene video-tape reporting	2.3	1.3	5.5	*	2.0	*
Total	11.2	6.0	11.6	3.9	5.0	1.1
Number of minutes (total news hole)	1,889		462		432	
Number of markets	10		5		7	
Number of stations	30		13		14	

* Less than 1 percent.

Although the sources of national and international reports are not identified, stations in the larger markets appear to be using more material from satellite news services. An examination of how national and international news is presented by stations in markets of different size reveals their emphasis on outside news sources. As table 2.1 shows, there is little difference in the proportion of the news hole devoted to anchor reports (straight "tell" stories that may be accompanied by a graphic or still picture in the background) among stations in markets of different sizes. But stations in large markets gave much greater emphasis to international news conveyed through their anchors than did stations in medium-size and small markets. Similarly, stations in large markets had a virtual monopoly on live interview or on-the-scene reports of national news, which would require a satellite feed.

Stations "localize" news reports by having a local reporter (usually an anchor) narrate a videotape, preempting the original reporter. Stations in large markets localized a much greater proportion of their video reports on national news than stations in medium-size markets did, although stations in both categories devoted similar proportions of their news hole (7.2 percent of large markets, 8.2 percent of medium-size markets) to national news. The focus on national and international news in small markets was about a third the amount for stations in the larger markets.

Although the stations in small and medium-size markets have news holes of similar size (462 and 435 minutes), the stations have different emphases on national and international news, no doubt reflecting lower profit levels and a competitive need to provide the diversity in news coverage that exists in larger markets. As other research has shown, local news has a higher priority in smaller markets.[20] Stations in the largest markets devoted much more time, particularly in video reports, to national and international news than stations in medium-size and small markets. In large markets, stations devoted 136 minutes to video reports on national news, compared with 38 minutes in medium-size and 3 minutes in small markets. Similarly, stations in large markets presented 76 minutes of video reports on international news, compared with 12 minutes in medium-size and none in small markets.

Stations in large markets, with their larger news holes, not only have more time to fill, but also have the greatest financial resources (and the greatest competitive incentive) to purchase SNG equipment and to send their reporters off to sites around the country or to other countries. Moreover, they tend to "localize" national and international news—a practice that is likely to give viewers the impression that these reports were originated by the stations' news departments.

THE FURTHER BLURRING OF NEWS SOURCES

As local news programs increase their coverage of national and international news, some members of the news profession have suggested that the networks may be reduced to serving their affiliates in the role of a wire service like the Associated Press (AP) or United Press International (UPI), with stations inserting network-generated stories into locally produced programs.[21] That possibility has even been suggested by the president of NBC News.[22] But the high cost of maintaining a local news operation large enough to respond to major national and international stories may well mitigate the demise of network news programs.[23]

NOTES

1. Alfred J. Jaffe, "Early News Surge Continues," *Television/Radio Age* (May 16, 1988): 39–40.
2. "Affiliates' Early Evening Local News Increases in Past Year," *TV Today* (August 8, 1988): 2.
3. "Affiliates Waking Up to Early Morning News," *TV Today* (September 19, 1988): 2.
4. Barbara Matusow, "Station Identification: Network Affiliates Loosen the Apron Strings," *Washington Journalism Review* (April 1985): 28–33.
5. "Key Satellite News-Gathering Players," *Electronic Media* (August 25, 1986): J-2.
6. Brian McKernan, "Star Trucks," *Broadcast Management/Engineering* (January 1987): 28.
7. Neal Koch, "Television Turns Its Back on the Statehouse," *Channels* (April 1989): 12.
8. Bob Puglisi, "Satellite News Feeds: Many New Sources," *RTNDA Communicator* (November 1988): 10–17.
9. Ernest Leiser, "*See It Now*: The Decline of Network News," *Washington Journalism Review* (January/February 1988): 51–52; Matusow, "Station Identification," 28–33.
10. James P. Forkan, "News Services Help Network/Affiliate Partnership Grow," *Television/Radio Age* (April 3, 1989): 29–31.
11. Ibid., 29.
12. Mike Clary, "Live from Anywhere," *Channels* (September 1989): 63–66.
13. Gary Cummings, "The Elephant in the Parking Lot," *Washington Journalism Review* (January/February 1987): 46; Dennis Holder, "Local Coverage on Ku: Direct Broadcasting, A Place in History," *Washington Journalism Review* (October 1985): 46–49.
14. E. Albert Moffett, "Satellite News Gathering at the National Conventions: The Coming of Age of Local Television News," paper presented at the Broadcast Education Association Annual Convention, Las Vegas, April 28, 1989.
15. "ABC News on Top of the World—And the Ratings," *Television/Radio Age* (June 13, 1988): 30, 32.
16. James G. Webster and Gregory D. Newton, "Structural Determinants of the Television News Audience," *Journal of Broadcasting and Electronic Media* 32 (Fall 1988): 381–9.
17. Robert H. Brown, "Atlanta CBS Affil Advances Local News to Open Double Access Slot," *Variety* (January 27, 1988): 60.
18. "ABC News on Top of the World—And the Ratings," 32.
19. Raymond L. Carroll, "Market Size and TV News Values," *Journalism Quarterly* 66 (Spring 1989): 49–56.
20. Ibid.
21. Peter Ainslie, "The Nieman Foundation at 50: The Curator Critiques Television News," *Channels* (June 1989): 10; Desmond Smith, "Is the Sun Setting on Network Nightly News?" *Washington Journalism Review* (January 1986): 30–33; Tom Matrullo, "What TV News Will Be Like in the '90s: Local Coverage," *RTNDA Communicator* (May 1989): 28.
22. Verne Gay, "Introspection at NBC: Is No News Good News?" *Variety* (April 5, 1989): 1, 4.
23. "Local TV News: Nipping at the Heels of the Networks," *Broadcasting* (May 5, 1986): 74–7; Diane Mermigas, "Local Stations Spur Network News Change," *Electronic Media* (August 25, 1986): J-3, J-18.

3

Super Tuesday and the Future of Local News

Robert M. Entman

The economic success of local television news and the predicted economic distress of network news have foreshadowed gloom and doom in broadcast journalism. The majority of Americans, it is said, may come to rely primarily on local television news even for coverage of national and foreign stories.[1]

As a result of my analysis of local news coverage of the presidential primaries on Super Tuesday, March 8, 1988, I believe that the networks have little to fear. Local stations either cannot or will not provide the coverage that the three networks have traditionally offered.

Super Tuesday was the largest one-day collection of presidential primaries in U.S. history, an event bound to exert great influence on the final selection of the nominees. Twenty states held primaries or caucuses and nearly one-third of the delegates to each party convention were at stake. Super Tuesday offered a perfect opportunity for local stations to "strut their stuff"—to deploy new communications equipment, specialized reporting staffs, and computer analyses on coverage of a national story of major importance and interest to their audience. In short, they could show whether they were ready and willing to take up the challenge thrust upon them by the decline of network news.

METHOD

The data for this study came from content analyses of Super Tuesday coverage on thirteen stations: WCBS (New York, market ranking no. 1); WBBM (Chicago, no. 3); WCAU (Philadelphia, no. 4); KPIX (San Francisco, no. 5); WBZ (Boston, no. 6); KDFW (Dallas–Fort Worth, no. 8); WUSA (Washington, D.C., no. 9); WAGA (Atlanta, no. 12); WTVJ (Miami, no. 14); KDKA (Pittsburgh, no. 16); KMOV (St. Louis, no. 18); KMGH (Denver, no. 19); and WFSB (Hartford–New Haven, no. 23).

To facilitate comparisons with network coverage, all stations chosen except one were CBS affiliates: The only usable tape available from Boston was of WBZ, an NBC affiliate. Results from WBZ were excluded from network comparisons but were used in other discussions. Most studies have found campaign coverage to be similar on all three networks.[2]

Taping was done by student and faculty volunteers from around the United States. As a volunteer effort, the project generated a sample that is neither random nor complete. The cities included were those where a person known to the author furnished a usable tape. As the text indicates, the selection should be representative of the largest markets, but given the imperfections, inferences here are tentative and readers are encouraged to check the results against their own impressions (or systematic studies) of local TV news. Whatever the shortcomings, this data base is one of the largest yet employed in a study of local TV news.

Wherever possible the programs analyzed were the early evening news shows for Monday through Thursday (March 7–10) and the late evening news shows for the night of Super Tuesday only.

The number of news programs actually recorded varied from city to city. Some volunteers missed one or more news programs. Thus, of the five possible programs to be recorded in each of thirteen stations, for a total of sixty-five, there were forty-five usable programs. To be included in the sample, a station had to be represented by at least three usable news shows, including those aired in the early evening of the Tuesday and Wednesday of Super Tuesday week. Most stations were represented by four programs.

To summarize the information the news contained, coverage was broken down into several categories. Beyond this categorization, each assertion by a reporter was coded for whether or not it explicitly mentioned a specific candidate. The categories were:

Pure horse race: Predictions or announcements of votes and outcomes; descriptions of candidates and their organizations' plans, hopes, activities, and tactics; and general strategic maps of the nomination contest.

Analytical horse race: Explanation of actual or predicted outcomes by reference to polls, voting breakdowns, or assessments of candidate coalition building.

Super Tuesday process: Mechanics of voting, apparent turnout, and discussions of the theory behind the creation of Super Tuesday.

Substance: Public policy issues and candidates' personal qualities, records, and qualifications.

STRATEGY, NOT POLICY

Content analysis of coverage during the week of the primaries by thirteen stations, each serving a different market among the top twenty-five, yields a discouraging picture of what we can expect from local news. When local stations covered the national election story, they, like the networks, stressed the comparatively trivial "horse race" factors—predicting and announcing votes and outcomes; describing candidates and their organizations' plans, hopes, activities, and tactics; and drawing general strategic maps of the contest. The stations made little or no effort to explain or analyze the actual or predicted outcomes by reference to polls, voting breakdowns, or assessments of coalition building by the candidates.

The mechanics of voting, voter turnout, and theories behind the creation of Super Tuesday received little attention. Public policy issues and candidates' personal qualities, records, and qualifications—the "substance" of an election campaign—were largely ignored.

Because the networks, newspapers, and newsmagazines cover the "horse race" aspects of presidential campaigns so thoroughly, local TV might have been expected to be different—to attract audiences by offering something distinctive. Far from it. When data from all thirteen stations were combined, 77 percent of the assertions made by local TV news reporters in covering Super Tuesday fell into the category of pure horse race, compared with 75 percent for CBS. Analytical horse-race material accounted for an average of 6 percent of the assertions by local stations, compared with 13 percent on CBS.

Viewers expecting the newly sophisticated local news operations to offer superior interpretations of the horse race were to be disappointed. Few stations offered more than the barest analysis of the reasons for the primary outcomes, and some offered almost none.

Super Tuesday "process" coverage—the mechanics of voting, voter turnout, and theories behind the creation of Super Tuesday— accounted for only 8 percent of local TV news coverage, compared with 1 percent on CBS.

Coverage of policy issues and the candidates' qualifications comprised an average of 5 percent of local TV reporting versus 11 percent on CBS, and this difference was more apparent than real. Neither the network nor the local stations devoted much attention to substantive matters. For example, on Thursday, March 10, CBS broadcast six substantive assertions but five of them were sound bites taken directly from campaign advertisements and shown as part of a report by Leslie Stahl on media tactics. None consisted of more than a few code words, such as "Congressman Dick Gephardt has flip-flopped on a lot of issues." Despite the inclusion in the sample of markets that had primaries coming up, for example, Illinois, Pennsylvania, and California, not one story dealt with questions such as "What if Bush becomes president?" or "Who is this Gore fellow?"

Table 3.1 displays the percentage of local TV reporters' assertions devoted to the horse race (pure and analytical) versus the percentage devoted to substance (candidates' records and policy stands) for each station separately. Especially noteworthy here are two points, developed more fully later. First, there is little variation among the stations; all but one devoted three-quarters or more of their coverage to the horse race and less than one-tenth to substance. This finding suggests that professional values, organizational goals, and practical constraints are similar from market to market.

Second, within this sample from the top twenty-five markets, there appears to be no relationship between size of market and focus on substance. The two stations that offered the most substantive coverage were the Denver and St. Louis affiliates of CBS. The flagship WCBS station in New York City was among those most obsessed with the horse race. If substance is a token of "quality," that characteristic does not correlate with market size. Presumably, the larger the market, the more intense the economic competition a station faces, and the more

Table 3.1

ASSERTIONS DEVOTED TO HORSE RACE VERSUS SUBSTANCE

Station	City	Horse Race (pure and analytical)	Substance
WUSA	Washington, D.C.	75%	5
KDFW	Dallas	88%	3
KDKA	Pittsburgh	100%	0
KMGH	Denver	69%	20
WTVJ	Miami	76%	3
KMOV	St. Louis	82%	8
WFSB	Hartford	90%	1
WBBM	Chicago	86%	6
WCBS	New York	90%	1
WAGA	Atlanta	83%	3
WCAU	Philadelphia	88%	3
KPIX	San Francisco	84%	7
WBZ	Boston	83%	6
Local Station Average		84%	5
"CBS Evening News"		88%	11

resources the station brings to the contest. The finding that market size is not correlated with quality therefore suggests that local TV journalism is not necessarily enhanced by either high levels of competition or deep pockets.

Despite the dominance of the horse-race framework, we might have expected that when stations aired candidate sound bites the candidates' assertions would tend to be substantive, that is, conveying information on candidates' records or positions. Yet the overwhelming majority of sound bites conveyed self-serving claims. The local programs sampled contained a total of 285 candidate sound bites, 82 percent of which were about the horse race. Only 9 percent had any substantive content. Most bites contained claims about the speaker's own success and support, exhortations of partisan crowds, or statements of the obvious. Here are some typical items broadcast by WUSA in Washington, D.C., on Monday, the day before the primary:

> Jesse Jackson: "And on Tuesday, roll the stone away. And on Wednesday morning have a resurrection: new hope, new life."
>
> Robert Dole: "I want to be certain to ask everyone for their vote, and I would just extend that invitation to Kemp supporters and Robertson supporters."
>
> George Bush: "No, we go right on to Illinois after this important, this most significant political event in the modern nominating process. There's no way anybody can deny that."
>
> Michael Dukakis: "I think we're going to do reasonably well in the South. It's very competitive and it's competitive state to state and primary to primary, but all I can say is that we're going to continue to work. There are still a lot of undecided voters in the South. I suspect a lot of people have only made up their minds in the last couple of days."

The bites broadcast by CBS were largely in the same vein. On the four evenings analyzed, the "CBS Evening News" broadcast twenty-seven sound bites, nineteen of which (70 percent) were horse-race comments. Five of the remaining eight bites came from a single story whose point was that all the candidates were mouthing the same clichés, and most of these assertions could be considered substantive only by the most generous of standards. For example:

> Gephardt: "You've really got to stand up for American workers and American businesses" (March 7).
>
> Jackson: "Whether a baby is white, black, or brown, hunger hurts: common ground!" (March 7).
>
> Gore: "We've got to have fundamental change" (March 10).

From this evidence, most sound bites do not convey new information. Their major purpose may be simply adding visual and aural variation to stories that consist largely of "talking heads." Secondarily, the bites legitimate and support claims that reporters or anchors make in their own words, and they often make sense only in the context of the narrative. For example, immediately before Jesse Jackson said, "And on Tuesday, roll the stone away . . . ." on WUSA, the reporter said, "Yesterday, at the church of slain civil rights leader Martin Luther King, Jackson told black voters they could carry on his struggle by voting Tuesday."

Given the difficulty most of the audience has in understanding and retaining the messages of television news, sound bites reinforced by a reporter's establishment of the context may be helpful. In addition, many bites bolster the symbolic portrait of the candidates that the media construct. The Jackson quotation urging black voters to "roll the stone," perplexing taken by itself, fits into the larger stream of images television conveyed of his candidacy. The quote supports the (perhaps accurate) stereotype of Jackson as a candidate whose appeal rested in part on his deft use of religious and emotional rhetoric. Although stereotypes can oversimplify and mislead, they can also help the mass audience (and journalists) process information and therefore may benefit viewers.

These findings suggest an irony. Technological progress notwithstanding, local TV and commercial network news have done little to diminish the value of personal attendance at speeches to hear the candidates express substantive policy views.[3] The one exception might be televised debates; however worthwhile, though, the format of debates is often too rigid to allow genuine probing of positions and records.

The findings also point to a related irony. In an attempt to demonstrate a commitment to "quality," many stations sent correspondents to report from remote locations and devoted resources to editing and incorporating feeds from the networks into their own shows. The result was the production of a narrative format that might be called "serial hype." Especially on Super Tuesday itself, much air time was turned over to candidates and their staff and supporters, who proceeded to hype their own candidate, saying things most viewers knew to be dubious, disingenuous, or self-serving. The consequence of serial hype may be to stimulate political cynicism and depress interest and voter turnout.

The horse-race framework may have suffused the coverage of both the local stations and CBS, but as table 3.2 shows, the network and

Table 3.2
ATTENTION TO CANDIDATES MEASURED BY
CANDIDATES' ASSERTIONS

Candidate	"CBS Evening News"	Average of Local Stations
Bush	30%	19%
Dole	6	9
Kemp	1	5
Robertson	3	5
Dukakis	16	11
Gephardt	2	5
Gore	12	9
Jackson	23	30
Simon	5	3
Hart	1	4

local stations diverged more in allocating time to the various candidates. Most noteworthy is that CBS gave assertions by George Bush 30 percent of the time devoted to campaign coverage, compared with 19 percent for Bush on the local stations; Jesse Jackson obtained 23 percent of the time devoted to candidate assertions on CBS and 30 percent on local news. Although a study including a full representation of local stations might have found smaller or larger differences, making generalization hazardous, it seems clear that Jackson did better than most candidates on both the network and the local news. That finding is bolstered by other research.[4]

Whereas Bush's domination of the other Republican candidates in the contest for coverage might have been expected, Jackson's success is a bit of a puzzle. On local stations he obtained about three times the coverage devoted to Dukakis and Albert Gore, Jr., each of whom did about as well as Jackson in the primaries. Jackson even received 50 percent more local station coverage than the triumphant Bush.

This is not the only distinction in Jackson's coverage. Jackson received by far the greatest share of the substantive assertions by reporters about candidates on the local stations. As table 3.3 shows, he was the subject of 42 percent of all such assertions; his closest rivals in the substantive category were Bush, with 15 percent, and Dukakis, with 14 percent. The typical local newscast contained a mere 2.5 substantive candidate assertions per show, so Jackson's strength here is more relative than absolute. Still, contrary to the assertions of some of Jackson's supporters, the evidence suggests that Jackson got more mileage out of his Super Tuesday successes on local TV than Dukakis or Gore got from theirs.[5]

Table 3.3
CANDIDATE DISTRIBUTION OF SUBSTANTIVE ASSERTIONS

Candidate	*Local TV Average*
Bush	15%
Dole	2
Kemp	2
Robertson	7
Dukakis	14
Gephardt	2
Gore	5
Jackson	42
Simon	7
Hart	3
Number of Assertions	121

Note: Varies slightly from 100 percent because of rounding.

Why did Jackson obtain such a large proportion of the coverage? One likely explanation is that local TV news stations cater to large segments of the audience who have an intense interest or preference. This sample included many stations serving central cities with large concentrations of African Americans who supported Jackson with near unanimity and considerable passion. Jackson received special attention because he was the only candidate to generate fervor among a large, identifiable audience block in a number of large markets. But Jackson also did well on CBS, where blacks form a small minority of the audience, so the attention he received on TV probably is also attributable to his telegenic presence, the unexpected scope of his electoral appeal, and his wide public recognition compared with the other major Democratic contenders.

The variation among the stations in coverage of candidates further suggests the influence of audience taste in shaping the local news. Table 3.4 shows that in each market where a candidate enjoyed local ties or a large group of intense supporters, the candidate obtained disproportionate coverage. Thus Bush, who calls Texas home, received by far his heaviest proportion of coverage on the Dallas–Fort Worth station and disproportionately heavy attention in Miami, where the city's large and influential Cuban-American community appeared to transfer to him an emotional loyalty previously reserved for Ronald Reagan. Similarly, Paul Simon received significant attention in Chicago and St. Louis, Gary Hart in Denver, and Richard Gephardt in St. Louis. Pat Robertson scored best in Atlanta, the biggest city in the Bible Belt.

Table 3.4
PERCENTAGE OF ALL CANDIDATE-FOCUSED ASSERTIONS ON EACH STATION

	Bush	Dole	Kemp	Robertson	Dukakis	Gephardt	Gore	Jackson	Simon	Hart
Boston (WBZ)	14	13	2	4	22	1	18	21	3	1
Hartford (WFSB)	26	10	11	6	23	2	8	13	—	—
New York (WCBS)	9	10	10	6	5	1	8	42	1	3
Phila (WCAU)	17	4	3	3	17	4	12	38	1	—
Pittsbg (KDKA)	19	10	13	—	10	3	16	52	3	6
WDC (WUSA)	15	7	8	2	14	4	9	37	3	1
Atlanta (WAGA)	12	4	2	23	11	3	17	24	1	2
Miami (WTVJ)	34	2	1	2	17	14	20	10	—	—
DallasFW (KDFW)	47	1	8	1	6	—	—	28	7	1
Chicago (WBBM)	15	19	4	7	7	1	5	28	11	1
StLouis (KMOV)	19	16	—	2	4	28	2	17	12	—
Denver (KMGH)	17	4	3	10	10	2	3	23	—	28
SFrncso (KPIX)	3	23	3	1	5	1	7	53	1	1
CBS Eve News	30	6	1	3	16	2	12	23	5	1

Note: Varies slightly from 100 percent because of rounding.

The local differences could indicate that local stations cover national news in ways that better serve the needs of local audiences, but the flip side of responsiveness to local audience groups is parochialism and isolation. Concentration on favorite sons may please large segments of the audience, but the local focus is more problematic as an aid to democratic citizenship. The citizens of St. Louis were ill-served by disproportionate coverage of Gephardt's campaign just because the candidate happened to live and have a lot of supporters there. Except for the handful who may have been determined to vote for the local candidate, what people in St. Louis needed was information about others who had some reasonable chance of gaining nominations.

Moreover, although some Super Tuesday reporting might have been expected to provide perspective about what it would mean to the particular community if one or another candidate were to become president, among the well over 1,000 assertions coded, only three touched on a local angle. Denver's KMGH broadcast two assertions on how the energy stands of two candidates (Bush and Dukakis) might affect the economy of Colorado. And Pittsburgh's KDKA noted that the Democratic mayor of Erie was supporting Robert Dole, because Dole had been helpful to Erie as Senate Republican leader. Material like this appears to be just the kind that networks usually ignore, and the kind that local stations would find both newsworthy and attractive to audiences, but such assertions were almost entirely absent during the sample period.

This situation leads us to suspect that "local" news is something of a misnomer. Local news is, in fact, virtually an interchangeable commodity, whether in the Super Tuesday story or other coverage. From city to city, form and content remain almost identical. A consistent professional culture may cause producers and reporters and station managers to produce similar fare from market to market. In a sense, this common culture shapes an implicit national "network," one that is probably reinforced by personal contacts like those that exist among professionals in most fields—people who meet at conventions, read the same trade magazines, and share the same occupational goals. Local news seems to be part of a national production system, with the common professional culture shaped by the news consultants that most stations employ (for example, Frank N. Magid Associates), the common needs of advertisers, the affiliations with network news organizations, and the increasingly homogeneous culture of the United States. Hence localism and diversity in broadcast news may be more apparent than real.

As one illustration of this implicit network of common practices, consider the choice of sound bites. Of the twelve stations that employed sound bites (KDKA had none), nine used the identical one of George Bush telling those gathered at his headquarters on the night of Super Tuesday, "And I'll repeat it, I'm going to be the next president of the United States."

Even the varying emphasis on candidates shown in table 3.4 suggests a deeper, common structure to the local news. Most stations made a similar journalistic decision: to emphasize coverage of candidates whom they believed to have the most intense appeal to key elements of their audience. Of course, that strategy led to some variation in content across the localities, but the common decision suggests the influence of a shared professional culture and similar organizational imperatives.

Two aspects of format were common to most stations. On eleven of the thirteen stations, black persons were coanchors of at least one half-hour segment of the program. Of the eleven black coanchors, nine were women. The choice of black anchors appears to reflect, again, an appeal to heavily black central city audiences. The pairing of black females with white males—there was no case of the converse—suggests continuing sensitivity to the white audience's prejudices and fears. Gender roles may help explain the racial distinctions. The female anchor was normally subordinate to the male anchor. The techniques of subordination were often subtle—differences in camera framing, in types of stories introduced and reported, and in the advertising campaigns used to promote the program, where men tend to get top billing. Pairing a black man with a white woman would fill the news program with signals of a black man dominating a white woman. White audiences probably view having a white man in charge as less threatening; the race of the female coanchor presumably matters little if the primary authority is white.

Another feature common to most stations was the surprisingly ordinary looks of their anchors. The sample included few women or men who would meet the standards of stardom in Hollywood. The appeal of most anchors in the sample seemed more a matter of demeanor and personality than physical appearance. In contrast to pure entertainment programming and advertising, the stories the anchors introduced and narrated were rarely, if ever, conducive to sexual fantasy or titillation. More important, the general function of local anchors appeared to be establishing a familial, "parasocial" relationship with the audience in order to induce viewers to think of them as friends they want to visit day after day. Hence the goal for local anchors is to be avuncular, reassuring, and authoritative (for the men) or upbeat and sincere (for the women)—not seductive.

THE FUTURE OF LOCAL AND NETWORK NEWS

The mere fact that local news is similar from city to city does not preclude the possibility that it is getting better. Certainly many observers seem to think it is, and if that were so, greater differentiation might follow as stations become increasingly aggressive and knowledgeable in exploiting their improved capabilities. The data from Super Tuesday, however, appear to belie this possibility.

One index of improvement would be the sponsorship of surveys designed to illuminate issues and opinions in the specific communities the stations serve. Super Tuesday provided an excellent opportunity for polling, especially by stations in the primary states. However, as the surprising paucity of analytical horse-race reporting suggests, the use of polls appears to be a minor practice on the local stations. In fact, none of the stations in the sample conducted its own Super Tuesday poll, and only five even cited polls of any kind. Only one of the stations used the CBS exit poll results for its state (WAGA in Atlanta).

A more common practice was to have a correspondent reporting from one of the primary states, usually Florida, Texas, or Georgia. Often the correspondents came from the local station's own staff; occasionally they represented other news organizations but were made available to the local station, perhaps in exchange for the local station's providing reports from its area to the cooperating station.

On Super Tuesday itself, most of the remote reports were broadcast "live," a point every station emphasized. Live reporting capitalizes on the presumed advantage of TV over print—its ability to place audiences at the scene in real time. Being on the scene theoretically might have allowed reporters to find some surprising material on candidates' records (say, a correspondent in Massachusetts covering Dukakis) or on their support coalitions (covering Dukakis in Florida). The data show a dearth of substantive or analytical horse-race material on all stations, however, regardless of whether they deployed correspondents outside their own markets. In fact, live reporting may handicap journalists who are forced to cover news in places where they do not know the turf, making it more difficult for them to discover patterns, understand context, or check factual claims with competing sources.

The evidence suggests that money spent on the technology that allows live and remote reporting offered few benefits to viewers seeking deeper understanding of either the campaign or the candidates. The local stations' deployment of correspondents around the country and their use of live satellite links seemed in this case to function largely as symbols designed to impress audiences that their local station runs a serious news organization—just like others in the market.

By reproducing network fare, these large urban-market stations proved that they could report Super Tuesday as the networks did—no better, perhaps, but neither appreciably worse nor much different. Thus the locals may be poised to handle the task that would confront them if the network news operations were to fade. The problem is that the networks themselves have not done a good job reporting presidential campaigns, as their own personnel often attest.[6] For the locals to offer more of the same does not promise much improvement.

If network news were to disappear, the mass audience might seek more extensive national coverage from local stations, which would then allocate more time to national news. In such a case, the networks might become "video wire services," producing batches of reports from which each local station could choose the most suitable. Alternatively, audiences relying on local broadcast television might simply settle for less national news.

The networks have prided themselves on minimizing the intrusion of commercial and ratings considerations into journalistic judgments, on giving audiences what they need, not necessarily what they want. If the network evening news fails to survive in its current form, it will leave the task of reporting national and foreign events to local stations whose news programming has been motivated more purely by audience and profit maximizing. The future is likely to bring heightened competition for the audience's attention, which will make local stations even more sensitive to mass tastes. Thus commercial imperatives may drive local stations and their news programs even more in the years to come.

If Super Tuesday is viewed as a harbinger of the kind of demographically targeted national news reporting that local stations may practice in the future, distribution of political information across the nation may suffer and the national political dialogue may undergo a perplexing alteration. For example, stations in Chicago may woo their large Polish-American and black populations by focusing heavily on news of Poland and of civil rights policy; stations in Seattle may neglect these to focus on environmental developments.

The social benefits of the network evening news may be worth preserving, even if the program is no longer profitable. If the network evening news vanishes, the nation will lose a common denominator, an integrative force in national political life. Simply by reaching tens of millions of homes each night, the networks impart some common data with which the public can participate in a widely shared political conversation.

The downside to the networks' integrative function, of course, is their great power to shape the national discourse. Some might argue that even if local television does a poor job covering national politics, the advantages to the country of no longer being under the sway of the three centralized networks would more than compensate. Still, if the nightly network news were to be supplanted by local TV, there is a danger that many ordinary Americans who are accustomed to receiving most of their news from television and are unlikely to switch to newspapers will find themselves cut off from the political world.

A more sanguine view also is possible. Judging by ratings, local television news does what it sets out to quite well. It attracts large and profitable audiences who watch programming labeled "news." We must simply acknowledge that, with occasional shining exceptions, local TV is unlikely to offer the sort of serious broadcast journalism on the local level that networks have traditionally provided on the national level. If the networks fade, other media can substitute: three newspapers employing diverse approaches (the *New York Times*, the *Wall Street Journal*, and *USA Today*) are available to most Americans every day, as are cable news services, National Public Radio, public television, at least one local daily newspaper, and many magazines. For local news, the public still has the daily newspaper, often joined by energetic weeklies—some of them free—and magazines and, in large markets, an all-news radio station. Communication and computer innovations may well add new options and sources of data on politics and policy. These and other forces may create a future news system better than the one we enjoy now. But from the evidence explored here, it is unlikely that local television stations will contribute much to that end.

NOTES

The data base used in this study was collected and analyzed with the aid of grants from the Annenberg Washington Program in Communications, the Markle Foundation, and the Media Studies Project of The Woodrow Wilson International Center for Scholars, in Washington, D.C.

1. See, for example, W. Drummond, "Is Time Running Out for Network News?" *Columbia Journalism Review* (May/June 1986): 50–3.
2. See, for example, Robert M. Entman, *Democracy without Citizens: Media and the Decay of American Politics* (New York: Oxford University Press, 1989); Doris Graber, *Mass Media and American Politics*, 3d ed. (Washington, D.C.: Congressional Quarterly Press, 1989); S. Robert Lichter, Daniel Amundson, and Richard Noyes, *The Video Campaign: Network Coverage of the 1988 Primaries* (Washington, D.C.: American Enterprise Institute for Public Policy Research, Center for Media and Public Affairs, 1988); and Lawrence W. Lichty, "Watergate, the Evening News, and the 1972 Election," in John J. O'Conner, ed., *American History/American Television: Interpreting the Video Past* (New York: Frederick Ungar, 1984), 232–55.
3. The "MacNeil/Lehrer NewsHour" on public television and C-SPAN and CNN on cable did offer frequent and substantial samples of candidates' policy pronouncements. Although none of these broadcasts garnered high ratings, their availability may have enhanced the ability of the most interested and motivated television viewer to hear candidates speak. Also, some candidates distributed videocassettes, which were shown by volunteers. Again, these could reach only a tiny fraction of potential voters.
4. Lichter, Amundson, and Noyes, *The Video Campaign.*
5. This point is supported by ibid., who found that for the precampaign year of 1987, Jackson generated twice as many stories as any other Democrat, and that for January to June 1988, he was the subject of about the same number of stories as any other Democrat, if not more. The authors also coded the tone of his coverage as substantially more "positive" than that of the other Democrats (see pp. 72, 79, 83, 111, and passim).
6. The best account of this is found in Martin Schram, *The Great American Video Game* (New York: William Morrow, 1987).

4

Learning from Television News

Mark R. Levy

Media researchers are fond of asking survey respondents, "Where do you get most of your news about what is going on in the world today—newspapers, radio, TV, magazines, or somewhere else?" Most Americans, and indeed most Europeans, usually reply, "Why, television, of course." The response helps explain why news has become a profit center for most local TV stations and why politicians and candidates are so eager to appear on TV news shows.

But the question really records only a subjective judgment about where people *think* they get their news. It does not measure what new information a person actually picks up in the course of the day. The question is fundamentally unanswerable for people who receive a daily barrage of information from radio, television, newspapers, magazines, books, and conversation with family, friends, and work colleagues.

For those interested in maintaining a healthy democratic dialogue among an informed public, it is more important to know which medium actually delivers the most understandable news to the greatest number of people. To answer that question, public opinion polls, laboratory experiments, and observation of people watching television in their homes reveal a remarkably consistent set of findings. TV news is not doing a very good job of informing the public. In fact, the typical viewer regularly fails to understand the main points in two-thirds of all major TV news stories. In other words, people who watch network TV news remember and comprehend only one out of three of the most important news stories reported by some of the world's most sophisticated news organizations.

Moreover, research clearly shows that television is not the public's main source for news. Because most people have multiple information sources, watching TV news adds little to the understanding of national and international events they already have from reading newspapers, listening to the radio, and talking with other people. Research also shows that people who watch TV news are only slightly better informed than people who do not watch; and, all things being equal, people who say they get most of their news from television are among the least-informed members of the public.[1]

Why is TV news an ineffective medium for conveying information? One explanation is that most people are not "news junkies"; they have many demands on their time and attention and do not follow news stories with the close interest of a professional journalist.

In addition, a number of characteristics about TV news lessen its impact:

- TV news is presented very quickly. The typical anchor delivers more than two hundred words a minute, and that is too fast for the typical viewer to absorb.
- Once a news story has been delivered, it is unlikely that the newscaster will repeat it or rephrase it. Only if the viewer sees the same story repeated on a later broadcast is there any reinforcement.
- Little explanation usually accompanies what appears on the screen. One of the cardinal rules of television journalism is, "Let the pictures speak for themselves." They seldom do.
- Similar stories are often reported back-to-back or serially. In a so-called linear medium like a newspaper, grouping stories about similar subjects makes sense. In television, it is a mistake to expect viewers to keep similar stories separate in their minds. Elements of different but related stories tend to merge in the viewer's memory as a kind of video soup.
- TV news stories usually report the most recent news first. That is like trying to get people to understand a joke by telling them the punch line first. Most people will not get the point of a joke or a news story without first hearing what leads up to the "laugh line."

Television, of course, does have some unique advantages in conveying information. When it slows down and repeats its message (much as TV commercials do), no communication medium can match it, particularly for conveying a sense of "being there," of experiencing a dramatic or historic event. Indeed, television is unsurpassed as a meaningful information source when its pictures are dramatic and unequivocal in the message they transmit—as with the *Challenger* disaster or the prodemocracy demonstrations in Beijing.

The problem, of course, is that TV's great power to provide drama and emotion is not matched by a capacity to inform in depth about complicated, serious matters. Even if television carried more documentaries than it does now, its ability to deal with complex issues would still be constrained by limits of the medium itself and by producers' flawed understandings of how to use that medium effectively.

What can TV newspeople do to improve the understandability of the stories they tell? First, they can pay more attention to their viewers and try to learn more about how audiences watch, learn, and fail to learn from their newscasts. When they do, TV news producers will discover that their viewers are less well informed than most journalists but intelligent enough to understand the news when it is presented clearly and succinctly. The local newscaster or network superstar who can figure out how to do that will capture both the audience's attention and its loyalty.

NOTE

1. See John Robinson and Mark R. Levy, *The Main Source: Learning from Television News* (Newbury Park, Calif.: Sage, 1986).

5

Talk-Show Journalism

Thomas B. Rosenstiel

John McLaughlin wanted to "get out," as they say in television—to end the discussion of President Bush's plan to bail out the savings and loan industry and break for a commercial:

> McLaughlin: "What's the embarrassment level?"
>
> Christopher Matthews: "I think it's a seven."
>
> McLaughlin: "A seven?"
>
> Matthews: "A negative seven." (Laughter all around.)
>
> McLaughlin: "Wow! What do you say?"
>
> Morton Kondracke: "Oh, it's about a three, but he's got to recover from things like this, and he should not have this kind of a story coming first thing out of the box."
>
> McLaughlin: "I think I have to say that he gets a five on this. We'll be right back."

With the rise of the political talk show in the 1980s, a sea change occurred in the culture of Washington journalism. Whereas in the 1970s the best-known and most-celebrated print journalists in America were investigative reporters, in the 1980s the mantle of the most famous and most influential moved to those members of the press corps who sat around in TV studios and offered quick opinions—high practitioners of the art of assertion.

Being on TV now is the most certain path for print journalists to book contracts, the lecture circuit, and greater clout with their publishers. Not surprising, print journalists in Washington now actively lobby to get on television shows, in some cases sending same-day faxes of their stories and videotapes of their past TV appearances to the program producers.

Publications also crave the visibility of talk-show journalism; many offer reporters bonuses for TV appearances. The *Chicago Tribune* even employs a media consultant to coach and promote its Washington correspondents on the air. *USA Today* regularly featured its newspaper reporters as experts on its own TV show, hoping one medium would sell the other. And so many of the major Washington bureau chiefs now are regulars on a TV talk show that some companies consider such participation an integral part of the job.

Taken together, the talk-show culture is changing print journalism, downgrading the traditional skills of reporting and a devotion to neutrality and objectivity while rewarding the skills that win talk-show audiences—a knack for asserting opinions, thinking in sound bites, and honing an attention-getting public persona.

The talk-show value system may well make public discourse more rancorous if the rewards in journalism increasingly go to those willing to stake out the most controversial opinions. The bitter tone of public debate over ethics in Congress and the nomination of Sen. John Tower to be secretary of defense are examples.

In a sense, the phenomenon mirrors the devaluation of substance that has occurred in politics. Just as the meaning of political events has come to depend heavily on their "spin," in Washington journalism the talk-show journalists' interpretation of events becomes more important than reporters' actual coverage of the events.

Moreover, as print journalists who appear on talk shows become as well known as the officials they cover, as has already occurred with TV correspondents and anchors, the press moves further away from the traditional, arm's-length, adversarial relationship with government that was underscored in the coverage of Vietnam and Watergate.

The appearance of print reporters on TV is hardly new. "Meet the Press" began using newspaper reporters to interview politicians back in the days of radio, and the show is NBC's longest-running program. PBS's "Washington Week in Review" started its roundtable discussion of the news with print reporters in 1967.

All this was born as part of TV's long-standing insecurity about the professional credentials of its own staff correspondents. As Edwin Newman put it upon leaving NBC in the 1970s, he needed to get a job in print to get back on TV.

But the culture of assertion journalism really dates back to 1980 when "Agronsky and Co." started asking its panel of journalists not merely to interview officials and offer some analysis but to assert their own opinions as well. Agronsky's success led ABC to incorporate a similar roundtable segment when it launched "This Week With David Brinkley," and freewheeling discussion became the show's distinguishing centerpiece.

Soon producers were including roundtables on "Face the Nation," "The Today Show," "Nightline," and others. By 1988, the *National Jour-*

nal's Washington source guide listed twenty-one public affairs programs that regularly used print reporters as guests. The success producers found in having reporters offer opinions has some connection to the humanizing of anchors that occurred with local TV's "happy talk" formats. As viewers come to identify with the personalities they see on TV, the viewers want to know more about what the TV personalities think and feel.

With time, it also became clear that the more gusto with which reporters gave their opinions, the bigger the audience. "Agronsky and Co.," with its sometimes arcane arguments, was quickly surpassed in ratings by "The McLaughlin Group," an opinion/entertainment show that replaces serious public policy debate with a brand of intellectual slapstick.

"The McLaughlin Group," in turn, has spawned offspring of its own. "McLaughlin" regulars Patrick Buchanan and Robert Novak launched a similarly Keystone Cops–style show on Cable News Network called "Capital Gang."

Even CBS's venerable "Face the Nation" has two kinds of roundtables, according to executive producer Karen Sughrue. With one, the panelists are asked to *analyze*: "Do you think (former House Speaker) Jim Wright will last?" In the other, they are asked to *advocate*: "Should he last?"

The culture of talk-show journalism is, admittedly still largely restricted to Washington, where the Sunday political talk shows originate. But as their success grows, it is likely that the format will be adopted by local stations in other cities.

Is talk-show journalism really so dangerous—a virus of distorted values infecting the pristine world of print? Defenders of such programming offer two principal defenses. The most common is, "Everything depends on the tone of the show," as *Washington Post* political writer David Broder puts it. Are reporters appearing as analysts to explain why events happened or "in the role of policy advocates," saying what should happen? The problem with Broder's argument is that it is dubious whether audiences really distinguish between advocates and analysts.

Moreover, the trend is toward more extremism. When the *Tribune* Company examined the possibility of airing a political talk show on its WGN Superstation, according to Washington bureau chief Nicholas Horrock, TV executives insisted that the program would have to be more in the "McLaughlin" mold to make money.

Perhaps the most curious defense of these programs is that they are harmless. Only about fifty print reporters regularly appear on TV.

Also, the programs will not pollute anybody, as "McLaughlin" regular Jack Germond put it, if those who appear on the shows "recognize that it is a half-hour of being a dancing bear to make a better living and . . . not a serious journalistic exercise."

One problem with Germond's argument is that not all participants consider the shows frivolous. "It is just a different kind of journalism," says Fred Barnes of the *New Republic*, another McLaughlinite. The other problem is that whether Germond takes it seriously or not, talk-show journalism already has changed who gets rewarded in print journalism and why, and that change in turn influences the values of the profession.

Although payment for a single appearance on most shows rarely exceeds $1,000 and may be as little as $200, appearing on TV is the surest way for a print reporter today to get rich. As noted earlier, appearing on TV makes it easier to get book contracts, which brings reporters status, clout with employers, and occasionally wealth. More certain, TV can lead to the lecture circuit, which is the primary source of income for such successful writers and TV performers as columnist George Will.

"The whole phenomenon of journalists' realizing that visibility can boost their careers in a number of ways has really taken off," says Sue Ducat, producer of "Washington Week in Review." The power of TV talk programs to bestow celebrity status on reporters has not been lost on the news organizations they work for, either. Reporters who appear on TV can command better assignments and higher pay.

TV can also be helpful in gaining the most prestigious jobs in Washington journalism. *Newsweek*, which gives reporters cash bonuses for TV appearances, hired Morton Kondracke as Washington bureau chief after he became a regular on the "McLaughlin" show, just as *U.S. News and World Report* found an editor in TV commentator David Gergen. (Kondracke has since returned to the *New Republic*; Gergen subsequently relinquished day-to-day responsibility for the magazine in part so that he could have more freedom to do television.)

Other Washington bureau chiefs also have become TV regulars, among them Jack Nelson of the *Los Angeles Times* ("Washington Week in Review"), Albert Hunt of the *Wall Street Journal* ("Capital Gang"), and Strobe Talbot of *Time* magazine ("Inside Washington," formerly known as "Agronsky and Co."). TV exposure clearly was critical in winning top jobs for some. Gergen, for example, had no real experience as a magazine editor.

Why is television so valuable to the print media? The assumption is that it helps promote print publications—that the exposure will persuade TV viewers to buy the magazine or newspaper. It is also argued that TV exposure helps reporters in their print jobs. The *Chicago Tribune* Washington bureau pays its TV coach, for instance, from its news budget. "We don't circulate heavily in this town," says Washington bureau chief Nicholas Horrock, but the TV talk shows do, so appearing on them, he argues, enhances access to sources.

Of all the talk-show panelists, Christopher Matthews of the *San Francisco Examiner* stands out for the extent to which his newspaper job seems subservient to his television appearances. In 1986, Matthews was a fairly obscure speechwriter for House Speaker Thomas P. "Tip" O'Neill, Jr.—a staff person reporters frequently encountered when they really wanted to interview O'Neill.

As his career as a Capitol Hill propagandist began to bore him, Matthews made no secret of his ambition to become a pundit on the Sunday political talk shows. He discussed his ambition with friends, and he described writing his book—a collection of Washington anecdotes titled *Hardball*—as a way to establish his credentials as a Washington insider.

In 1987 Matthews and *San Francisco Examiner* executive editor Larry Kramer struck a deal. "He needed to be a journalist," Kramer explains, "to have the kind of respectability to be on TV. That's what we brought to the table." What Matthews brought to the table for the *Examiner*, Kramer says, was visibility from "any one of the fifty shows he is on morning, noon, and night with our name under his picture." So valuable is such exposure, Kramer gave Matthews the title of Washington bureau chief, which seems a bit inflated for a bureau that consists of Matthews and one reporter.

Kramer even arranged to have Matthews's column syndicated by King Features. It was, says Kramer, "the only way [for Matthews] to get even half" of what the former speechwriter was making as a Washington consultant. By 1989, Matthews had more than sixty client papers, many of them picked up when the King syndicate's only other liberal, Nicholas Von Hoffman, stopped writing his column.

This approach has worked like a charm. Matthews's column is not published in Washington, and his paper does not circulate widely even in hometown San Francisco. Nonetheless, Matthews, who talk-show producers agreed was the most aggressive self-promoter they had dealt with, had become such a familiar face on talk shows that early in 1989 *Washingtonian* magazine named him "one of the top fifty journalists" in the city. Says his editor Kramer, a Harvard Business School graduate, "I should be paying him out of the marketing budget." *Washingtonian* magazine's top fifty journalists included only nine print reporters who did not appear on television.

Peanuts, *by Charles M. Schultz (Reprinted with permission of United Feature Syndicate)*

Even the strictest print news organizations have at most an ambivalent attitude toward the talk-show culture. The *New York Times* asks that reporters not "appear with the frequency that you have become a regular" on any one program, said assistant managing editor Warren Hoge. Yet those who book the talk shows say that this policy is actually applied case by case, and it gets particularly fuzzy in the case of really big-name reporters such as R. W. Apple, the paper's chief Washington correspondent, who appears frequently on several programs.

The *Washington Post, Philadelphia Inquirer*, and *Wall Street Journal* have similar policies. The *Los Angeles Times* also asks that reporters not become regulars on any program, according to editor Shelby Coffey III, but Jack Nelson's appearances on "Washington Week in Review," according to Coffey, comply with company policy.

"What bothers me is the message of what it is we value and esteem," says the *Washington Post*'s David Broder. And the values of television are not necessarily those that make a good print reporter. Karen Sughrue, executive producer of "Face the Nation," says, "I need someone who is glib, colorful, whose thoughts can be condensed into a conversational style."

Producers on other shows mention irreverence and wit as important. And crucial to all these shows is the ability to spark conflict. "A good fight," says "McLaughlin" producer Allyson Kennedy, "someone who is not afraid to go out on a limb." In the miniaturized logic of television, where emotions are conveyed better than ideas and where words become metaphors, staking out a position on the political spectrum that provokes conflict is more important than the substance of one's argument.

What is "the effect on public discourse, generally," wonders Hodding Carter, if our national pundits are those who perform well on television? And what is the effect on audiences? "Do Americans think they are getting anything of substance from any of this?"

In the *New York Review of Books* in 1987, James Fallows argued that talk-show journalism was drumming "the subtlety and complication out of public issues and [encouraging] journalists to think as predictably as politicians." It was also contributing to "a strange snobbish wave in Washington writing" and a meanness in public debate, Fallows argued, because the conflict-loving talk shows were increasingly taking on a "bullying tone."

Since then, if anything public debate has gotten rougher. Consider the 1988 presidential campaign, the fight over John Tower's nomination to be secretary of defense, the scandal involving House Speaker Jim Wright, and the rise of "attack ads" in political campaigns. Talk-show journalism is hardly to blame, but it may be part of a trend toward sensationalism, vitriol, and personal attacks in politics generally.

"McLaughlin" regular Eleanor Clift of *Newsweek* believes that the move toward advocacy by journalists on television is part of a more general trend away from traditional, and possibly mythical, ideas of objectivity. Newspapers are becoming more interpretive, so newsweeklies are getting more advocative.

For the people who appear on talk-show programs, the most obvious concern is that the more lucrative part of their activities is that which does not involve reporting. The more time spent building celebrity status and wealth, the less time there is to cover the news. As Paul Duke, moderator of PBS's "Washington Week in Review," told me, "We both know there are a lot of people in this town who write columns and engage in journalism on the run."

"I can't prove this," says Barbara Matusow, a student of Washington journalism for *Washingtonian* magazine, "but I really think that you find young people in print journalism hustling themselves as a product in a way that you wouldn't have before. The pot of gold is so much bigger today, it is just unimaginable." Columnist Robert Novak, one of the most ubiquitous stars of talk-show journalism, agrees that the shows reflect a devaluation of the printed word. "The depressing thing is that I am not remembered for the coherent prose I work hard at, not always successfully." Instead, "the stuff that I just throw off the top of my head gets more currency than the stuff I really work at. . . . Reading is not a lost art, but it is certainly a failing practice." People who appear on the programs talk about how they have a sense that their words vanish into thin air, and of how fans unfailingly remark on "seeing" them on TV but rarely on hearing what they had to say.

"It invites a sort of lazy opinion mongering," says *Rolling Stone* Washington editor William Greider, another occasional practitioner of talk-show journalism. "My sense is that some people are confusing it with reporting."

Matthews is quite open about what he does and does not do. He says he rarely does any reporting for the twice-weekly columns and weekly analyses that he writes, a statement that is borne out by a review of his work. (This comment might come as a surprise to CBS's morning program, which hired him, according to the program's producer, because his experience as a former Washington speechwriter gave him special access to sources.) "I don't think interviewing people or doing basic snooping is that much of a pure form of information gathering," Matthews explained in an interview. Instead, "Every time I give a speech I get challenged, or every time I talk on TV. The process of writing is formative, and to say that you are not thinking, not developing information, I don't think that is valid."

A journalist who does not believe in reporting sounds like a contradiction in terms, but Matthews goes further. He describes what he does on TV, in lectures, or in print as providing audiences with a "colorful exposé." The syntax is revealing. The term *exposé* once referred to investigative reporting.

Matthews's view reflects what has occurred in political campaigns, where the way an event is interpreted can have more effect than the event itself. In the new culture of assertion journalism, in which reporters are more highly rewarded for their opinions than for their ability to uncover what has happened, the "spin" that reporters put on events becomes more important than the events themselves.

Another aspect of talk-show journalism is evident in the way that the programs are further helping blur the lines between journalists and the officials they cover. In a speech after the 1988 presidential campaign, Broder in particular spoke out about journalists' "allowing themselves to become androgynous Washington insiders . . . all of us seeking and wielding influence in our own ways." Robert Novak has described his experience in trying to cover a Richard Gephardt campaign stop in Iowa this way: "People ignored Gephardt and gathered around me, whose views they hated, . . . It wasn't that they thought I was good, or liked what I said, or defended my right to say it. It was just that I was on TV."

The journalist as Washington insider, a celebrity with special information and insight, is integral to the ethos of the talk show. On David Brinkley's show, after the guest politician departs we get the last word from our trusted translators, Brinkley, George Will, and Sam Donaldson, who muse freely about what is really going on. McLaughlin's program goes one step further. It mixes journalists with ideological apparatchiks or latter-day pamphleteers such as Patrick Buchanan (currently a host of CNN's "Crossfire" program) and McLaughlin himself, a former White House aide.

And the trend is further in that direction. On CNN's offshoot of "McLaughlin," "Capital Gang," not only is no distinction made between Pat Buchanan and Al Hunt, Washington bureau chief of the *Wall Street Journal*, but each week a different politician joins the panel, not as a guest to be queried but as an equal kibitzer. "Welcome Charlie," Buchanan says to Congressman Charles B. Rangel, Democrat of New York, insider to insider.

Even on the more staid programs, the symbols of distance between reporter and officials are no longer considered important. Gone are the desks that once separated the supposed interrogators from their subject on "Meet the Press" or "Face the Nation."

The worry, widespread in Washington, is that the ethos of Washington insider-celebrity onscreen "translates into a sort of social corruption" offscreen, as Greider put it, with journalists becoming social equals of the officials they cover, and thereby more distant from the public the press supposedly represents.

This celebrity spawns a fragile euphoria, and it is fair to ask whether journalists are as likely to question the status quo when they are among its most prized beneficiaries. John McLaughlin has conceded, "There is no doubt in my mind that when you develop special relationships that there are times when you are willing to turn a blind eye to minor criticisms." The reporter does that, McLaughlin contends, "in order to preserve a source for a major exposé of a major policy issue. . . . It is a question of preserving the connection for the greater good." But what major exposé or policy issue comes from talk-show journalism?

Some journalists have expressed concern that such relativist utilitarianism indicates that the press is becoming weaker and less responsible. Benjamin C. Bradlee, executive editor of the *Washington Post*, has decried the press's "return to deference" toward the presidency during the Reagan years. In a speech after the 1988 presidential election, columnist Anthony Lewis argued that the established press in this country has, to a large extent, reverted to an old relationship with government that predates Vietnam and Watergate. "We are an adversary only on the margins, not on the fundamentals that challenge power," Lewis said.

The celebrity status of the press is only one factor, Lewis went on. Other factors include Reagan's popularity, improved techniques for manipulating the press, a revisionist attitude that blames the news media for America losing the war in Vietnam, and fears within the press about its credibility—fears about its alleged liberal tilt.

If Lewis is right, the phenomenon of talk-show journalism is really linked to even larger trends that deserve further study. It is already clear that the talk shows are leaving their mark and altering some traditional values of the print media.

II

Newspapers

6

The State of the Industry

Leo Bogart

As the 1990s began, American daily newspapers showed both dynamism and strain in a media marketplace that had become progressively more competitive and complex.[1] Here are some examples:

The nation's second-largest market, Los Angeles, was left with only a single metropolitan daily when the *Herald-Examiner* ceased publication. Once the country's biggest afternoon paper, it had required a repeated infusion of capital from its owners, the Hearst Corporation.

In New York City, the *Daily News* almost disappeared after a disastrous strike and was bought by British press tycoon Robert Maxwell who died in November 1991. The *Post* dropped a short-lived Sunday edition, reducing to three the number of papers engaged in a head-to-head, seven-day, free-for-all for readers and advertising. The Long Island *Newsday* continued to make inroads with its New York City edition.

In York, Pennsylvania, two small competing dailies, the *Daily Record* and the *Dispatch*, sought a joint operating agreement under the controversial Newspaper Preservation Act.

In Detroit, after a long battle through the courts, two of the country's largest and best papers, the Gannett-owned *News* and Knight-Ridder's *Free Press*, merged their business operations under a joint operating agreement. The two papers had for years been locked in a death struggle that kept their rates uneconomically low, both for advertisers and readers.

In Little Rock, the independently owned *Democrat* charged Gannett's *Arkansas Gazette* with predatory pricing, the latest battle in a bitter war for survival. Gannett sold the *Gazette* in 1991.

In Miami, Cox Enterprises' *News*, a steady money-loser, was killed off despite a long-standing joint operating agreement with Knight-Ridder's *Herald*.

Newspapers exemplify a typical nineteenth-century industrial product. (Photo by Rick Friedman, New York Times)

In Bladen, North Carolina, the *Journal* (circulation 4,186) increased its publication frequency from three to five times a week, joining the ranks of the nation's 1,645 dailies.

Amid such dramatic changes in individual communities, daily newspapers maintained their position as the leading advertising medium and as a highly profitable business, though they were severely hit by the recession of 1990–92. Newspapers' production and distribution methods have been transformed. Huge investments have been made in plants and equipment. Newspapers remain an important voice in politics and a vital element in the civic fabric of American communities. A new sensitivity to reader interests has infused and altered editorial practices.

Table 6.1
GROWTH OF TOTAL CIRCULATION VERSUS ADULTS AND HOUSEHOLDS, 1970–88

Increase in daily circulation	+0.3%
Increase in Sunday circulation	+26.8
Increase in number of adults	+44.1
Increase in number of households	+44.5

SOURCES: Newspaper Advertising Bureau estimates based on Audit Bureau of Circulations. Census statistics.

At the same time, the number of competing dailies has continued to drop, and more and more morning-evening combination papers have gone to a single edition. The reduction of choice reduced the number of two-paper readers, but the effect on circulation was somewhat offset by the emergence and growth of national dailies. But circulation, the basic source of newspapers' advertising might, also reflects the changed habits of readership brought about by rapid and far-ranging changes in American work and living patterns.

Newspaper penetration of American homes is down. Weekday circulation has inched up, but as table 6.1 demonstrates, daily circulation between 1970 and 1988 did not keep pace with the nation's growth in households, which are becoming smaller, or with the increase in the number of adults (persons over age eighteen), the universe of potential newspaper readers.

Throughout the 1970s and 1980s, as can be seen in table 6.1, the increase in circulation for Sunday newspapers at least approached the increases in numbers of adults and households. Indeed, table 6.1 indicates that, compared with weekday papers, Sunday newspapers demonstrated a healthy growth in circulation figures but still did not match the overall increase of population and households.

Daily Newspaper Household Penetration 1920–87

From Leo Bogart, Press and Public, 2d ed. (Hillsdale, N.J.: Lawrence Erlbaum Associates, 1989). Reprinted with permission.

Figure 7

The strength of Sunday newspapers has been demonstrated in advertising as well as in circulation. Sunday papers today count for 38 percent of all newspaper advertising volume, compared with 32 percent ten years ago. The increased ad volume has meant a corresponding growth in the bulk of the average Sunday newspaper and helped sustain the growth of daily papers. Newspapers now average 55 percent greater bulk on weekdays than they did a decade ago, and 98 percent greater bulk on Sundays. (For example, the daily *New York Times* grew from an average of 71 pages in 1977 to 113 pages in 1987; the Sunday *Times* from 648 pages, counting the tabloid-size elements, to 1,037 pages; and the Bergen (New Jersey) *Record* went from 70 to 84 pages daily, and from 337 to 576 pages on Sunday.)

This increase in size has important implications. First, there is more physical weight for circulation departments to handle and for carriers to distribute. Because the news hole has grown even faster than advertising, there are more pages for editors to fill. And there are more pages with which readers must contend. The shift of much retail advertising and a large portion of national food advertising from run-of-the-paper into inserts has also changed the character of the package that is presented to readers, particularly in the case of food advertising.

Apart from the vast increases in size, newspapers have been changing significantly in other ways that affect appearance and content. In response both to a new editorial sensitivity to reader interests and to the opportunities opened up by computerized composition and makeup, many papers introduced new graphics, new typefaces, and new layouts. An industrywide shift to Standard Advertising Units (SAUs) led to uniform page and column dimensions. Gannett's *USA Today*, launched in September 1982, spurred the upgrading of color quality in newspapers across the United States.

How is the new newspaper organized? The effort to package editorial matter in clearly definable and identifiable sections has continued. At the same time, the number of newspapers that regularly (at least once a week) offer special interest columns and features appealing to particular groups of readers has continued to decline.

Two other trends became evident in the 1980s: more emphasis on features relative to news, and increased emphasis on local rather than national and world news. The typical paper has changed its structure not by cutting out information but by reformatting additional information. Curiously, both these observable content trends (more features, more local news) run counter to what readers tell survey researchers that they want in their daily newspaper. When questioned, readers say they desire more hard news (as opposed to features), and more national and world news (relative to local news). But editors believe that what readers actually read and respond to most warmly are features and local news.

The restructuring of newspaper formats has not been the only significant change; there have also been important changes in the ways newspapers are delivered. Computers are now widely used to manage comprehensive subscriber information systems that permit more efficient solicitation of subscriptions, better customer service, and, perhaps more important, the development of nonsubscriber lists to which TMC ("total market coverage") products can be sent. Centralized control permits office billing and has supported the substitution of adult for juvenile carriers.

Subscriptions account for nearly three-quarters of sales on any given day, with another one-fifth sold as single copies and the rest pass-alongs at work or from someone else. Although the majority of newspapers still rely mainly on juvenile carriers, these newspapers do not account for the majority of circulation. In a national survey by the

Newspaper Advertising Bureau in 1987, more than half the newspaper subscribers reported that their paper was delivered by an adult, and many reported that they did not even know who that adult was. Most subscribers pay by mail, and of these, most pay in advance in the same way they might pay for a magazine.

The economics of the newspaper business has also led to fewer choices in terms of the number of papers from which the typical reader can choose. With more and more chains abandoning evening newspapers, fewer papers battle for readers' attention, for the big scoop. The surviving papers show "less bite" and idiosyncrasy, less of a difference to catch readers' attention.

The ten newspapers with the largest circulation take on more and more importance. Led by two national dailies, the *Wall Street Journal* and *USA Today*, the "top ten" are concentrated in the country's biggest markets. As table 6.2 shows, many have stagnant or declining circulations. (In 1990, the *Los Angeles Times* became the largest local daily.)

HOW READERS USE TODAY'S PAPER

How do most readers "use" today's newspaper? People read a daily paper and a Sunday paper in different ways. Half the readers go through the weekday paper methodically, page by page. But on Sunday they typically skip around, going directly to the sections in which they have the greatest interest. This is particularly true for young people who, more than others, read only what interests them.

Virtually everyone reads the main news section of the Sunday paper. This section, the magazine section, and the television guide are the most popular parts of the average Sunday paper. The Sunday paper also has a long shelf life; it is often kept around the house for the entire following week to be read at leisure.

Readership on Saturday is 10 percent below that of the other five days of the week. To boost interest in Saturday papers, some newspaper executives have proposed that certain special sections be shifted from the Sunday paper. The *Washington Post*, for example, puts its real estate section in the Saturday paper. (In Canada, a number of major papers have moved sections from their strong Saturday papers to Sunday. Traditionally, papers were not published on Sunday, and the weekend package appeared on Saturday.) When surveyed, most readers said they preferred special sections to continue to appear in the Sunday paper, but this statement may simply reflect a predictable leaning to what is familiar.

Table 6.2

TOP TEN NEWSPAPERS' CIRCULATION, 1988 AND 1991

	September 30, 1988		September 30, 1991		Percentage Change	
	Weekday	*Sunday*	*Weekday*	*Sunday*	*Weekday*	*Sunday*
Wall Street Journal	1,869,950	—	1,795,448	—	−4	—
USA Today	1,338,734	—	1,418,477	—	+6	—
New York Daily News	1,281,706	1,568,862	762,078	911,684	−41	−42
Los Angeles Times	1,116,334	1,394,910	1,177,253	1,529,609	+5	+1
New York Times	1,038,829	1,601,085	1,114,830	1,700,825	+7	+6
Washington Post	769,318	1,112,349	791,289	1,143,145	+3	+3
Chicago Tribune	715,618	1,098,127	723,178	1,107,938	+1	+1
Newsday	680,926	706,440	763,972	875,239	+12	+24
Detroit News	677,385	686,787	446,831	1,202,604[a]	−34	
Detroit Free Press	629,065	710,112	598,418		−5	−14

SOURCE: Audit Bureau of Circulations.

[a]An operating agreement in November 1989 initiated a joint Sunday newspaper.

One factor contributing to the decline of afternoon newspapers was getting delivery trucks through traffic to the suburbs. Increasingly, satellite transmission will be used to transmit newspaper copy even within the same urban area. (Los Angeles Times Archives)

The biggest problem for readers—and for newspaper executives—is the pull of other media. In a 1987 Newspaper Advertising Bureau survey, about one-fifth of the adults in subscribing households reported that on a typical day they did not get to read the paper. Reading the Sunday paper is a more regular habit than reading the daily paper every day of the week. One-third of the readers surveyed said that, if forced to make a choice, they would give up weekday papers for the Sunday paper. This preference is expressed most strongly by younger adults, 85 percent of whom read the newspaper but are less likely to have developed a daily reading habit.

The typical newspaper today competes with a multitude of news outlets, various entertainment media, and all sorts of leisure-time activities. Two-thirds of the people in the 1987 survey claimed to have watched one hour of television news on the day before the interview, but this television viewing included a variety of shows, ranging from local news to "News at Sunrise," "Today," "Good Morning America," the network evening news, and "Nightline."

Television news is not the only news competitor the newspaper industry faces. In the Newspaper Advertising Bureau's survey, some 45 percent of those interviewed said that on a typical day they received some news from the radio; 13 percent subscribed to one or more newsmagazines, while only 30 percent read a weekly paper for which they paid. Some 55 percent reported that they read a "shopper" or other free paper.

Despite time pressures most people say they try to "keep up with the news," but it is difficult to know precisely what that means. Television apparently helps people distinguish the "big" story from less important ones. For political news and sports, with pictures from Washington or abroad and from sports arenas around the nation, television supplies vivid images that remain in the viewer's memory. Television, with its growing interest in news, is increasingly providing more details of the big news stories—or at least, so viewers believe. In 1982, when the Newspaper Advertising Bureau asked whether respondents got enough details from television news, only 30 percent said yes. In 1987 the proportion had increased to 42 percent. On major stories, more people regard television than newspapers as their main source of information.

Newspapers, according to the survey, are considered preferable to television as a source for local news. The newspaper has the greatest comparative advantage when it is reporting on happenings in the city, town, region, and, to some extent, the state. Television's time constraints limit this type of coverage in most markets.

For other types of stories, such as news about the economy or sports, survey respondents rated newspapers and television news about even. Surprisingly, people have reported that they rely more on television for international news, entertainment news, and news of politics.

Given this news environment, how do people today read their newspapers? The answer is—selectively. A Newspaper Advertising Bureau survey in 1987 revealed that 80 percent of readers turn to pages of editorial opinion and analysis and pages made up of national and international news, and 79 percent to pages that carry advice columns. Seventy-five percent open pages featuring local, state, and regional news or a calendar of local events, 74 percent the comics, and 73 percent health or science pages. The typical sports page is opened by 72 percent of male readers and 46 percent of female readers. Seventy-eight percent of women (and 61 percent of men) open the average "lifestyle" or "society" pages, and 75 percent of women readers turn to the fashion pages. The lowest "opening levels" are registered for pages made up entirely of classified advertising.

The bulkier the newspaper, the lower the "page opening" score. Not surprisingly, the smaller the number of pages in a newspaper, the higher the level of "page opening." For this reason, "page opening" is higher in newspapers with circulations below 50,000 than it is in fat papers such as the *Los Angeles Times* and *Washington Post*. And because surviving evening newspapers are most often published in small towns and have smaller circulations, their readers, on average, scan more pages.

Table 6.3 gives some indication of readers' preferences for newspaper content and the intensity of their interest.

The percentage of people who read particular parts of the newspaper is not a reliable guide to the *intensity* of their interest. Newspaper readership is made up of many varied constituencies, and a feature with little readership may be very important to a small minority. Magazines may be directed to clearly defined special interests,

Table 6.3
READERS' PREFERENCES AMONG NEWSPAPER CONTENT

Section	Usually Read	Like Most
Local community news	84%	30%
International news	75	25
News briefs and summaries	74	15
Presidential and congressional news	72	9
Local politics and governmental news	69	14
Economic news	68	9
Celebrity and famous people news	65	7
TV listings	60	8
Advice columns	59	16
Comics	58	17
Calendar of local events	57	5
Sports news	51	23

but newspapers do not include more material than could possibly be of interest to any reader; they try to reach a common denominator, because they seek to be a mass medium.

Because readers are so familiar with their daily newspaper, few report any difficulty in locating content that matters to them. They "know" the daily newspaper, much as they "know" the schedules of local television stations. It is therefore not surprising that the majority of readers do not read the newspaper's own published summary index regularly.

Advertising is a growing part of daily newspapers, particularly ad inserts. The Newspaper Advertising Bureau's surveys show that a majority of readers are satisfied with the amount of advertising they get. Nearly one-third say that they would prefer less advertising in their newspaper, compared with 6 percent who said they wanted more. Advertising is an important component of what attracts people to a newspaper. More than half the readers clip advertising coupons. And on any given day, classified advertisements are scanned by far more people than those who are actually seeking to acquire a job, house, car or other advertised item.

The mix of news and advertising varies in different sections of the paper, but there is some news on three-quarters of all pages. One-quarter of newspaper pages consists exclusively of editorial content, slightly more than one-quarter consists entirely of advertising, and the rest contain some mixture of the two. The typical two-page spread offers at least some editorial content.

People read the average newspaper for a great variety of reasons, and when the Newspaper Advertising Bureau listed eleven of them in its 1987 survey, they all seemed to apply to some readers. Motivations include a desire to follow up on news obtained elsewhere (50 percent), to read an interesting news story or particular feature (48 percent), to help form opinions (41 percent), to acquire conversational topics (38 percent), to discover where to shop (35 percent), and to feel in touch with events (25 percent). As for the news versus entertainment question, most respondents leaned to the news side, except for younger readers, who seemed to be attracted primarily by features like the entertainment section, advice columns, and comics.

Only a minority of those surveyed thought that their newspaper showed consistent editorial bias, but more than half had a mixed (46 percent) or critical (16 percent) view of the paper's editorial position. Politically, newspapers were generally seen as middle of the road, but somewhat more people considered them conservative than liberal. Finally, most respondents gave the typical newspaper a high rating, compared with television, for its value in shopping and in planning the readers' use of leisure time.

CONTENT CONSIDERATIONS

During the 1980s the content of the American press had changed under the pressures of increased suburbanization, the explosion of television news, and technological changes in the news industry. The extent and character of these changes have been tracked by a series of surveys of daily newspapers conducted by the Newspaper Advertising Bureau over a span of twenty years. These surveys reveal changes in newspaper content and design. The larger the paper's circulation, the greater likelihood of editorial and graphic changes, but even papers with circulations under 10,000 have seen substantial changes. For example, on July 1, 1984, climaxing a trend toward uniformity of page layout that had been under way for several years, American newspapers adopted a standard six-column, thirteen-inch-wide page designed to facilitate the placement of advertising. Other transformations in the look of the average paper include changes in the masthead, greater use of photography, and new typefaces.

The typical newspaper on a weekday has, on average, three separate sections. (The smallest-circulation papers have two, larger-circulation ones, five.) Photos and illustrations make up between 10 and 20 percent of the news hole for the typical paper but nearly one-quarter use more than 20 percent of their news hole for graphic material. Even before the launching of *USA Today* in 1982, color in editorial matter had been increasingly evident in the American press. In 1987 only 17 percent of all papers reported to the Newspaper Advertising Bureau that they used no editorial color at all.

One important development has been the introduction of geographically zoned editions that include editorial matter as well as specialized advertising. The launching of zoned editions was in large part a response by metropolitan papers to growing suburban competition, and by dailies generally to the rise of free weekly "shoppers."

News coverage has increased substantially in two areas: sports and business, particularly in the larger-circulation, big-city papers. Although readership studies show that sports and business sections do attract female readers, both have traditionally been thought of as subjects of special interest to males. Like sports and business programming on television, these sections offer advertisers of tires, automobiles, and financial services specific opportunities for reaching specific customers.

Op-ed pages are another phenomenon that has been increasing in importance as editors of newspapers in communities where there is no competing paper seek to present an assortment of viewpoints. In

1979 about one-third of U.S. papers were running op-ed pages at least once a week. By 1987 this practice had expanded to half the papers, representing nearly three-quarters of the circulation. Two out of three Sunday papers were also carrying an op-ed page. Such pages have become favorites for institutional advertising.

As already indicated, the trends that emerge from the surveys of the Newspaper Advertising Bureau about actual content often directly contradict the findings of what people *say* interests them most. Readers seem to like certain subjects more than others, but they expect newspapers to offer them both facts and fun, to encompass both the trivial and the earthshaking. Every subject in the paper draws some readers, but few readers respond to all subjects the paper offers. Readers say that they want more hard news, but changes in recent years favor softer news, especially among papers of less than 25,000 circulation.

The typical paper has also increased local news rather than international and national news. Many editors may have decided to emphasize local news in the belief that people want "chicken dinner news" from their newspapers at a time when television is bringing them battle scenes live from the Middle East and Central America. Some may also have become discouraged at the thought of competing with the TV networks, expanded local news coverage, and now two round-the-clock news services from the Cable News Network (CNN), offering authoritative reporting on national and world affairs.

As the ratio of hard news to features has decreased, how have these changes been reflected in the physically separate or otherwise identifiable, or labeled, sections of the newspaper? Seventy percent of all daily newspapers run a main news section and a sports section, but only 25 percent have a labeled business section. After sports and main news sections, daily newspapers (about 40 percent of those surveyed) are mostly likely to carry a second news section and a lifestyle/women's section. Entertainment or television sections follow, appearing in about a third of all papers every day. No other section (be it food, fashion, home, farm, travel, or science) runs in more than 10 percent of papers daily.

Among newspapers with circulations of more than 100,000, which represent more than half the nation's total circulation, almost all have a main news and a sports section every day, and more than half run a business section. Entertainment, food (on Wednesdays), lifestyle, second news sections, and business sections each run in the vast majority of papers, with fewer having special home, fashion, farm, travel, or science sections.

By presenting content in a predictable and routine fashion, packaged in a convenient and manageable form, sections make the newspaper more accessible to readers. Surveys show that newspaper readers expect to find a certain element in a certain place, whether that element is a comic strip or a political column. This predictability develops readers' emotional ties to certain features and brings them back to the daily paper, day after day. Consistent packaging makes the paper's content seem familiar and comfortable amid the endless turmoil and daily turnover in subject matter of the (predominantly unpleasant) hard news.

In five surveys of content, the Newspaper Advertising Bureau has taken an inventory of the standing features or columns that appear daily. With a few changes the survey has tracked about seventy different subjects in 1967, 1974, 1979, 1983, and 1987. Regular coverage has diminished on almost every single subject of special interest, especially those that do not readily fit into the new "Home," "Style," or "Entertainment" sections. Of the thirty-two special-interest columns that have been tracked by the Newspaper Advertising Bureau since the early 1970s, only "Astrology" has shown an increase, while nearly all the others have sharply declined. Table 6.4 depicts the highlights of the data. Note that the decreases demonstrated since 1967 would actually be greater than indicated if the nonresponding (and smaller) newspapers had been included in 1974 and 1979.

Newspapers representing substantial chunks of the total U.S. newspaper circulation continue to provide columns and features that speak to an enormous assortment of segmented concerns on a scale beyond the scope of other mass media, particularly television. For example, less than 50 percent of all newspapers regularly offer a movie timetable or movie reviews, but those that do represent 70 percent of all copies sold. The same is also true for papers that regularly review records, tapes (audio and video), and books, and regularly carry travel news. (These features, it should be noted, have special appeal for young readers, whom newspapers ought to attract for future prosperity and growth.)

During the 1980s nearly 10 percent of newspapers started a feature for personal computer buffs; about the same number began publishing features on science. But although the population is aging and people are retiring sooner, less than 25 percent of papers regularly carry a retirement feature.

On many subjects, features tend to come predominantly from syndicated sources. Thus the reduction in regular coverage of some subjects may represent an attempt by editors to increase the amount of staff-

Table 6.4
PERCENTAGE OF DAILY NEWSPAPERS CARRYING FEATURES AT LEAST ONCE A WEEK

Feature	1967	1974	1979	1983	1987
Astrology, horoscope	NA	75	78	84	85
Automotive news	18	18	18	13	16
Beauty	45	36	36	23	15
Bridge	60	62	57	55	57
Business, financial	77	78	66	67	69
Child care	36	22	17	11	10
College	30	33	16	10	8
Etiquette	31	22	13	12	16
Farm news	53	43	40	34	34
Fashion, men's	18	20	26	16	15
Fashion, teenagers'	25	28	27	16	14
Fashion, women's	57	47	41	26	23
Gardening	53	47	43	37	30
Health and medical	68	71	66	63	55
Home decoration	39	35	28	18	17
Home repair	47	37	29	22	16
Movies	61	60	46	46	49
Outdoors	64	60	47	44	39
Personal advice	76	82	74	71	68
Pets	18	21	14	14	14
Radio	43	29	22	16	13
Recipes	81	78	78	74	71
School news	73	66	61	52	55
Science	34	24	14	9	11
Sewing patterns	62	57	50	44	31
Society news	93	95	85	80	77
Stock information	67	66	56	48	46
Television	91	91	85	87	83
Theater news	56	56	54	41	44
Travel	23	22	19	11	8

SOURCE: Newspaper Advertising Bureau.
Note: Percentages are not strictly comparable. The figures for 1967, 1983, and 1987 were weighted to compensate for below-average response rate from small-circulation newspapers, whereas 1974 and 1979 figures are based on responding newspapers only.

generated content. It may also be that, as part of the "sectional revolution," newspapers have been covering subjects of special interest on an individual assignment basis and varying the content from one week to the next, rather than trying to publish identifiable, labeled features week in, week out.

Whatever the causes, the trend toward irregular coverage of special subjects runs counter to the increasing segmentation of people's interests in a complex and mobile American society. This segmentation of interests is what fueled the growth of specialty magazines and of selective programming on cable television and radio, and the phenomenal popularity of home video. Newspapers' mass appeal derives from the fact that they deal not only with common interests, but with innumerable idiosyncrasies. Readership surveys may show that relatively few people share any one particular interest, but the surveys are not likely to show how intensely people feel about these interests.

FUTURE DIRECTIONS

The substantial changes just documented, in both the appearance and the content of U.S. newspapers, have been stimulated by the introduction of new technology, a growing sensitivity to readers' interests, and the acutely competitive marketing pressures that newspapers face as a business. Changes in editorial emphasis that run counter to the conclusions of research on readers' interests came about as the result of innumerable decisions made in small day-to-day competitive situations. Collectively, they may significantly affect the future of U.S. newspapers.

As bigger papers switched from juvenile carriers to adult carriers and office billing, there was more professionalism and efficiency, but the downside of this trend has been the loss of personal contact that characterized the "little merchant" system at its best. In an age of impersonal telemarketing and computerized information systems, the newspaper industry must maintain the personal touch and not allow its product to become simply another magazine that arrives in the mail. Newspapers have had a unique niche, which they should not lose.

During the 1980s newspapers grew tremendously in size, but readers are not spending any more time with them than they did in the past. The principal news section, which continues to have universal appeal, makes newspapers one of the last *mass* media left in an era of increased specialization or narrowcasting. But as individual parts become identified with separate subjects, it seems inevitable that many busy readers in the future will not venture beyond a glance at certain sections. Thus the principal newspaper audience will become more segmented.

Segmentation raises some interesting questions about the prospects for spinning off separate products, with savings in newsprint and perhaps increases in circulation revenue. But disassembling the newspaper as currently formatted poses great risks.

The model for successful segmentation of the newspaper audience is the Sunday paper. Advertisers can pick and choose among various sections. Resort advertisers have the travel section, movie theaters, the entertainment section, developers, the real estate section. All understand that not every reader of the massive Sunday paper will turn to their particular advertisement, but the prime prospects who are really interested will. And these are the members of the community the advertiser wants most to reach.

Newspapers have long built their audiences from a composite of both generally shared and innumerable minor interests found in any community. Editors have never assumed that every item would be read by every reader, but rather that every reader would be able to find some items that make the whole paper worth buying. Traditionally, newspaper columns and features aimed at the special interests of pet owners, stamp collectors, and bridge addicts appeared regularly where their fans could find them. Despite their vastly expanded news holes, newspapers are running fewer and fewer of these regular features than they used to. That may be a mistake.

The surveys of the Newspaper Advertising Bureau still indicate that readers look to newspapers primarily for news, but that the definition of what is *big news* is more and more provided by television. Television news has in recent years expanded its news hole (time on the air) with new cable networks (CNN, C-SPAN, FNN) and new network news shows ("Nightline"). Local television stations typically now run between two and two-and-one-half hours of news per day, more in larger markets. In addition, there are the national syndicated shows such as "A Current Affair," "Hard Copy," "Entertainment Tonight," and others.

Television more and more defines the "big" stories, the significant dramas of world events. When such stories fit into a dramatic story mold—such as the hijacking of an airplane or the rescue of a child from a well—they appear live on television from every corner of the globe. President Ronald Reagan's advisers made him the central figure in any number of dramas that were closely followed by television news.

Newspapers should not sacrifice their unique franchise as the local news medium, but they must also struggle to recapture the edge they seem to be losing in the domain of national and international news.

Even more essential to the future of the newspaper industry is the reestablishment of the daily newspaper-reading habit. Some 85 percent of all adult Americans are newspaper readers, but far fewer regard reading the daily newspaper as the kind of necessity it was even a few years ago. The first step is to make sure that newspapers get the fullest possible readership among present subscribers. Newspaper editors (and circulation managers) must not become too complacent. They must retain the readers they have *and* then go after new ones.

This task will not be easy. Newspapers have to work hard to keep their readers. They have raised prices, but at a slower rate than the general inflation rate. The news hole is getting bigger, but the regularity of reading is on the decline.

One reason for the decline in readership is the decline in the number of metropolitan daily newspapers. In 1980, 57 percent of the American population had access to two or more locally published daily newspapers, including combinations and suburban papers. Today only 46 percent has such access.

Fewer newspaper titles lead to a drop in readership primarily because of the heterogeneity of public tastes. In most major American cities a generation or two ago, different papers served different constituencies. In New York City, for example, a reader could choose a Protestant paper, a Catholic paper, or a Jewish paper. Readers chose a paper that reflected and expressed their identity in a way that a surviving single-ownership newspaper cannot do.

When there is one daily left in town, it must try to be all things to all men and women—an impossible task in a complex metropolitan region. Everyone's paper is no one's paper, or at least not one that anyone is likely to feel very strongly about.

While the harsh realities of business life bring about daily newspaper deaths and mergers, the circulation of "shoppers" increased by 65 percent between 1977 and 1988. Shoppers and alternative weeklies are reaching the very kinds of people whose readership of dailies is most irregular. Shoppers can deliver advertising just as daily newspapers can. They cannot replace newspapers' editorial functions. Except for a handful of alternative weeklies catering to the entertainment interests of young adults, the nondaily press exists only to serve the interests of advertisers, not of readers.

The emergence of desktop publishing technology has drastically reduced the cost of entry into the newspaper market. Anyone can now compose and make up a newspaper on a shoestring and have it printed by a job press. But the publisher of a small shopper who wants to turn it into a daily in a metropolitan center is not easily going to develop technical solutions to the problems of mass distribution. It is certainly not in the interest of any established paper to make life easy for new would-be competitors. Yet it is in the *collective* interest of the newspaper business to develop and disseminate the technology that facilitates such market entry, because an increase in the number of daily papers in the market will spur readership of newspapers generally and therefore spur the interest of advertisers in the press.

The question remains, Is the advertising marketplace large enough to support more daily newspapers in the metropolitan areas that have most of the people and most of the newspaper circulation? With $126 billion being spent on advertising in 1989, there should be enough money to go around, although it may mean less revenue for other competing media. A medium that is growing, feisty, exciting is going to get a bigger piece of the pie.

A century ago a publisher proclaimed that he was "almost disappointed" when his newspaper investment yielded a profit. He said, "I went into the *Daily News* not to make money, but to advocate principles." In today's hard cruel marketing world, newspapers that cannot make money will not be advocating principles for long. But more than ever, making money depends on having principles to advocate and on facing off with competitors who have principles too.

NOTE

1. See Leo Bogart, *Press and Public: Who Read What, When, Where and Why in American Newspapers* (Hillsdale, N.J.: Lawrence Erlbaum Associates, 1989), and *Preserving the Press: How Newspapers Mobilize to Keep Their Readers* (New York: Columbia University Press, 1990).

Commentary

Richard Harwood

The inauguration of President John F. Kennedy symbolized, as he said on that occasion, the coming to power of a "new generation of Americans—born in this century, tempered by war [and] disciplined by a hard and bitter peace . . . ." This generational change was not limited to politics and government, as I wrote in 1979 after revisiting islands in the Pacific where many of us had gone to war:

> Out of these Pacific wastes covering one-third of the surface of the earth, out of these islands with strange and half-forgotten names—Tulagi, Vella Lavella, Vona Vona, Kwajalein, Yap, Tarawa, Saipan, Bougainville—and out of Europe, too, came the young American men who were to dominate for decades the principal institutions of American life.
>
> They are the captains of Coca-Cola, Weyerhauser, Sears, Allied Chemical, J. P. Morgan, Pepsico, Citicorp, Chase Manhattan, First Chicago, Boeing, Lockheed, Chrysler, Ford, General Motors, Bank of America, TRW, American Airlines, Anheuser Busch, ITT, and dozens more. The labor unions, philanthropic foundations, newspapers, international banks, the Pentagon, the CIA, and political bodies of every description came under their control.
>
> They have been the last five presidents of the United States (if you count Carter's Naval Academy years). All were young naval officers and all of them (Carter excepted) did their time in the Pacific. In Congress even today, half the senators and 45 percent of the representatives are veterans of the war. Another number: of all men between the ages of 50 and 60 in the United States, 83 percent served in World War II.
>
> Most of them, of course, didn't make it to the mountaintop. They went back to farming and bartending and pumping gas and to the Legion Hall. Others are wheezing out their days in VA hospitals and rooming houses.
>
> Nevertheless, it all fits. The war is the tie that binds in the American establishment, the shared experience of the middle-aged American male. Their next common experience will be re-

tirement and death; their average age approaches 60 and already they are going off at the rate of 300,000 a year. But for now, they remain the Establishment which young journalists and sociologists seek always to discover.

Since that was written, we have had two more presidents, both veterans (Reagan being a special sort) of World War II. George Bush, another navy man, will be the last. The "torch has passed to a new generation of Americans," Kennedy said in 1961, and nowhere is that more evident than in the business of newspapers. The editors and publishers who were Kennedy's comrades or contemporaries and who have shaped American journalism and built its great institutions over the past thirty years have been overtaken by time—Allen Neuharth of Gannett; Bill Thomas of the *Los Angeles Times*; Eugene Patterson of Atlanta and St. Petersburg; Allen Gould and Wes Gallagher of the Associated Press; Ed Cony and Vermont Royster of the *Wall Street Journal*; Mark Ethridge of Louisville; John Knight, Lee Hills, and Alvah Chapman of Knight-Ridder; Harry Ashmore of Little Rock; Bill Attwood of *Newsday*; and Abe Rosenthal of the *New York Times*. Ben Bradlee of the *Washington Post*, John Quinn and John Siegenthaler of *USA Today*—possibly even Katharine Graham and Punch Sulzberger— are about a step behind.

These people brought to the enterprise of journalism life experiences—a common world view—that were clearly reflected in the newspapers they produced. They had participated in the emergence of the United States as a world power and were internationalist in their outlooks. They had fought in a war in which the rhetoric of freedom was dominant, and they were sensitized to issues of civil liberty and civil rights at home and around the world. They were exposed to scientific and technological change on a vast scale: revolutions in medical care, transportation, mass production, nuclear physics, agriculture, communication, and the exploration of space. They had seen an enormous expansion of educational opportunities in the United States, the creation of endless suburbs, the decline of the central cities, the turmoil of racial integration, new American wars, assassinations, riots, a cultural revolution, government scandal, an erosion of faith in the old American verities, and perhaps even an occasional loss of nerve.

The American newspaper industry today is, to a large extent, the product of the generation I described and of the social forces that have swept the world in the postwar years. These men and women have significantly raised the vocational standards of journalism, with the result that today the range, accuracy, fairness, and literary quality of the American press are unmatched in the world. They have tested and litigated the meaning of the First Amendment in important cases—the Pentagon Papers and *New York Times* v. *Sullivan,* for example—that have expanded press freedoms to an extraordinary degree. They have built on our major newspapers large foreign and national staffs whose work has made possible the creation of successful supplemental news services that provide diversity to newspapers around the world and that have brought competition to domestic and international reports once dominated by the wire services. They have presided, sometimes reluctantly and always cautiously, over the introduction of computer technology to news operations, a technological change that has had a profound influence on labor relations (strikes, for example, no longer pose an important threat to the industry) and on newspaper profits. They have encouraged the development of new communications and research systems and have created a host of new products—magazines, special sections, reference services, books, national and international editions. They have introduced the Standard Advertising Unit (SAU), which has contributed to improvements in newspaper graphics and design. They have also introduced, on a lavish scale in some cases, the use of "run of press" color in hundreds of newspapers.

Midcareer training is not yet commonplace, but it is more common than at any time in the past. The Nieman Fellowship program at Harvard, created in 1939, is now but one of several programs for the intellectual enrichment of journalists. Stanford, Columbia, Michigan, Massachusetts Institute of Technology, Maryland, and other universities have entered the business as well. At the same time, there has been an exponential expansion of formal journalism training in schools of higher learning; there were four schools of journalism in 1900, fifty-four in 1927, more than two hundred in 1971, and more than three hundred today with enrollments exceeding ninety thousand. In addition, graduate programs for future journalists in fields such as agriculture and the environment are being introduced at a number of schools.

Leo Bogart has emphasized the concern in the newspaper industry about the decline in regular readership as a percentage of the population. The problem is real and the concern is justified. Nevertheless, newspapers are incomparably more healthy in a financial sense than ever before. Eight newspaper companies last year had revenues exceeding $1 billion; their profit margins are spectacular. They have provided investors with average annual returns that are a multiple of the return on oil industry investments.

The market value of these companies, measured in terms of outstanding common stock prices, ranged in mid-1988 from roughly $2.2

to $2.6 billion (the *New York Times* and the *Washington Post*) to well over $5 billion (Gannett and Capital Cities). Investor confidence in the future of newspapers is reflected in the price run ups of newspaper stocks in recent years and in the investment patterns of newspaper companies themselves. They are buying back their own stock and spending billions on new plants and equipment. The *New York Times* has completed a $400 million printing facility with color capabilities in Edison, New Jersey; a $400 million expansion of this plant is scheduled for 1993. The *Washington Post* is planning a similar investment in the near future; the *Los Angeles Times* and *Chicago Tribune* recently completed very large expansion programs. Overall, newspapers invested $1.2 billion in new plant and equipment in 1987 and about $1.6 billion in 1988. And although the number of American newspapers has declined over the past eighty years from 2,600 to a little over 1,600, employment in the industry, including its newsrooms, has nearly doubled since the end of World War II.

What is now in place—the institutions and the people who run them—defines what the American newspaper will be through at least the first decade of the twenty-first century. The computers, printing presses, and other factory equipment now being installed or on order will determine the size, configuration, and color content of tomorrow's newspapers; the useful life of a press is at least twenty years. The editors and publishers newly in command will determine the content, range, and distribution patterns of their publications. The existing population and literacy levels, by and large, will determine the market size, because babies born hereafter will not reach the traditional newspaper-buying age until at least the second decade of the coming century.

What can we say about the new generation of leaders? First, they are fairly well-known commodities and given their present ages—early to mid-forties in most cases—their managerial careers have, on the average, twenty years or so to run. Most of them already have spent roughly twenty years in apprenticeship under the direction of the men and women they are replacing. They have acquired from these tutors habits of mind and taste and institutional values that will predispose them to produce the kinds of newspapers on which they have trained and which have proved thus far to be so financially successful. Some may wish to rebel against the departed "father figures" and produce radically different newspapers, but they will not be able to indulge that wish. They have been exposed, far more so than their predecessors at the same age, to the corporate values and financial imperatives of the "media giants" and "media conglomerates" that have engulfed the industry over the last twenty years. The newspaper is no longer a mom-and-pop operation responsive to the whims and quixotic impulses of eccentric individualists, including editors. The likes of Horace Greeley and James Gordon Bennett will not be seen again. In the corporate world where company values are calculated daily on the stock exchanges and where boards of directors, consultants, and the gurus of opinion and market research are major players in the decision-making process, innovation and change occur slowly.

For all these reasons it is highly unlikely that the content of the newspapers of 2010 will differ greatly from that of today's newspapers. The same trio of "national newspapers" we have today—the *Wall Street Journal*, the *New York Times*, and *USA Today* (if Gannett can get over the advertising hump)—will continue to exist. There will be a powerful newspaper in the nation's capital—the *Washington Post*—and a number of strong and conventional regional papers such as the *Philadelphia Inquirer, Los Angeles Times, Miami Herald, Baltimore Sun, Minneapolis Star Tribune, Des Moines Register, Dallas Morning News, Chicago Tribune, Newsday,* and *Boston Globe.*

These newspapers will continue to sustain the corps of foreign correspondents, but a significant expansion in its size is unlikely; the same will be true of the domestic bureaus these papers maintain. As a result, large expansions of the foreign and national news holes are unlikely. A greater emphasis on local news, meaning expanded staffs, news holes, and zoned editions, is likely. The trend toward specialization in newsrooms is likely to continue; more and more people will be hired with law and medical degrees and with graduate training in major areas of interest such as the environment, consumer affairs, and business and finance. Midcareer training will become more commonplace. White men already are a minority in some newsrooms, and that trend will continue; women within the next two or three decades may well be the new newsroom majority.

Greater sexual and ethnic diversity may affect newspaper content to some degree. But again, the principal executives of the major newspapers already are in place and, barring upheavals or turns of fortune beyond our knowing, will remain there into the next century: Donald Graham at the *Washington Post*; Arthur O. Sulzberger, Jr., at the *New York Times*; Chandler heirs at the *Los Angeles Times*; Jim Batten and Dave Lawrence at Knight-Ridder; Benjamin Taylor at the *Boston Globe*; and Jim Hoge at the *Tribune* Company. I hedge my bet by quoting an old colleague, Richard Wald of NBC:

> Because the mass media of our day are so big, there is a tendency
> to think of them as immutable. Because commerce and caution

have tended to make our media respectable, we think of them as unchanging institutions. Because the people who are important now seem so important, we think the basic points are settled. The truth, though, is that we are on the edge of change we can only dimly perceive.

Shoe, *by Jeff MacNelly (Reprinted with permission of Tribune Media Services)*

7

Unbundling the Daily Newspaper

William B. Blankenburg

Not everyone reads all of the newspaper all of the time. Nor do all advertisers want all of the readers all of the time. Having learned these lessons, publishers are responding with marketing strategies that subdivide the newspaper and its readers into segments. In large markets, the next temptation will be to take the newspaper apart and sell the right pieces to the right people. Some people will be left out.

The 1989 American Newspaper Publishers Association (ANPA) convention took the theme "Readership and Circulation," prompted by the long stagnation of daily circulation and a sense of urgency about retaining readers and advertisers. But how to go about it? Two years later the convention theme was "Reinventing How Newspapers Go to Market," and the ANPA chairman said newspapers should help people use information by "customizing and targeting the message to specific audiences."[1]

The alarms were real enough. The number of households in the United States increased more than 40 percent from 1970 to 1990, but daily circulation went up by only 1 percent. The ratio of copies to households has steadily declined since World War II.[2] In many communities, less than half of all households received a daily newspaper. In 1970, 78 percent of U.S. adults read a newspaper on a typical day. Twenty years later only 62 percent did.[3]

Today's subscribers are fickle. In some locales, the turnover rate of subscriptions is 100 percent a year. A 1987 study, aptly titled *Love Us and Leave Us*, found that subscribers liked their newspaper a lot, yet dropped it with ease. Only 53 percent of new subscribers in that study still took the paper at the end of a year. Among those who did subscribe, 14 percent skipped at least one issue a week even though they had paid for it. Nearly one-third said there were times when they didn't read an issue before the next one arrived.[4] In the 1980s, weekday editions grew 50 percent in number of pages, and the size of Sunday papers nearly doubled. But readers spent no more time with them than in the past.

These are sorry numbers for publishers, who make their money by selling readers to advertisers. In times past, their response was to blame the reader for faithlessness and then try out some new syndicated features. The daily newspaper became a bazaar of information and features because it was relatively cheap to add them in order to attract and keep readers. More readers meant more advertising at higher prices. In its bulk and variety, the daily newspaper was well suited to large, home-centered American families that had few diversions other than church and politics.

Today there are myriad diversions and many kinds of households. The whole newspaper is not needed or used. In the study mentioned above, the two most frequent reasons given for stopping subscriptions were "had no time to read" and "papers kept piling up." For many years publishers thought "lack of time" was merely a polite excuse. Now they take it seriously as meaning the newspaper is not worth taking the time to read. The rise of the "nontraditional family," meaning single parents or two earners with few kids, has been cited by Leo Bogart and others as fundamental to the circulation malaise.[5]

On the supply side, the price of newsprint rose sharply in the 1970s. It was $173 a ton in 1973, then $430 a ton in 1980. Ten years later it was about $650. Recycled paper cost even more. At such prices, it makes sense to give subscribers only those parts of the paper they want, and only when they want it.

This would mean unbundling the daily newspaper as we know it and fundamentally altering both its methods and character. Such a profound change seems to be under way, made possible by significant changes in technology and attitudes—the latter as crucial as the former. The oldest moral question in journalism asks how best to serve the readers: Should we give them what they want or what they ought to have? The argument has been resolved in favor of marketing. In February 1989, in Miami, representatives of 450 dailies convened to discuss "Keys to Success: Strategies for Newspaper Marketing in the '90s." Both God and Mammon attended. Editors were in the thick of it with circulation managers, advertising and marketing executives, and publishers. Attendees emphasized giving readers what they want, "not what we think they need to have," said the conference chairman, Phil de Montmollin of the *Miami Herald*.[6]

This attitude took hold around the country. It positively blossomed in Florida, where Knight-Ridder's *Boca Raton News* launched what it called the "25/43 Project" in October 1990. The redesigned *News* hoped to captivate readers twenty-five to forty-three years old by slicing and dicing and garnishing itself even more relentlessly than *USA*

Today. It was the product of $2 million worth of research, including a year of prototypes and twenty-one focus groups of readers and advertisers. Among its early features were a full page of weather data and a "Critter Watch" column about local beasties.

Something called the "total newspaper concept" was preached in the late 1970s, mainly by promotion managers, and was accepted widely in the 1980s. The idea was that all departments, including news, should pull together to sell the newspaper. Coordination became common, and cross-training made sense. For example, the editor of the *Billings Gazette* also became its circulation director.[7] Consultants came into vogue. Marketing committees emerged on most large newspapers. In early 1989 the *New York Times* announced a new marketing department "that will consolidate the paper's efforts in news, advertising, and circulation."[8]

As retail advertising sagged in the early 1990s, some companies added nontraditional information services, with fair success. In places as diverse as Baltimore and Cedar Rapids, newspapers offered "audiotex," voice information by telephone, sometimes in conjunction with other companies. Many such services—featuring restaurant reviews, sermon previews, and movie summaries, for example—were free, but publishers also joined the growing 900-number industry. The *New York Times* started "Clue Line" and charged readers for answers to the daily crossword puzzle. The weekly *Boston Phoenix* began a voice-mail system for people who would like to meet. This grew out of its classified personal ad section. By 1991, three hundred newspapers offered 900-number lines. Touch-tone telephones permitted interactive access to newspaper information, and with computers in about one-fifth of American homes, a revival of videotext seemed likely, allowing newspapers to sell information on demand, in tailored packages if desired.

Newspaper companies also branched further into delivery services, elaborating on the "total market coverage" (TMC) products they established many years before. In the 1970s such large, powerful advertisers as Sears and K Mart wanted saturation coverage of the newspaper's market. Publishers responded with TMC papers delivered free to homes that did not subscribe to their regular newspaper. The publishers hoped to keep these major advertisers from using direct mail or free "shoppers." Thus many newspaper companies found themselves in the throwaway business that they previously had scorned.

By the 1990s, a good many advertisers decided they did not want total market coverage at all. An upscale retailer, for example, might wish coverage in certain neighborhoods only. Such a retailer is tempted to use direct mail and catalogs instead of newpapers or TMC.

Rather than lose customers to Advo and other mass mailers, some publishers started their own alternate delivery systems, to bypass the mails. The new ADS could carry the old TMC publication and other products to specific neighborhoods.

This suits the rising number of advertisers who are target shooters. "Micromarketing is the media buzzword for the '90s," said *Advertising Age*. "The trend toward highly refined target marketing is a result of audience fragmentation."[9] Even grocery ads, once a newspaper staple, have become target-conscious. *Progressive Grocer* magazine reported that since the mid-1980s, the emphasis in supermarket advertising has shifted dramatically from newspapers to circulars, supplements, and mailers—all of which permit target marketing.[10]

In aid of targeting, firms like Claritas, of Alexandria, Virginia, sell "geodemographic" profiles of small regions. Using Claritas's "PRIZM" technique, marketers can carve the nation's 36,000 ZIP codes into forty neighborhood types, each with its own propensities.[11] Categories include "Norma Rae-Ville," "Old Yankee Rows," "Shotguns and Pickups," "Money and Brains," and "Blue-Blood Estates." Armed with knowledge about these specialized markets, an advertiser will seek a medium that can deliver on target. To such an advertiser, a traditional daily newspaper looks like a marketing blunderbuss.

Thus in the 1990s newspaper companies feel centrifugal forces pulling on their once-comprehensive daily product. One response has been to start new product lines, like audiotex and alternate delivery systems. Another response, now under way, is to take apart the traditional newspaper itself.

Some rudimentary tools of partitioning the daily newspaper have been in place for a long time: editorial sectioning and circulation zoning. Together, sectioning and zoning can target relatively small clusters of readers. A zoned edition is typically aimed at a set of suburbs or districts of an urban area. It contains some coverage of that area, perhaps in a four-page section, and carries some advertising to that area only, also in the special section. Target marketing creates pressure for even finer segmentation, and new technologies are making it possible.

With advanced presses and computer-aided pagination, editorial and advertising modifications during press runs will become more feasible. Sophisticated collation devices can assemble sections for particular neighborhoods. Adult carriers, who are rapidly supplanting the "little merchants," can provide reliable delivery. Computers help keep track of it all. Bar codes and scanners tell advertisers what sells, and where.

The Hartford Courant

Target Markets

West Hartford
Farmington Valley

Hartford (North)
Bloomfield

Hartford (South)

New Britain
Bristol
Southington

Enfield
Windsor Locks
Stafford

Middletown,
The Shore

East Hartford
Manchester
Vernon

Figure 8

As market research identified desirable audiences and their needs, the traditional newspaper developed special sections featuring content that is mutually attractive to the advertiser and the target audience. Hence the rise of whole pages in color devoted, say, to cooking artichokes. Albert Scardino, media writer for the *New York Times*, once mused on the rise of the food section: "Was that caused by an outbreak of concern about our dietary habits? . . . No, editors became aware through their advertising departments that grocery stores had become supermarkets and supermarkets had become their biggest advertisers. The big advertiser wanted compatible news wrapped around his ads. So we developed food sections."[12]

Beside the now-ubiquitous food, business, and science sections are pages on fitness, child-rearing, health, education, pop music, computers, and children's TV programming. In 1985, the *Orange County*

Register (California) started a Friday entertainment section, a tabloid with a regular photo spread on the youth nightclub scene.[13] In the 1990s it began covering shopping malls as a full-time beat. The *Register* abolished traditional beats—city hall, for example—in favor of such new assignments as relationships, making money, houses, learning, hobbies and pets, aging, and transportation.

The outburst of features on running shoes and home medical test kits and dead rock stars, *inter alia*, lent newspapers a frothy tone usually found in consumer magazines. These features and sections signify the adoption of marketing by dailies and remind us that advertising influences editorial content through symbiosis, not extortion.

Editors who may have squirmed in their new role as caterers were comforted by Ruth Clark, a market researcher with the firm of Yankelovich, Skelly, and White. In a 1979 study, Clark perceived that readers felt alienated, and she called for a "new social contract" with newspapers.[14] She reported hearing complaints of "cold, unfeeling writing." She said readers "want to know the editors and writers. They want stories told in terms of people and with human feeling, even compassion." She said readers were self-interested and craved good news as well as the bad. No matter that her sweeping advice was based on "focus-group" interviews with only 120 readers in only twelve cities. Her admonitions were widely hailed and implemented, for they were sponsored by the American Society of Newspaper Editors and they offered a plan of action. Thus ensued a new round of cheery, helpful feature stories and ads for the newspapers depicting genial editors and sensitive reporters.

In 1984 Clark was again hired to probe readers. This time she reported that they wanted hard news: facts about such things as health, technology, and science.[15] She attributed this rather sudden reversal of interest to domestic and foreign crises. She advised newspapers to go back to the basics. But editors who might have been relieved to hear this had a new problem—*USA Today*, born in 1982 wearing spangles and exuding bonhomie. Confronted with this new competitor, editors clung to upbeat features and adorned their pages with colorful graphics.

The addition of specialized content did not necessarily mean a reduction in traditional news, because newspapers increased substantially in bulk during the 1980s.

But space and money ebbed after the economic crash of 1987. More mergers among large retailers meant less advertising. Publishers identified three threats for the 1990s: fragmentation of media and markets, audience targeting, and "bypass." The last meant that retailers were finding ways to reach their customers without using newspapers—direct mail, telemarketing, coupons, and catalogs.[16] Frank A. Blethen, chief executive officer of the *Seattle Times*, explained: "The cost to advertisers of reaching a specific target audience through the newspaper is climbing, while the costs for reaching a far more tightly defined audience directly are rising at a much slower rate."

So now the newspaper business is at a point when advertisers can seek specific audiences by alternative means, when newsprint is increasingly expensive to buy and dispose of, when readers are irregular, and when content is shaped by marketing teams.

The stage is set to break down the form and functions of larger dailies. The result is likely to be a basic package with options, like an automobile or cable TV. Most readers will be able to buy what they want, but some will be excluded.

To glimpse the emerging daily, think about the present Sunday newspaper, a compendium of attractions that has long shelf life and special pricing and availability. Spot news is a relatively small part of its content and appeal. Bogart describes the Sunday paper as "the model for successful segmentation of the newspaper audience." It is also the prototype of the unbundled daily newspaper, at least as to pricing and delivery. It is sold separately from other days, or in a variety of combinations. This suggests the possibility of home delivery in any combination of days the customer wants. The *Toronto Star* began doing this in the 1970s after perceiving a special demand for Wednesday (food) and Saturday (weekend) editions. Computers and adult carriers make this feasible. George Cashau, vice-president/technical for ANPA, forecast that in the 1990s "customers will call by touch-tone phones to numbers published in the previous day's newspaper for specialized sections or deletion of certain sections in an otherwise tailored product."[17]

Unbundling delivery is one thing; unbundling content is another. The many-faceted Sunday paper is comprehensive in the sum of its parts. To sell the parts separately is tempting, yet dangerous for a publisher. Doing so would save newsprint and attract dedicated subscribers but it might mean forsaking a broad franchise. Therefore a core of general news and features will remain. The extent of this core is uncertain because its domain has been invaded. Bogart points out that television lops off the audience for "big" stories. At the other end of the scale, urban and suburban weeklies, many circulating free, cover Little League and chicken dinners.

Steering through these shoals, editors will maintain a package of news for general distribution: major news from a distance, consequen-

General-Circulation Newspapers Published in New York City

Paper	Circulation: 1949	1990[a]
New York Times	543,943	1,108,447
Daily News	2,254,644	1,097,693
New York Post	366,286	510,219
Staten Island Advance	38,911	76,006
Mirror	1,020,879	Ceased publication 1963
Journal-American	707,195	Combined in 1966 to form the
World-Telegram	373,034	World Journal Tribune, which
New York Herald-Tribune	340,430	ceased publication in 1967
Sun	294,128	Ceased publication 1950[b]
Long Island Press	151,602	Ceased publication 1977
Brooklyn Eagle	130,479	Ceased publication 1955
Long Island Star-Journal	79,709	Ceased publication 1968

The 10 suburban papers with the highest circulation in 1990

Paper	Circulation: 1949	1990[a]
Newsday Melville, L.I.	96,421	714,128[c]
The Star-Ledger Newark, N.J.	163,658	476,257
Asbury Park Press Neptune, N.J.	22,088	159,629
Record Hackensack, N.J.	43,896	159,550
North Jersey Herald and News Passaic, N.J.	50,235	88,113
Times Herald-Record Middletown, N.Y.	10,155	85,607
Daily Record Parsippany, N.J.	9,123	54,708
Central New Jersey Home News New Brunswick, N.J.	27,212	53,011
Jersey Journal Jersey City, N.J.	49,998	52,205
News Tribune Woodbridge, N.J.	24,952	51,800

[a] Preliminary figures subject to audit; 6 month average circulation for the period ended September 30, 1990.
[b] The Sun merged with the World-Telegram in 1950.
[c] Includes New York Newsday, with a circulation of 230,000 in 1990.

Sources: Editor and Publisher, 1950 and 1990; N.W. Ayer and Son's Directory, Newspapers and Periodicals, 1950; Audit Bureau of Circulation; New Jersey Herald and News.

Figure 9

tial news from nearby, and human-interest features of wide appeal. These topics could constitute one section supported by the kind of advertisers who seek a broad reach.

Beyond this general section begins the tailoring. The fineness of the fit will depend on technology and advertisers. Existing sections could subdivide the sports section into women's or prep or pro sports only for delivery to those who want it or to those who are wanted by advertisers. Considerable opportunity awaits syndicators who can supply highly focused material, and a cost advantage will accrue to chains that share specialized content among their papers.

Apprehensive publishers have opportunities for both retreat and growth. They can diversify into weeklies and shoppers, thereby joining the trend that nags them. They could even start new dailies, as suggested by Leo Bogart and Christine Urban at the 1989 ANPA convention. Their point was that the general-circulation daily is missing certain segments of the audience, leaving a demand unserved. Urban said that if an existing newspaper operates in a market with two distinct population segments, such as white-collar and blue-collar, "then you've got to have two separate products."[18] This would be much the same as unbundling the present comprehensive newspaper into two demographically focused dailies. But why stop at two segments? The newspaper will become as divisible as the market itself. If the newspapers of the 1990s follow a cable-TV model, a basic subscription will provide the main news section and perhaps a section that lists scores, vital statistics, and coming events. The reader who wants more may get some sections free of charge, courtesy of advertisers who like his or her market profile. Other sections will bear their own subscription prices, like pay-TV channels.

As they grope their way toward the millennium, publishers can continue to lobby against telephone companies that want to generate and distribute information and advertising, or they can join them as suppliers. Cooperation is likely, and it will inspire publishers to distinguish more clearly their business lines: creation, selection, production, and distribution of information. These, too, can be unbundled, resulting, perhaps, in a publisher who gathers information but no longer prints and distributes it, or vice versa.

Whether all this will be good for society depends on your feelings about economy, democracy, and authority. Surely a reduction of waste newsprint would be good for the environment, and the cost savings could be shared with consumers. But tailoring content trims the civic menu and thwarts the serendipity that rewards the browser.

A shift of sovereignty to the consumer, which marketing professes to promote, is democratic on its face and may be a shield against an authoritarian publisher.

And yet we want authority from the news media, though we would prefer to call it leadership. Here is the paradox. We complain about the agenda-setting power of the big media but fear that trivialization due to marketing may be even worse. The traditional newspaper has been prodigal toward its readers and optimistic that they could sort things out. An editor's guesses about what the readers wanted and needed produced a stew more nourishing than the marketer's confections.

In the 1990s the diversity of content will be greater than ever, but it will not be available to everyone. Segmentation allows exclusion as well as inclusion. Claritas's "Norma Rae-Ville," "Hard Scrabble," and "Public Assistance" neighborhoods are candidates for red lining. The process that brings readers what they want is likewise a process that shuts out readers who are not wanted.

NOTES

1. M. L. Stein, "Upbeat Advice Against a Gloomy Backdrop," *Editor and Publisher* (May 11, 1991): 12.
2. These and other trends are presented in the work of Leo Bogart. In particular see *Press and Public*, 2d ed. (Hillsdale, N.J.: Erlbaum, 1989).
3. Mary Alice Bagby, "Transforming Newspapers for Readers," *Presstime* (April 1991): 19.
4. Virginia Dodge Fielder and Beverly A. Barnum, *Love Us and Leave Us: New Subscribers One Year Later* (Reston, Va.: American Society of Newspaper Editors, 1987).
5. Bogart, *Press and Public*, 18.
6. "Circulation Summit in Miami Focuses on Giving Readers What They Want," *Presstime* (March 1989): 25.
7. This happened on four dailies and was discontinued after a few years. "'Editor as Circulator' Ends Run," *Presstime* (June 1989): 66.
8. *"New York Times* Reorganization," *Editor and Publisher* (April 1, 1989): 16.
9. "Media Moving toward More Precise Targets," *Advertising Age* (March 27, 1989): 48.
10. "1988 Nielsen Review of Retail Grocery Store Trends," *Progressive Grocer* (October 1988).
11. "Your ZIP Tells a Tale on You," *Boston Globe*, November 22, 1989.
12. "Press Critics Criticize," *Editor and Publisher* (April 15, 1989): 14.
13. "Luring the Young: For Papers, Generation Is Missing," *Los Angeles Times*, March 15, 1989.
14. Ruth Clark, *Changing Needs of Changing Readers* (Reston, Va.: American Society of Newspaper Editors, 1979).
15. American Society of Newspaper Editors, *Proceedings of the 1984 Convention* (Washington, D.C., 1985): 107–21.
16. "Telecommunications Technology Beckons, but Is It a Boon or a Bane?" *Presstime* (May 1989): 56–57.
17. "Newspapers in the Year 2000 Envisioned," *Editor and Publisher* (June 23, 1990): 28.
18. "Newspapers Should Start New Papers," *Presstime* (May 1989): 44.

8

News Workers and Newsmakers

Douglas Gomery

The latter half of the twentieth century will be remembered for the emergence of the news reporter as media star. There have always been famous columnists—the Walter Winchells and Joseph Alsops—but few of them achieved the fame and fortune of today's media stars who command national television audiences and salaries well in excess of $1 million a year.

In the past it was assumed that the typical news reporter could identify with the average citizen because they lived in similar neighborhoods and their children went to the same schools. No longer. Reporters like Jack Nelson, Cokie Roberts, Jack Germond, and Roger Ebert are recognized and ogled in public as if they were professional athletes or movie stars.

No wonder thousands of college and university students jam classes in journalism. The numbers are staggering. The Association for Education in Journalism and Mass Communication estimates that throughout the 1980s between 15,000 and 20,000 college seniors graduated each year with a degree in journalism. Approximately half found work in the media—in newspapers, television, and increasingly in public relations. But becoming a public relations "flack" is hardly what the aspiring journalist has in mind when signing up for a course in investigative reporting or broadcast news. No, the goal is to become the next Bob Woodward or Connie Chung.

The odds of achieving that goal are exceedingly low. According to Department of Labor estimates, between 1970 and 1980 only 45,000 persons were hired to be newspaper reporters in the United States, most for community papers like the *Augusta* (Kansas) *Daily Gazette*, not the *Washington Post* or the *New York Times*. New positions opening up each year in broadcast journalism in cities larger than Milwaukee or Omaha can be counted on the fingers of two hands. Rod Gelatt, chairman of the broadcast news department at the University of Missouri, has estimated that only two-thirds of the students who sign up for his prestigious program ever get jobs in the news media.

What, then, is the future for the nearly 200,000 graduates of journalism and mass communications programs, as well as the thousands more with degrees in history, political science, communications, and English who aspire to join the fourth estate?

The salaries for the average news worker are lower than might be expected. In the 1980s, in all but the twenty-five biggest markets the typical salary of a radio newscaster never went above $20,000, while the TV anchors there earned less than $30,000. Median salaries for rank-and-file reporters were about $20,000 for TV and $15,000 for radio. It is the top scale that keeps students flocking to small-town stations so they can gain experience and move to a station in the top twenty-five, where the average television anchor earns about $75,000.

When print reporters join the staff of a certain handful of newspapers, they are often told they must join a union, frequently the Newspaper Guild. (Those exempted from union membership usually work under union-negotiated contracts.) The guild has helped seasoned *New York Times* reporters earn more than $50,000 a year, but the guarantees at the *Chattanooga Times*, the *Utica* (New York) *Observer-Dispatch*, and the *Massillon* (Ohio) *Independent* barely reach $20,000 a year. Salaries for beginning reporters are far less. Those at nonunion papers are no higher, either for beginners or for experienced reporters.

At papers with Newspaper Guild contracts the number of entry-level staff is determined by the number of "journeyman" positions. Papers cannot add a low-paid beginner to the staff until an experienced reporter leaves—no openings, no jobs, even if the aspiring journalist is willing to work for almost nothing. Moreover, because salaries are set by Newspaper Guild contract, the fresh journalism graduate is in a "take it or leave it" position. Such provisions may protect long-time workers, but in a world of eager, aspiring "Woodsteins," the Newspaper Guild, a union of professional writers, and the largest union of reporters, seems almost out of place. The thousands of university-trained reporters of the 1980s do not want job security—they want a chance to become media stars.

Thus it is not surprising to learn that although 400,000 people worked in the newspaper industry as the 1980s drew to a close, the Newspaper Guild claimed only 34,000 members. Nearly half worked in the business as reporters, photographers, librarians, or artists (the creative side), while the others handled more mundane tasks in advertising sales or accounting.

From its headquarters in suburban Silver Spring, Maryland, eight long miles from the corridors of Washington power, the Newspaper Guild oversees some eighty local guild chapters, with contracts at 150 news organizations in the United States and Canada. The union also serves as the bargaining agent at *Time* and *Newsweek*, as well as at the two major wire services, the Associated Press and United Press International.

The problem of Newspaper Guild leaders is that they are representing elite white-collar workers who want access to fame and fortune, not just job security and an adequate wage. Moreover, the economics of the media business are such that the guild has less bargaining power than at any time in its nearly sixty-year history. With computerization, newspaper supervisory personnel can operate the necessary electronic equipment and automatic presses so that, in the event of a strike, the paper can still publish, albeit in a somewhat smaller version. Only the drivers, who transport the papers from the publishing plant to the carriers, can truly bring a large metropolitan daily to its knees, and the drivers are not members of the Newspaper Guild.

As a consequence, although the newspaper industry, in particular large monopoly papers in major cities, has earned substantial profits, the leadership of the Newspaper Guild has had to accept contracts that, despite their best efforts, deliver few benefits that nonunion reporters do not also enjoy. It is not from lack of effort. During the summer of 1988, for example, after months of negotiations, the Washington-Baltimore chapter of the Newspaper Guild launched an offensive against the *Washington Post* that included a "byline" strike, in which reporters withheld their names from articles; a wave of formal complaints to the National Labor Relations Board; and additional filings of race, sex, and age discrimination complaints to the appropriate agencies. Still, contract negotiations dragged on until August 1989, and the agreement ultimately signed was far closer to what management had in mind than what the Newspaper Guild demanded.

Indeed, the trend has been toward the elimination of newspaper jobs. Whenever a new owner assumes control of an existing newspaper, the deal usually calls for the elimination of a specified number of editorial and other positions. When Rupert Murdoch, for example, sold the *New York Post* to Peter Kalikov in 1988, part of the sales agreement called for the elimination of 130 positions. The economic principle is simple. As more and more daily papers become de facto monopolies, the primary goal of management is not to increase sales but to reduce costs.

As Eric Philo, newspaper specialist for Wall Street's Goldman Sachs, put it, "The [*New York Daily*] *News* does about $450 million in revenue and just about breaks even. . . . If the *News* could save $40 or $50 million in labor costs, it could get a 10 percent operating margin."

This tough anti-union stance represents the latest U.S. import from Britain. In 1986, in a highly publicized, dramatic confrontation, Murdoch, owner of the *Times* of London and several mass-circulation British papers, took on the powerful British press unions at "Fortress Wapping," the modern printing plant he had built behind a moat and barbed wire in a former dock area of London. For years it had been assumed that the British unions would win any battle over the introduction of new technology that cost workers their jobs. But Murdoch held fast and the unions eventually backed down.

Fortress Wapping became a model for American newspapers. James Hoge, publisher of the *New York Daily News*, took his executives to England to see what Murdoch had wrought. Hoge later commented, "The main thing we learned is that getting management control of the production and distribution operation allows for all the things we want at the *Daily News*—papers that come off the presses on time every night and are delivered on time every morning."

The truth about the modern newspaper is that although reporters see themselves as the heart and soul of the enterprise, management thinks that reporters make little difference in the bottom line. One or two writers might have to be pampered, but the typical reporter can easily be replaced by one of the thousands of recent journalism school graduates at a rock-bottom wage. The modern newspaper business has become one of creating an attractive editorial package to compete effectively with television for advertising dollars. A competent graphic artist or layout designer is as important as a skillful city hall reporter.

Ironically, although Woodward and Bernstein may be more famous than TV newsman Gordon Peterson, of Washington, D.C., or Jerry Dunphy, of Los Angeles, those two local news anchors, and many others around the nation, are paid far more and have vastly greater bargaining power. TV creates stars far more effectively than any newspaper, even a *New York Times* or a *Washington Post*.

As the 1980s drew to a close there was a move to make some news readers the stars of their own prime-time television programs. The Diane Sawyers and Sam Donaldsons of television do not pursue or dig up news stories but, rather, "perform" dramatic interviews, read lines written for them, and awkwardly try to ad-lib intelligently on shows like "Yesterday, Today, and Tomorrow" (NBC), "Primetime Live" (ABC), and "Saturday Night With Connie Chung" (CBS).

Television news has long had its stars, from Chet Huntley to Walter Cronkite and Barbara Walters, but until the late 1980s they operated within the bounds of accepted journalistic conventions. With the rise of Fox's "A Current Affair" (a direct clone of a popular Rupert Murdoch show in Australia), the networks (all with new owners) have been inspired to create offerings structured around their star personalities, following the same principle as "The Tonight Show," starring Johnny Carson and Jay Leno.

This "news making as show business" has long troubled network and local news departments. Being a skilled reporter ceases to be a path to success. Good looks, skill at reading scripts, and the ability to express emotion on the air become valuable traits and the requisite characteristics of stardom. Reviews of these programs speak of "chemistry" in the same terms that might have been used to praise a Hepburn-Tracy comedy. These shows function as star vehicles in the Hollywood tradition of Charlie Chaplin, Mary Pickford, and Joan Crawford.

The Deborah Norville–Jane Pauley affair of 1989, in which the mid-twenties blonde Norville replaced the late-thirties brunette Pauley on NBC's "Today" show, illustrates how important the star system has become to the news business. After the tears and travail passed, many outsiders cynically asked, "Why would the choice of a news reader and interviewer be so important to a huge network like NBC?" The answer surely did nothing to gladden the hearts of American feminists. The word spreading through NBC hallways was that the news division had a new motto: "Stop the ratings slide with peroxide." Jon Katz, former executive producer of "CBS Morning News," analyzed the situation this way: "The people who make the decisions in network news are all white middle-aged men, and in their desperate attempt to keep audiences from shrinking, they've turned to the Hollywood star system of the 1930s, to the era of dazzling blondes such as Jean Harlow."

By the same criteria, newspaper reporters whose looks qualify them for TV success seek "proper vehicles" for exposure on television. Cokie Roberts is America's most famous congressional correspondent, not for her fine work on National Public Radio, but for her appearances on ABC-TV. Jack Nelson, Washington bureau chief of the *Los Angeles Times*, once was rejected as a speaker because an unknowing booker insisted on the Jack Nelson of "Washington Week in Review" (PBS), unaware that they were one and the same. Jack Germond, distinguished columnist of the *Baltimore Sun*, is far better known as the foil for John McLaughlin on the latter's talk show than he is as a columnist. Chicago-based movie reviewers Roger Ebert and Gene Siskel are surely the best-known movie writers in the United States. Thousands have read their columns, but millions have seen their long-running TV show.

The path to wealth and recognition—equal to that of any movie or TV star—is for a print journalist to make regular appearances on television, not to publish exposés in the style of Woodward and Bernstein. News work changed fundamentally in the latter half of the twentieth century as the star system came to dominate. News workers have now become newsmakers.

9

From the Heartland

Jean Folkerts

In 1916, William Allen White, editor of the *Emporia* (Kansas) *Gazette*, rated the *Kansas City Star*, the *Chicago Tribune*, and the *St. Paul Pioneer Press* as three of the top ten newspapers in the United States. If an editor less committed to the Republican Party than White had been making the selection, newspapers such as the *St. Louis Post-Dispatch* and the *Milwaukee Journal* also might have ranked among the top ten.

Throughout this century, a number of midwestern metropolitan newspapers have earned a reputation for excellence. They have often been owned by outspoken, independent publishers who challenged corruption and championed civil service reform, public ownership of utilities, and increased city services. These newspapers were integrally involved with their developing cities. Some favored Republican politics, some Democratic, and some, such as the *Kansas City Star*, professed an independent stand in the mugwump tradition. (By the 1930s the *Star* had become strongly Republican.) During the early twentieth century, when presidents and members of Congress wanted to test grass-roots sentiment—to know how the typical voter thought the republic was faring—they consulted the editors of these newspapers.

Although today's critics often measure journalistic quality against eastern circulation leaders such as the *Washington Post*, the *New York Times*, and the *Boston Globe*, only about 2.25 million of the nation's 63 million readers see one of those newspapers. Other metropolitan dailies, small-town newspapers, and community weeklies make up the bulk of America's newspaper circulation. These are the newspapers that affect local politics and wield influence in state legislatures and congressional elections.

Despite the readership figures, newspapers on the eastern seaboard are far more often seen as leaders than are midwestern papers. Do presidents and members of Congress still consult the local newspapers for political sentiment or are they more influenced by eastern seaboard newspapers? What is the current state of newspapers in the nation's heartland? Are they economically and editorially healthy?

Critics have argued that, with the continuing transition to chain ownership and a desire for increased profits, newspaper editors have sacrificed hard news for feature fluff.

During the past ten years, the growth of suburban, or community, newspapers in cities such as Detroit, Chicago, and Cleveland has more than offset the decline of metropolitan dailies. Many of these suburban newspapers are investing heavily in coverage of traditional local news, such as local sports and school board news. At the same time, many of the leading midwestern papers have grown, paid less attention to specific local audiences, and converted to chain ownership. With these changes, large midwestern dailies have sacrificed not hard news but devoted community audiences, and suburban newspapers and small-town papers struggle to compete with the large dailies for advertising dollars based on cost per thousand readers. Some large, midwestern newspapers have abandoned their commitment to metropolitan improvement and have chosen to compete with the eastern leaders from a nationally based concept of news.

The *Chicago Tribune*, for example, considers itself to be a national, rather than a local, newspaper. Its Washington bureau of about twenty-three is headed by a bureau chief who has never worked in the Midwest. A former member of a *Tribune* Pulitzer prize-winning team, Kathleen Burns, notes that the *Tribune* used to emphasize local coverage, especially through a triweekly supplement called *The Trib*, staffed by young, aggressive reporters. However, the triweekly was dropped several years ago and has not been replaced with a solid metro supplement.

Because the major midwestern papers have long been independent voices, the switch to group ownership has often provoked intense resistance from media critics and subscribers. Of the midwestern leaders, only the *St. Louis Post-Dispatch* and the *Milwaukee Journal* remain independent. The *Kansas City Star* and *Kansas City Times* lost their independent status in 1977 when they were bought by Capital Cities. In 1985 Gannett acquired the *Des Moines Register* and Tribune Company as well as the *Detroit News*; Gannett and the *Washington Post* Company own stock in the Minneapolis *Star Tribune*.

Because the change to group ownership often is accompanied by new management styles and attention to market research, reporters can easily become alienated from management and echo the sentiments of those who decry group ownership. Newspapers in midwestern cities have encountered many of the same problems that have plagued newspapers throughout the country, and cities such as Milwaukee have been severely affected by a lagging economy. Furthermore, the decline of big-city afternoon papers has accelerated, with Detroit's afternoon paper surviving only on the basis of a joint operating agreement under review by the U.S. Supreme Court.

The quality of midwestern newspapers is not specifically related to group ownership or to management dependence on market research, but quality is related to size, and midwestern newspapers tend to have fewer pages than their counterparts in the rest of the nation. The smaller size realistically reflects a smaller retail base, and therefore a smaller advertising base, than is the case for major metropolitan dailies on either seaboard.

Midwestern newspaper editors should be credited for fairness, but most rely too much on wire copy and generate too little staff-written copy. Limited resources are a major reason for wire-service dependence among smaller newspapers. Publishers such as Bruce Buchanan of the *Parsons* (Kansas) *Sun* recognize that only a small portion of their readers subscribe to a larger newspaper. Buchanan therefore feels obligated to provide the readers of his 7,500-circulation newspaper with some national news. His most convenient and cheapest source of national news, given his limited subscriber base, is a standard wire service. Buchanan's affiliation with the Harris Group gains him access to a statewide group-owned wire, which provides thorough state coverage.

Owners of the leading midwestern papers have upgraded graphics and tried to broaden the appeal of their front pages. In many cases, group ownership has improved the product, but at a cost to the newspaper's identification with its own community. If these midwestern leaders are losing their influence, such a loss may be attributable not to lower quality but to a lack of direction. In abandoning their strong city orientations and commitment to local improvements, metropolitan midwestern leaders try to compete on a national basis with the *New York Times* and the *Washington Post*, and in doing so they sacrifice their traditional strength as regional voices.

Objective measures of newspaper quality include polls, prizes awarded, and scientific analyses of broad samples of newspapers. Polls and prizes tend to recognize larger and historically popular newspapers. Quantitative analyses of random samples provide broader and more complete information about newspapers in general but little information about a particular newspaper over time. In a content analysis of 114 newspapers in 1984, Stephen Lacy, an associate professor at Michigan State University, analyzed such factors as circulation, relationship of local news to circulation size, and percentage of the news hole dedicated to national, international, and local news. His goal was to devise an objective method for measuring the quality of newspapers and to eliminate subjective factors. The results of his analysis allow some comparisons among regions, among independent versus group-owned papers, and among papers of various sizes.[1]

Comparing twenty-eight midwestern newspapers with eighty-six others from around the United States, Lacy found that newspapers in the Midwest tended to be smaller than the national sample, and that most of the regional differences were accounted for by size rather than by geography. Larger newspapers with greater resources consistently ranked higher in all quality measures used. Nevertheless, after circulation differences were taken into account, some significant differences in news content remained. Midwestern newspapers allocated less space for staff-written stories, hard news, photos, and graphics, and allocated a greater percentage of the news hole to wire copy. Stories appearing in midwestern newspapers, particularly hard-news stories, were shorter than those in the national sample.

In another analysis—to compare independent newspapers with those that belonged to a newspaper group—Lacy and Frederick Fico, also of Michigan State University, devised a newspaper quality index based on a survey of 746 daily newspaper editors conducted by Leo Bogart in 1977.[2] In the Lacy-Fico index, a newspaper was considered to be of "higher" quality if it carried a high ratio of staff-written copy to wire service and nonlocal feature copy, and a high ratio of illustrations to text. Staff-written copy indicates that the newspaper is generating independent, usually locally based copy instead of relying on wire service boilerplate. A high ratio of illustrations usually indicates a graphically attractive paper.

In the 1977 survey, editors said a commitment to publish local copy over wire copy represented a concern for local audiences, which they regarded as the primary reason for publishing a newspaper. News interpretation and background information, or attempts to put the news in context, took priority over spot-news coverage. Longer front-page news stories also earned points for providing context. In addition, newspapers were given points for subscribing to a large number of supplementary news services and for maintaining a high ratio of nonadvertising to advertising copy. Supplementary wire and news services provide a wider range of information from which editors can choose to give a complete and accurate account of the day's news. The amount of copy produced by each reporter and the total amount of nonadvertising copy also were considered.

Applying these criteria, midwestern newspapers had a lower news quality index than the typical newspaper in the national sample. Mid-

Newspaper (City, year founded)	Audited Circulation		
	1980	1985	1990
NY Amsterdam News (New York, 1909)	81,200	50,000	31,584
Michigan Chronicle (Detroit, 1936)	41,712	32,000	24,516
L.A. Sentinel (Los Angeles, 1933)	34,100	29,356	23,886
Afro-American (Baltimore, 1892)	26,400	12,500	11,614
Mobile Beacon (Mobile, Ala., 1954)	7,560	4,678	4,672
Louisiana Weekly (New Orleans, 1926)	17,370	9,600	4,651

Declining Readership at Some Black Weeklies

Source: Editor and Publisher

Figure 10

Courtesy the Wall Street Journal

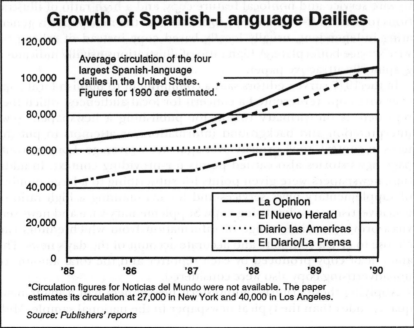

Growth of Spanish-Language Dailies

Average circulation of the four largest Spanish-language dailies in the United States. Figures for 1990 are estimated.

— La Opinion
- - - El Nuevo Herald
...... Diario las Americas
·—··— El Diario/La Prensa

*Circulation figures for Noticias del Mundo were not available. The paper estimates its circulation at 27,000 in New York and 40,000 in Los Angeles.

Source: Publishers' reports

Courtesy the New York Times

Figure 11

western papers rely more on wire services and spend less money on staff-generated stories than do newspapers across the nation. The reliance on wire copy also may explain the higher emphasis on spot news, rather than on news background and interpretation.

In a 1986 study of the fairness of local, controversial, bylined stories about law enforcement, government, education, and business, Lacy, Fico, and Todd Simon found that metropolitan midwestern newspapers rated high. In a study of twenty-one newspapers, the *Minneapolis Star Tribune* tied for third place, the *St. Louis Post-Dispatch* ranked fourth, the *Cleveland Plain Dealer* ranked fifth, and the *Detroit News* ranked seventh. At the bottom of the rankings were the *Chicago Tribune* and the *Chicago Sun Times*. Lacy and his colleagues counted the number of controversial stories published in a given week and computed the percentage of stories that reported two sides of an issue or dispute.[3]

In the Lacy and Fico studies, whether a newspaper was group-owned or independent, privately held or public, had no systematic effect on news quality, but some of the data do reflect on the midwestern newspapers. Capital Cities, owner of the *Kansas City Star*, ranked fifth in news quality among fifteen newspaper groups studied. Gannett, owner of the *Des Moines Register* and the *Detroit News*, ranked seventh. Knight-Ridder, owner of the *Detroit Free Press*, was not included in the sample.[4] At the bottom of the rankings were Stauffer Communications, Ottoway Newspapers, Lee Newspapers, and Thomson Newspapers. Both Thomson and Stauffer have significant holdings in the Midwest. The quality of the particular group has significantly more effect on newspaper quality than does the mere fact of group ownership.

Complementing the kind of quantitative data gathered by Lacy, Fico, and Simon are various surveys of editors, publishers, and educators—a subjective technique at best. William Allen White, for example, would never have included the *Post-Dispatch* in his list of the top ten newspapers because he hated the Pulitzer family, despised Missouri Democratic politics, and regarded sensationalism as cheap trickery of the reader.

Nevertheless, such surveys from 1960 to 1984 have consistently placed the *Chicago Tribune*, owned by the *Tribune* Company, and the independent *Milwaukee Journal* and *St. Louis Post-Dispatch* in the top ten. During that same period, despite some changes in their relative positions, the *Kansas City Star* and *Times*, *Chicago Daily News*, *Des Moines Register*, *Minneapolis Star Tribune*, *Chicago Sun Times*, and *Detroit Free Press* have consistently ranked in the top ten or twenty newspapers in the country.

Another measure of quality is the number of Pulitzer prizes and Sigma Delta Chi awards a newspaper and its staff have received. These honors are not free from bias. Critics charge, for example, that Pulitzer prize judges tend to be far too representative of the eastern establishment. Pulitzers, of course, except for the medal for meritorious public service, which goes directly to a newspaper, are awarded to individuals. An exceptional person can lend distinction to an otherwise undistinguished newspaper, as photographer Brian Lanker did for the Stauffer-owned *Topeka Capital Journal* in 1973. Also, obscure newspapers win Pulitzers as well. If Pulitzer prize winning were the sole criterion of excellence, papers like the *Hungry Horse News* in Columbia Falls, Montana, and the *Hutchinson News* in Kansas would make the top ten list.

Despite the drawbacks of using awards such as the Pulitzers as measures of quality, consistent award winning generally indicates that a newspaper is willing to grant time and resources to reporters and photographers who are trained and eager to turn a good idea into a great story. An analysis of Pulitzer prizes given since 1950 reveals that the *Chicago Tribune* has received the most awards (twelve) of any midwestern newspaper, winning in a variety of categories including reporting, commentary, editorial writing, and editorial cartoons. The *Des Moines Register* also ranks well, earning ten Pulitzers, most recently in 1985 and 1987. The *Register* has been particularly successful in the category of national reporting, winning six Pulitzers in this category since 1954. The *Chicago Tribune* and the *Des Moines Register* (formerly *Register* and *Tribune*) both were ranked among the top ten U.S. newspapers by *Time* magazine in 1984. *Time* used as its criteria imaginative staff coverage of regional, national, and foreign issues; liveliness in writing, layout, and graphics; national influence achieved through general enterprise; and command of some particular field of coverage or a track record of training top-ranked younger journalists. *Time* clearly used national focus as a major criterion, chiding the *Chicago Tribune* for lack of influence outside its own circulation area.

The records of the *Kansas City Star* and *Times*, the *Milwaukee Journal*, the *St. Louis Post-Dispatch*, and the *Detroit Free Press* have been less illustrious but certainly not shabby. The *Star* earned three awards since 1950 and shared one with the *Times*. Its last Pulitzer was in 1982. The *Journal* won three, the last in 1977; the *Post-Dispatch* won five—the most recent in 1972 except for its 1989 photo award, earned by a nonstaff furniture salesman for his first published picture. The *Free Press* also won six awards, including a 1990 photo award.

Objective measures of quality—quantitative analyses, polls, and prizes—indicate that midwestern newspapers could be better but have not deteriorated as much as their detractors claim. Why, then, is there a perception of decline that prompts critics to question the quality of these newspapers? The answer may lie in the recent trend toward chain ownership, which seems to be at odds with the midwestern newspaper's traditional close community ties.

Changes in ownership clearly affect how a community views a local newspaper. Chain or group ownership often signals the importation of reporters from other regions of the country to the local paper—reporters who are alien to a community's culture and politics.

The *Kansas City Star*, for example, known as an independent voice in part because it had been employee-owned since 1926, was so capital-poor by 1976 that it had little choice but to sell out to Capital Cities for $125 million. Capital Cities immediately brought in a new publisher, James H. Hale, who was born, reared, and trained in Texas. Hale brought new management to all divisions of the company—editorial, production, circulation, and advertising.

Hale replaced W. W. Baker, the fifty-eight-year-old president and editor of the *Star*, who had started with the paper as a reporter in 1947. Resigning a month after Baker left was executive editor Cruise Palmer, who had worked there since 1932, when he began as a high-school correspondent. Within the first year more than seventy news employees left the paper, voluntarily and involuntarily.

Admittedly, Capital Cities modernized the newspaper's formats and production plants, raised employee pay scales, and created a new vibrancy in news coverage. But critics charge that Capital Cities' emphasis on profits killed the afternoon *Star*. (The morning *Times* has been renamed the *Kansas City Star*.) The massive firings and more liberal political realignment earned Hale harsh criticism from local media and from long-standing *Star* employees, particularly those who regarded themselves as members of the Kansas City community. While the *Star* has improved, some believe that it has lost its ties to the community, and many mourn the death of the famous afternoon paper.

In Des Moines, Iowans faced a similar situation. The *Des Moines Register* calls itself the "Newspaper Iowans Depend Upon." Nearly half the people in Iowa read the daily *Register*, and three-fifths of the state's citizens read the Sunday edition. Sale of the paper to the Gannett Corporation in 1985 ended three generations of Cowles family ownership. Staff members have described the *Register* as leaner and meaner since Gannett took over, but some longtime readers criticize the paper for being less aggressive and less innovative editorially.

Group ownership changed the relationship of the *Kansas City Star* and the *Des Moines Register* to their communities. As outsiders came in to run the family- and employee-owned papers, the lament was of a loss of individuality—of midwestern local values giving way to the values of a national or international media conglomerate. The feeling that a newspaper has become a little less a part of the community makes it easier to criticize chain ownership, even if it provides a viable, and perhaps even more aggressive, product.

Given the preference of most editors, publishers, and journalism educators for independently owned papers, it is not surprising that the *Milwaukee Journal* and the *St. Louis Post-Dispatch* remain at the top of the top ten lists, despite the *Chicago Tribune* and *Des Moines Register*'s greater success in earning Pulitzer prizes. The employee-owned *Milwaukee Journal* has been described by one Milwaukee press club member as a good newspaper in a dead town. The paper also suffers from a lack of employee turnover. The benefits of employee ownership encourage long-term employment and stifle creative change that could occur from a healthy influx of young, aggressive reporters. Critics also charge that the *Journal* spends too few resources outside Milwaukee. The *Post-Dispatch*, which has successfully resisted one takeover attempt, remains in the hands of the Pulitzer family, although the publisher is no longer a Pulitzer family member. From 1937 to 1952 the *Post-Dispatch* won five Pulitzers for meritorious public service, a record it has not matched in recent years.

Any comment on midwestern newspapers would be incomplete without further attention to the small weekly and daily papers that receive little recognition but are often well edited, important forces in their communities. Of the 7,500 nondaily U.S. newspapers with paid circulations, recent surveys show that 54 percent are published in agricultural-industrial communities; another 35 percent are published in suburban areas; the remaining 11 percent are resort community newspapers, primarily outside the Midwest. Added to these are thousands of small dailies.

Most small-town editors have strengthened their coverage of local issues during the last decade. The future of these smaller papers will depend on the use of new technology, such as desktop publishing equipment, and on the ability of small towns to revitalize themselves and halt the out-migration of their citizenry. There are indications that good small-town newspapers will survive and continue to perform their vital function.

Chains such as the Harris Group have initiated management training programs for young publishers. Such newspapers, although small in circulation, are strong voices in their communities with vibrant editorial pages that make them far more than community bulletin boards.

In the coming years, critics of heartland journalism will consult the polls, count the prizes, and decry the homogenizing effects of chain ownership. And they will probably measure the performance of the nation's newspapers by their national influence rather than by regional importance. But the successors to the William Allen Whites, the Cowles, and Pulitzers will continue to make their voices heard, whether through group-owned or independent newspapers. Newspaper editors who compete on a national level will always be measured against elite leaders such as the *New York Times* and the *Washington Post*, but those who choose to remain a solid voice in their communities may find renewed importance as strong regional voices.

NOTES

1. The author wishes to thank Stephen Lacy for computing the midwestern data specifically for this chapter. See also Lacy and Frederick Fico, "Newspaper Quality and Ownership: Rating the Groups," a paper presented to the Midwest Association for Public Opinion Research, Chicago, November 1988; and Lacy and James M. Bernstein, "Daily Newspaper Content's Relationship to Publication Cycle and Circulation Size," *Newspaper Research Journal* (Winter 1988).
2. Leo Bogart, *Press and Public: Who Reads What, When, Where and Why in American Newspapers* (Hillsdale, N.J.: Lawrence Erlbaum Associates, 1981).
3. These computations were provided specifically for this chapter. The complete results will be published separately.
4. The newspapers mentioned here were not necessarily included in the samples for each group.

10

The Daily Newsweekly

James Devitt

"The new *New York Times*—It's a lot more than the news." This marketing slogan was intended to highlight the new weekly sections—"Weekend," "Living," and "Home"—the *Times* began offering its readers in 1976. The slogan might just as well have been, "It's a lot more than the newsweeklies," because by adding these sections the "new *New York Times*" was beginning to resemble a daily newsmagazine, giving *Time, Newsweek,* and *U.S. News and World Report* another competitor.

The *New York Times* now offers articles every day of the week similar to those found in the newsweeklies. In addition to "The Week in Review," the *Times* Sunday edition has long contained sections that encroach on the domain of the newsweeklies. The "Travel," "Arts and Leisure," and "Book Review" sections arrive on subscribers' doorsteps a couple of days before *Time, Newsweek,* and *U.S. News and World Report* hit the newsstands. In fact, the *Times* has even begun advertising its Sunday paper as better than the newsweeklies. One *Times* advertisement reads, "The Sunday *New York Times* gives you more information on more different subjects than any news magazine. . . ."

During the week, the *Times* continues to provide the reader with a steady diet of newsweekly-style material in the form of special sections. The reader begins the workweek with "Sports Monday," which recaps the weekend's sports news and includes a few feature articles. On Tuesday there is "Science Times," with story topics ranging from medicine and rain forests to outer space and personal computers. Wednesday's offering, the "Living" section, is just as broad; while including articles on entertainment and food, the section also has stories on daily living. The August 30, 1988, "Living" section, for example, had a piece on different ways of tying neckties. Thursday's "Home" section offers tips on upgrading one's living accommodations as well as features on the home improvement efforts of individuals. The "Weekend" section on Friday contains articles on leisure activities and provides a calendar of events in the New York area.

But the paper has not limited its competition with the newsweeklies to content. The *Times* is also challenging the newsmagazines for distribution turf. By the end of 1988, the paper's national edition, which premiered in 1980, represented more than 16 percent of the *Times*'s daily circulation.

The *Times* has even begun to resemble the three newsweeklies graphically. Stories are broken up into chapters, with parts of each story highlighted by subheads. Front-page pictures are accompanied by captions that encapsulate the story. The front page also features charts, graphs, and boxes. "I steal shamelessly from the newsmagazines," former assistant managing editor Allan M. Siegal told the *Columbia Journalism Review* in 1988.[1]

It is difficult to measure the effect the changed *Times* has had on the newsweeklies, but in 1989, when he was *U.S. News* editor, Roger Rosenblatt admitted to the *Columbia Journalism Review*, "The question it has suddenly become quite urgent for newsmagazines to ask is, 'What are we giving readers that they can't get anywhere else?'"[2]

From 1969 to 1979, the combined circulation of *Time*, *Newsweek*, and *U.S. News* rose by more than 1 million. From 1979 to 1989, however, the combined circulation increase was only 400,000. The total combined advertising pages for the newsweeklies has significantly decreased in the past ten years, dropping from more than 8,600 pages in 1979 to less than 7,000 in 1988.[3]

Although the special sections are new to the weekday editions of the *New York Times*, the paper has hardly revolutionized the newspaper business. Since the nineteenth century other dailies have been using similar sections to increase circulation. Indeed, the *Times* itself has been running Sunday's "Week in Review" section since 1935.

The *Chicago Tribune* beat the *Times* on the weekday special section innovation by about one hundred years. In December 1852, the *Tribune* began producing each week a few pages labeled "The Home Journal," which provided tips on cooking and home care. These few pages, according to Colleen Dishon, an associate editor at the *Tribune*, eventually became an entire, or freestanding, section in 1876. "There've always been [special sections]," Dishon says. "They have existed with newspapers for a long time."[4]

The *Milwaukee Journal* led the post–World War II special section drive, producing freestanding men's and women's sections in the 1950s. The *Chicago Tribune* introduced its "Weekend" section in 1965, and added a "Homes" supplement in 1973. The *Washington Post*'s daily "Style" section began appearing in 1969.[5]

Although the *Times* did not originate weekday special sections, it introduced all of them rapidly; all five special sections were added to

the paper in less than three years. Why the rush? The *Times* was looking to boost its average daily circulation, which had fallen nearly 10
percent between 1970 and 1975,[6] while advertising linage had shown a
similar drop.[7] "The *Times* almost went under," J. Kendrick Noble, Jr., a
media analyst at Paine Webber, Inc., told *Business Week* in 1986.[8]

The 1975 recession and increasing operating costs added to the
Times's woes, as did competition from other New York–area papers,
which were covering the suburbs more extensively than the *Times*. In
1976, the Long Island–based *Newsday* was reaching 62 percent of all
Long Island households, and the *New York Daily News* 31 percent; the
Times was reaching only 11 percent of all Long Island homes. In the
New York City metropolitan market—the fifty-mile radius surround-
ing New York City—the *Times* was received by only 14 percent of all
households.[9]

The *Times*, by the mid-1970s, was also facing competition from news
media outside the New York area. "There was a time when the *Times*
had little competition," then–executive editor Abe Rosenthal told *Time*
magazine in 1977. "TV didn't exist, the newsweeklies weren't much,
the *Washington Post* was a nonpaper."[10]

After the introduction of its first three special sections, the *Times*'s
circulation began to grow rapidly. By August 1977, 35,000 more people
were buying the *New York Times* on days that the "Weekend," "Living,"
and "Home" sections appeared than when the paper had no supplements.[11] The paper's advertising numbers rose with circulation. In
May 1977, two months after the third section, "Home," had been introduced, the *Times* sold more advertising than in any previous month in
the paper's 126-year history.[12] Pretax earnings, after dropping 58 percent to $4.6 million in 1975, grew to $10.4 million in 1976, and to
$17.7 million in 1977. By the end of 1978, the *Times* had special sec-
tions every day of the week, adding "Sports Monday" in January of
1978 and "Science Times" in November of that same year.

"We knew we had readers out there who had tasted the *Times* and
given it up," publisher Arthur Sulzberger told *Newsweek* in 1977. "We
needed a product the reader in the suburb was interested in."[13]

The addition of these sections was not the sole reason for the *Times*'s
increased earnings and circulation. The recession was over, and the
Times lowered its production costs by switching to computerized typesetting in 1974. The paper also began changing its appearance in
1976. The *Times* reduced its news columns on a page from eight to six,
returning to the format the paper had used in its debut in 1851.
Sulzberger told the *Wall Street Journal* that the change was intended to
give the reader "a more open, easier-to-read format."[14] The *Times* also

increased the number of display advertising columns from eight to nine, allowing for greater revenue on each advertising page.

Circulation figures were boosted when the *Times* created a two-section national edition in 1980 for distribution in the Midwest. The paper was produced in New York City, then sent by satellite to a printing plant in Chicago. This edition emphasized national, international, and business coverage. The *Times*'s daily circulation totals jumped from 863,500 in 1979 to nearly 915,000 in 1980. Throughout the first half of the 1980s, the *Times* began producing the national edition in other U.S. cities. In April 1988, the *Times* added a third section to its national edition, "The Living Arts." This edition, originally distributed in the San Francisco area, expanded to the Los Angeles area in October 1988. Daily circulation exceeded 1 million in 1985 and continued to climb in the latter half of the 1980s.

Although the addition of special sections to the *New York Times* does not necessarily account for the higher circulation figures, the paper has continued to add similar material to its daily editions. Since Max Frankel replaced Rosenthal as executive editor in November of 1986, the *Times* has added weekly special pages. The topics range from law, education, and fashion to health and the media.

Although the *New York Times* is, in part, competing with the newsweeklies in content and appearance, its use of special sections may be a preview to a profound change in the way daily newspapers are sold. As William Blankenburg noted in chapter 7, the newspaper business could attract more advertisers and more readers by "unbundling" the current daily newspaper, providing a section of news for general distribution, with the remaining sections delivered separately only to those who wanted them.

Colleen Dishon of the *Chicago Tribune* sees readers of daily newspapers primed for such a change and newspapers beginning to cater to readers' tastes. "I think what you're seeing is the segmentation of readership," Dishon says. "You want the type of readers that buy specialized magazines. [Newspapers] now do things that magazines would have done in the past. You can afford to do that if you already have your mass audience."[15]

Dishon believes that the creation of these sections has boosted newspapers' advertising revenue because advertisers can target a specific audience by appearing in a special section. "You can only run so many ads in your A section," she explains. "The question is, how do you find the vehicle to expand that? You give the client more of a reason to be in your paper [by creating a special section]."[16]

The "unbundling" Blankenburg suggests has already begun in Canada, where the *Toronto Star* offers home delivery of the newspaper on any combination of days the customer wants. If other daily news-papers begin to make the changes Blankenburg has proposed, the *New York Times*, with its daily special sections, appears ready to present all the news that's fit to unbundle.

NOTES

1. *Columbia Journalism Review* (November/December 1988): 30–1.
2. Quoted in *Columbia Journalism Review* (March/April 1989): 24.
3. *Time* magazine's marketing and information systems department.
4. Personal interview with author, August 10, 1989.
5. *Washington Monthly* (December 1984): 13.
6. *Newsweek* (April 25, 1977): 84.
7. *Business Week* (August 30, 1976): 42.
8. Quoted in *Business Week* (April 28, 1986): 46.
9. *Business Week* (August 30, 1976): 43.
10. Quoted in *Time* (August 15, 1977): 80.
11. Ibid., 73.
12. Ibid.
13. *Newsweek* (April 25, 1977): 84.
14. Quoted in the *Wall Street Journal*, June 15, 1976.
15. Colleen Dishon, personal interview with author, August 10, 1989.
16. Ibid.

III

Wire Services

11

The Associated Press and United Press International

Richard A. Schwarzlose

By the time Samuel F. B. Morse opened his first intercity telegraph line to the public's business on May 24, 1844, that line had already carried a significant news dispatch from Annapolis Junction to Washington, D.C., announcing the national ticket of the Whig Party, then meeting in Baltimore.[1] Even before telegraphy was formally underway in the United States, a partnership of sorts had sprung up between this new "lightning" technology and journalism's need for news from distant cities.

Telegraphy, telephony, and the computer and satellite sciences have, since the 1840s, made it possible for the American wire services— Associated Press, United Press International, and their predecessors— to gather news on a widening global scale and to deliver the reports of that news to a growing audience of newspapers, broadcast stations, cable television subscribers, foreign wire services, and even government offices. Technology's crucial contribution to the birth and growth of wire services in the nineteenth century, however, has become a major challenge to the wires' continued operation, at least on traditional principles, in the late twentieth century. As the wires cope with changing technological and journalistic forces today, they must also keep the content of their news reports in flux, seeking both to satisfy newspapers' traditional needs for spot news and to find new niches for their report in an ever-more-crowded news market.

After briefly reviewing the historical roles of technology and the newspaper industry in the growth of the wires, this chapter traces the technical and economic fortunes of the major American wire services since 1965 and discusses the effect of these developments on the wires' news reports. The past quarter-century has been difficult for the wires. Spearheading journalism's rush into the terminal-computer-communication satellite technology, the wires by the mid-1970s faced major expenses associated with converting to computer processing of news. Meanwhile television news was challenging the wires' historic lock on spot-news reporting and diminishing the significance of newspapers as a source of national and foreign news to readers in their local communities. Although neither wire escaped the stresses of competition and innovation, UPI's path has been especially rocky since 1980, strewn with ownership and management changes, a bankruptcy proceeding, and growing doubts in the industry about the wire service's survivability.

BACKGROUND

After having modest and sporadic success for two centuries using land and water transportation to deliver news dispatches from distant communities to their offices, newspaper editors gratefully embraced telegraphy in the mid-1840s as a fast, efficient, albeit expensive, alternative.[2] The value of a news report in a community is directly proportional to the number of people who do not know that news before they encounter that report. Editors and reporters survive by controlling the flow of information to their audiences; if you monopolize the news, the public will pay to know what you know. As long as ships, wagons, post riders, and trains brought newspapers and letters as quickly to a community's citizens as to its local newspaper editor, that editor could not monopolize the news, and the newspaper was viewed largely as a record of, and a journalistic reaction to, information that was already known by a large portion of the community.

Telegraphy, in contrast, gave the nineteenth-century editor the opportunity to bring news into the community ahead of transportation systems, even though the volume of news had to be sacrificed to gain telegraphy's speed and distance (as measured by the extent of the growing network of telegraph lines). With amazing alacrity a new kind of news agency sprang up along the newspaper-telegraph interface, doing for many newspapers what was too expensive for each paper to do for itself: delivering a brief dispatch of distant news for the common use of all participating papers. The Associated Press traces its origins to two such early agencies, one being the efforts of editors in 1846 to gather news cooperatively on a pioneer telegraph line in upstate New York, and the other being the sporadic efforts between 1846 and 1849 of New York City's leading editors to gather news from Washington, D.C., and Europe.

After a series of wire service competitors unsuccessfully challenged AP's supremacy in the second half of the nineteenth century, the nation's two most powerful newspaper owners, William Randolph Hearst and E. W. Scripps, set out to provide alternative wire services for their own papers and for those kept out of AP because of cost or stringent AP membership requirements. Scripps's United Press (UP), founded in 1907, and Hearst's various wire service ventures, notably International News Service (INS), which appeared in 1909, rapidly expanded into international news gathering and delivery, ventured into brighter and more entertaining news writing, and eagerly served broadcasters when they began to appear. UP and INS were merged into UPI in May 1958, as a subsidiary of the E. W. Scripps newspaper company.

For the first thirty years the wires' news reports were transmitted by telegraph companies on lines also used for the public's messages at times when the company's business was slack. After 1875, however, the wires gradually came to control more of their own news-delivery network by leasing telegraph circuits for their exclusive use and by placing their own telegraphers at both ends of these circuits. After World War I, the wires automated their delivery systems, gradually replacing operators with teletype machines that delivered typed, all-capital-letter news reports to the newspaper at about sixty words per minute. As World War II ended, the wires' news monopoly was still largely intact with newspapers and broadcasters relying on AP or UP or both wires for the nuts-and-bolts coverage of spot news from around the world. Radio's bulletin news reports were making inroads on that monopoly only for the most obvious breaking stories.

Since the early 1960s, television coverage of breaking stories—whether local, national, or foreign—has largely established a monopoly on the bulletin and picture dimensions of spot news, forcing the wires to emphasize depth and analysis in addition to speed.

Neither of the major American wire services makes a profit, one by design, the other by default. Arising from a handful of regional corporations and local newspaper partnerships, AP has been a national membership cooperative since the 1890s, assessing its members only for the expense of gathering and delivering the news to them. Profits from UPI's operation, although welcomed by the parent company, have been almost nonexistent since 1965.

ECONOMIC AND TECHNICAL CHANGE

As of 1965, the relative status of Associated Press and United Press International in the industry had not changed significantly for a half-century.[3] AP, according to industry wisdom, was the backbone of journalism—the great reliable conduit of spot news, complete and accurate in its reporting. Perhaps somewhat predictable and flat, AP was nonetheless the indispensable news service for a local editor striving to produce a complete and credible newspaper and able to afford AP's cost. UPI's value to an editor was traditionally as a second wire that could deliver a faster bulletin, cover an event with an interesting angle, or write a story in a brighter manner. Some editors subscribed only to UPI because it was cheaper than AP or because it offered an alternative to a competitor's steady diet of AP copy.

Table 11.1
NEWSPAPERS' WIRE SERVICE AFFILIATIONS, 1960–90

Year	AP and UPI	AP Only	UPI Only	None
1960	436 (25%)	750 (43%)	481 (27%)	88 (5%)
1970	393 (22)	783 (45)	467 (27)	115 (7)
1980	307 (18)	920 (53)	483 (28)	40 (2)
1985	200 (12)	1,030 (61)	415 (25)	40 (2)
1990	100 (6)	1,313 (81)	156 (10)	56 (3)

SOURCES: For 1960, Michael W. Singletary, "Newspaper Use of Supplemental Services: 1960–73," *Journalism Quarterly* 52 (1975): 750; for 1970, Edward J. Trayes, "News/Feature Services by Circulation Group Use," *Journalism Quarterly* 49 (1972): 135; for 1980, 1985, and 1990, the author of this chapter. All sources used *Editor and Publisher International Yearbooks*, which note major and supplemental wire service affiliations for all daily newspapers, usually as of January of the year indicated. These entries are provided by the newspapers and doubtless contain a small percentage of error.

Several tabulations (table 11.1) of newspapers' wire service affiliations reveal rather consistent patronage of the major wire services during the 1960s (and even through the 1970s). If we focus here on the newspapers' use of the major wire services (supplemental wires such as those of the *New York Times* and *Washington Post* are discussed later), slightly more than 40 percent of the dailies relied exclusively on AP in the 1960s, and slightly more than 25 percent relied exclusively on UPI. Another 25 percent received both major wires, and 5 percent operated without a major wire service report.

Both wires gathered and sold news around the world, and both provided news reports for broadcasters. The two wires' technical systems were almost identical in 1965, both still relying on the teletype system that was fifty years old. The big corporate news in 1965 was that the wires were about to convert their all-cap teletype reports to capital and lowercase letters to make these circuits computer-compatible, anticipating the eventual computerization of the news reports. As of 1965, however, computers in the news business were largely confined to assisting in justifying and hyphenating lines in typesetting and to processing and transmitting to a handful of newspapers the closing stock market quotations.

Late in the 1960s both wires exceeded $50 million in annual expenses for the first time, with AP, traditionally the wealthier wire, reaching this mark three years ahead of UPI. Scattered reports of comparable annual expenses for the wires over the years reveal that UPI expenses had regularly reached 85 to 90 percent of AP's expenses in the same years. And whereas AP depended heavily on U.S. newspapers for its revenue and UPI received substantial support from U.S. broadcasters, both had regions of strength and weakness in gathering and marketing news in the international community.

In sum, the nation's two major wire services in the mid-1960s were in roughly comparable situations in terms of financial security, technological innovation, and customer relations, and they had been for four decades. UPI's financial weakness was occasionally discussed in the industry with some concern, but nothing more drastic than adjustments in the news report and in the wire service's pricing structure seemed necessary to remedy UPI's malaise. The total number of America's daily newspapers—the foundation of both wires' revenue—had remained at about 1,750 since the 1950s, and since World War II the wires had capitalized on the appearance of many new foreign subscribers and the rapid growth of the domestic broadcast and cable TV markets. Trends in totals of wire service members and subscribers remained relatively stable as the years went by, AP's strength growing at an extremely slow pace. And disturbances in the gradual cost-of-living climb of expenses were always attributable to the uncommon costs of covering an Olympics, a presidential campaign, or a distant war.

By 1970, however, this situation was disturbed by three forces that, for the next two decades, would dramatically alter the way both wire services operated and would threaten UPI's existence:

1. Several waves of technological innovation required massive expenditures for terminals, computers, and satellite stations and thus strained relations between the wires and their members or subscribers;
2. Aggressive global coverage of news by the broadcast networks and by cable news systems drew the public's attention from newspapers and forced the major wire services to reassess their devotion to spot-news coverage; and
3. Declines in the numbers and financial strength of local daily newspapers, the heart of the wires' financial resources, forced the wires to seek out new sources of revenue.

Technological innovation was undertaken to eliminate the wires' costly old technology. The mounting expense of keyboarding the news report onto AT&T landlines leading to teletype and teletypesetter machines in local news offices forced the wires to explore the feasibility of linking all reporters and editors via terminals to central computers that would store, process, and transmit news copy, and of linking terminals in small bureaus to regional computers that would be connected to the central computers at headquarters. As electronics specialists explained in the late 1960s, reporters would do the only keyboarding of the news story; the wires' editors would merely call up the story for editing and routing. The flood of paper so common in the traditional newsroom would be replaced by the images of words on video display terminals.

UPI had pioneered in the use of computers in 1962 when it began delivering stock market data via computer to metropolitan newspapers. AP followed suit within a year. In 1969 both wires at their annual spring meetings in New York City proudly previewed their terminal-computer systems that would centralize and speed up the handling of copy and reduce the cost of leasing landlines and employing telegraphers. In 1970, AP became the first to try out the scheme, having its reporters in the Columbia, South Carolina, bureau write and file their stories on terminals linked directly to a regional computer in Atlanta.

This was the modest beginning of what would become a tidal wave of electronic innovation sweeping over the entire news business in the next ten years—terminals replacing typewriters, data bases replacing paper, and electronically produced offset "cold type" replacing hot lead and the linecasting machine in newspaper plants. Thousands of craft jobs were eliminated across the industry, and reporters woke up to the realization that their keystrokes on their terminals had replaced the high-priced, often unionized, keyboarding of typesetters and telegraphers. On March 18, 1974, the reporters' Wire Service Guild struck UPI—the wire's first union walkout in history. Officially, the dispute was over wages, but the trade press reported that the real issue was reporters' unhappiness with having to adapt to video display terminals.[4]

Between 1974 and 1982 both wires underwent periodic upgrading of their systems and occasionally introduced new computer- or satellite-based services. AP's Laserphoto service appeared in 1974, as did its DataStream service, which fed copy at high speeds directly from AP's computer into members' computers. UPI's DataNews went straight into subscribers' computers in 1976, the same year that UPI expanded its satellite network to deliver copy from abroad faster. UPI's special cable news service was reaching 275 cable systems in 1977, and UPI was delivering an audio news report to 900 broadcast stations. In 1981, both wires began delivering their news reports to customers and members via satellite, and both were beginning to find new revenue by delivering the reports of their supplemental wire competitors via the wires' satellite systems on a time-sharing basis.

As a counterpoint to this steady stream of innovation, however, ominous signs of financial stress and uncertainty became apparent at the wires. In the summer of 1974, UPI established a fifteen-member Newspaper Advisory Board to chart "common management goals, principles, and policies for the benefit of all UPI subscribers," as UPI President Roderick W. Beaton put it.[5] Looking a lot like AP's board of directors, which dated from 1900 and numbered eighteen newspaper publishers, this UPI board of newspaper publishers could generate loyalty for the wire among some of its wealthiest subscribers. Two years later AP increased its board of directors by three seats, all reserved for broadcast members of AP. Each wire was courting customers more commonly aligned with the competing wire. In January 1977, UPI increased its subscriber rates by 9.5 percent and announced it would end its long-standing practice of charging bargain-basement rates on some contracts in order to get or to keep the subscriber.

Meanwhile, AP was not escaping the cost of new technology. Although emphasizing the savings realized by converting from landlines to satellite links, AP regularly increased members' assessments by hefty amounts. The wire's equipment needs rose from $2.3 million annually in 1973 to $16.2 million in 1983. While announcing a 9.5 percent special rate assessment for 1983, Frank Batten, chairman of AP's board of directors, spelled out AP's unique situation as a not-for-profit cooperative:

> In recent years the AP has financed the bulk of its escalating equipment needs with expensive, short-term debt. It can no longer do so. As a nonprofit cooperative, the AP has not accumulated earnings. Its equity capital is insignificant. Thus, AP does not have access to long-term debt markets at realistic interest rates. Now, the banks have insisted that a higher proportion of AP's capital spending come from internally generated funds rather than debt.
>
> These factors have forced the board to turn to the members to provide part of the capital required to maintain a reliable competitive and efficient communications system at the AP.[6]

Despite the occasionally large increases in annual assessments, newspapers were, by the 1980s, supplying less than half of AP's revenue for the first time in history. For example, U.S. newspaper members contributed $91.2 million, 48.5 percent of AP's total $188.1 million in revenue in 1983. Domestic broadcasters contributed $40 million (21.3 percent of the total), and foreign sources and customers using AP technology provided the remaining 30 percent. Nonetheless, AP's members, after facing 9.5 percent increases in assessment in 1982 and 1983, began to feel the pinch, and one publisher complained publicly about the increases.[7]

AP could weather this storm of expensive innovation because newspaper publishers would rather pay for AP than switch. Over at UPI, however, where profits were already rare and newspaper loyalty could be fickle, conditions grew critical under the stress of competitive innovation by the late 1970s. The extent of UPI's plight became apparent in February 1978, when, during negotiations with the Wire Service Guild, the wire service asked for a wage freeze of nine and one-half months to help offset a $2.2 million annual jump in landlines leasing costs. By a meager 32-vote margin out of 642 votes cast, the union agreed to the request.

Nearly two years later, however, such stopgap measures gave way to a UPI ultimatum to American journalism. For years editors and publishers had asserted that the competition between AP and UPI was healthy and that the industry needed both major wires. So, in September 1979, UPI issued a prospectus seeking forty-five news organizations to become partners in UPI at an annual investment of $100,000 each. After losing $5 million on UPI in 1978, the E. W. Scripps company, with the backing of UPI's five-year-old Newspaper Advisory Board, told the industry to put its money where its mouth was. The response was insufficient and a year later the Scripps company announced that UPI was for sale.

The British-based Reuters News Agency showed some interest in acquiring UPI, but months passed without an announcement of a sale. At its spring meeting in April 1982, UPI's officials sounded more optimistic about the wire than they had for a decade. "We cleared some high hurdles in 1981," UPI President Beaton told the advisory board, and "we are moving confidently in the right direction."[8] Seasoned business watchers might have concluded that such uncommon optimism signaled drastic changes ahead, and they would have been correct. Two months later, on June 2, 1982, the Scripps company sold UPI for one dollar to Media News Corporation, a company formed to acquire UPI. It was subsequently reported in the trade press that Scripps had given UPI to Media News, along with $12 million in cash and forgiven debt, to rid itself of the wire. Media News's principals were Len R. Small, vice-president of a newspaper chain; Cordell Over-gaard, president of a cable system; and Douglas Ruhe and William Geissler, officers of a chain of low-powered television stations. Industry observers expressed the view that the new owners represented too little newspaper experience, and this impression was strengthened by Ruhe and Geissler's eventual emergence as the sole owners.

The sale, however, was Scripps's last desperate attempt to dump a money-losing wire that the parent company could not continue to subsidize. Four years after the sale, Larry Leser, a Scripps executive who had been involved in the sale, explained his company's dilemma:

> We underwrote UPI for a lot of years. We couldn't continue to underwrite it alone. We went to the industry in the late 1970s and asked for help in keeping it alive. We asked for rate hikes—and got a lot of resistance to that. We went to the UPI advisory board and asked if they wanted to turn UPI into a cooperative. The board members said "No" because AP was already operating that way. We went to the newspaper and broadcasting industries to see if they'd be interested in a limited partnership with UPI. Some were interested. Some agreed. But the total offering was not enough.

At a meeting of major U.S. newspaper companies, Leser continued, no one jumped at the chance to acquire UPI, and nine months of negotiating with Reuters ended without a sale.[9] Media News was apparently the only buyer around.

Despite pledges to bring UPI out of its financial quagmire, Media News could not stop the deficits and debts from piling up. Extremely patient amid this uncertainty, the Wire Service Guild, by a surprisingly wide margin (454 to 164) in September 1984, approved a management proposal for a 25 percent pay cut for three months, followed by a gradual restoration of salaries to 100 percent over the next twelve months. The agreement also permitted the wire to fire one hundred guild members at UPI. Calling it the "worst agreement" he had ever recommended that his membership accept, the guild's president William Morrissey said, "This places a tremendous burden on UPI owners and managers. It is UPI which must now swiftly and diligently seek additional capital support to secure the future of its employees and the company."[10]

But concern about security at UPI was overshadowed in press reports by turmoil and bickering at UPI. Ruhe and Geissler fired two presidents in six months and then, in March 1985, abruptly agreed to give control of UPI to a board representing owners, management, and employees. Meanwhile, as was later disclosed, the wire lost $14.8 million in 1983 and $11.1 million in 1984. On April 25, 1985, UPI told its 1,850 employees not to cash their paychecks because the wire service had insufficient funds to cover them. Within three days UPI was in court filing for protection from its creditors under chapter 11 of the federal bankruptcy code. The filing documents presented a disturbing picture: liabilities of $45 million, including $20 million in accounts payable; estimated assets of only $20 million; a list of 1,500 creditors; and $1.77 million past due in payroll taxes owed to the Internal Revenue Service. Although the wire was able to report a profit of $334,000 in 1985, the surplus reflected the effects of the bankruptcy proceedings and the sale of some UPI assets to other companies.

Since that dramatic moment, UPI has been purchased by new owners, has had numerous changes of editors and management teams, and has continued to limp along financially. Millionaire Mario Vázquez Raña, publisher of sixty-two profitable daily newspapers in Mexico, and Joe Russo, a Houston real estate developer and financier, proposed in November 1985 to buy UPI for $41 million. After numerous hearings in bankruptcy court on the proposal and a challenge from an investment group, Vázquez gained control of the wire in July 1986. In his first year, Vázquez spent almost $7 million on eight hundred new terminals, more than one thousand new printers, new satellite receiving dishes, and an entirely new $4.75-million computer system to replace UPI's four existing computers, which ranged from three to twenty years old.

As the wire service entered 1988, it was reportedly losing $1 million per month with no apparent way to stem the losses except for Vázquez to dig deeper in his own pockets. In February 1988, Vázquez, while retaining his 95 percent ownership of UPI, handed over the operating control of the wire to World News Wire (WNW), a spin-off of the Financial News Network, the investment group that had vied with Vázquez to own UPI in 1986. Headed by Earl Brian, an investor who specializes in corporate turnarounds, and Paul Steinle, a broadcast news executive and an adviser to the government's Voice of America, the WNW group was brought into the picture in response to $18 million in UPI losses in 1987. Two months later WNW unveiled its turnaround plan: cut 150 jobs, fewer than 100 of which would be editorial; cut $10 million in administrative costs; and inject $5 million of WNW's money into UPI operations. By July 1988, WNW was seeking $15 million in European and American investment capital for new equipment and operating expenses. In 1991 the industry eagerly awaited signs that UPI might be on the mend.

Between 1975 and 1985, UPI lost 221 daily newspaper subscribers, according to my tabulations from *Editor and Publisher Yearbooks*. At the same time, the supplemental news services' clients grew from 710 to 1,134. The defections from UPI have continued up to the present, according to fragmentary occasional accounts in *Editor and Publisher*. In an effort to recover lost revenue, UPI began to sue former subscribers for breach of contract. A defendant in one such suit estimated in December 1988 that UPI had actions of this type pending against thirty-seven newspapers.[11] The cancellation in 1988 by the *Atlanta Journal* and *Constitution* of the papers' contract with UPI cost the wire an estimated $200,000 annually.

If daily newspaper journalism is the financial backbone of the American wire services, publishers' decisions about wire affiliation over the years have had a profound effect on the wires. Table 11.1, presented earlier, depicts newspapers' choices between AP and UPI, without regard for supplemental wires. The proportion of U.S. papers taking UPI alone (25 to 30 percent) has shown modest decline, and as expected most of that decline occurred between 1980 and 1985. The significant trend in table 11.1 is the newspapers' switch from subscribing to both major wires to subscribing only to the Associated Press. Between 1960 and 1985 the total of AP's members taking UPI decreased 54.1 percent.

The norm of one major wire service for 85.7 percent of the dailies in 1985 (as compared with 70.1 percent of dailies twenty-five years earlier) is only one of several important trends. Papers with one major wire are much more likely to receive one or more supplemental wires now than in 1965. Among dailies taking one major wire, 33.9 percent also took one or more supplemental wires in 1985 (compared with only 8.8 percent in 1965), according to my tabulations. The dailies taking both AP and UPI (primarily metropolitan papers, which, as a group, are declining in number) have always used supplemental services heavily. Among these papers, the proportion using supplementals rose from 35 percent in 1965 to 78 percent in 1985. A total of 65 of the 200 dailies taking both AP and UPI in 1985 (32.5 percent) subscribed to three or more supplemental news services. Clearly the growing use of supplements since 1965 is partly attributable to improved service and more aggressive marketing and partly to the rich variety of news and features the supplements offer.

Between 1960 and 1985, the total contracts for major wire services fell by 12.3 percent, whereas contracts for supplemental wires grew by 196.9 percent. Meanwhile, only a few U.S. newspaper publishers subscribed to any of the three other international wire services—Reuters,

Agence France Presse, and TASS. The number of U.S. dailies subscribing to Reuters declined from forty-four in 1960 to sixteen 1985; in 1985, Agence France Presse served only four dailies and Tass served only two.

Despite arguments that American journalism needs two major wire services and that each needs the other to keep it honest and on its toes, the American daily newspaper industry has clearly opted for one major wire service (which is AP for 60 percent of all dailies) and for one or more supplemental services (for 38.7 percent of all dailies).

The reasons for these trends are not easy to identify; publishers contract for news services on the basis of personal preference and perception and in response to competitive forces in the local news market. Although each is an individual decision, two contributing forces suggest themselves. First, UPI's seven-year journey into bankruptcy and turmoil has lowered the confidence of publishers and the public in the wire's news reports. Second, daily newspapers in some regions and metropolitan evening papers across the country are feeling the financial pressures of declining local economies and stagnant audiences, with the inevitable adverse effect on advertising revenue. After remaining stable at about 1,750 since the mid-1950s, the total number of daily newspapers in the United States began to fall again in the 1980s. Since 1980 one hundred dailies have ceased publication—a loss of 6 percent. Meanwhile, total daily circulation in the United States refused to grow beyond about 62.5 million in the 1980s. Although AP and UPI, under such conditions, are looking elsewhere to make up the loss of revenue from a stagnant newspaper industry, the wire services' alternatives to newspaper revenue are unattractive and even nonjournalistic.

Broadcasters have never been willing to purchase more than the abbreviated news reports they need for their newscasts, and the services of various broadcast networks threaten to make AP or UPI service redundant in the eyes of local broadcasters. The major wire services rent their technological channels to other news distributors, but such business ventures require only the wires' technology, not their massive news-gathering organizations. The wires must find ways of broadening the use of their news product or of repackaging that product for new markets; otherwise, the labor-intensive apparatus for generating a news report will eventually face drastic cutbacks.

In the final analysis, UPI's travail, duplication by AP and UPI of traditional news services, and a sluggish newspaper industry contribute to the pessimistic statistical picture presented here. John Morton, a former newspaper reporter and a newspaper analyst for Lynch, Jones, and Ryan, recently offered a fitting overview of the wire service–newspaper relationship:

> Much of UPI's failure ensues from the nature of the wire service business in this country. UPI has always been a profit-seeking enterprise whose chief competitor is a nonprofit association supported by its member newspapers, which underwrite its expenses. Thus the AP has always had more money, more people for more coverage, and an assured supply of customers. Moreover, the rise of supplementary news services, such as those offered by the *New York Times*, the *Los Angeles Times*, and the *Washington Post*, put pressure on editors: why spend money on UPI's sometimes inferior duplicates of what the newspaper is already committed to receiving from AP when the money could buy supplementary wires that offer something different?[12]

ADJUSTMENTS IN CONTENT

Wire service news reports are the stories journalists love to hate, even though the news industry could not survive without them. The conventional wisdom about the differences between AP and UPI (and UPI's predecessors, UP and INS) has been self-perpetuating since World War I, when UP's premature armistice story led to the view that UP was faster than AP but not so accurate. Also at that time the unveiling of INS's foreign news staff as largely nonexistent, the British denial of cable service to INS because of the wire's German sympathies, and the U.S. Supreme Court's decision that INS had plagiarized copy from AP's wires led to the view that INS's news could not be trusted.

Similar judgments of the wires periodically resurface in journalism. Leo Rosten, interviewing Washington, D.C., news correspondents in the mid-1930s, found that the respondents were equally divided in their preference for AP and UP stories, commenting that AP was "more reliable" and UP was "better written" and "more liberal."[13] The author, conducting a mail survey in 1963, found that fifty managing editors, who saw AP as the "essential" wire service offering complete, accurate coverage, including good regional coverage, saw UPI as a "fill-in" wire service offering less accuracy but also having good regional coverage, more interpretive reporting, good writing, and colorful stories.[14]

A 1971 survey of 1,300 practicing U.S. journalists listed AP second and UPI third behind the *New York Times* in overall performance among the top news organizations in the country. As the fairest and most reliable news organization, the journalists picked AP second to the *Times*, but dropped UPI to fifth behind the *Washington Post* and the *Wall Street Journal*.[15] In February 1980, when UPI was searching for partners in the industry, *Business Week* carried the following assessment of the wires' performance:

> Editors who work with both services are equally critical of each. The news editor of one major daily claims that "UPI is faster, livelier, and less accurate than AP." He adds that UPI is consistently superior in its Washington coverage, particularly of the Supreme Court. "Both," he says, "are good on hurricanes, floods, and other natural disasters, but not on anything subtle or anything that will shake up a client. It's a case of the bland leading the bland." Nevertheless, he adds, "I wouldn't want either of them to fold; it would be a lot worse if there wasn't a UPI out there."[16]

Regardless of what an independent, scientific analysis might discover about the content of the wires' news reports, the impressions reported in these studies add up to the industry's views of the wires' performance. These impressions are unlikely to change soon, and they are the stuff wire affiliations are made of.

To understand the content of the wire services, it is important first to know the historical relationship between wires and newspapers. The wires have always been a news-gathering extension of member or subscriber newspapers. Newspaper publishers needed the wires to cover the regional, national, and international world at the lowest possible cost. The wires listened to and accommodated newspapers' coverage needs and occasionally introduced local editors to new subjects in, and approaches to, news coverage. Walter R. Mears, AP vice-president and political columnist, observed in 1989 that AP still sometimes leads the industry in coverage and sometimes follows it. But as Mears pointed out, at AP the newspaper publishers are the wire's owners, and both wires at minimum will provide those services that the newspaper clients expect and will pay for.[17]

Even though the wires' news reports have been expanded to accommodate radio, television, cable, and access by personal computers, the historical relationship between the wires and their newspaper members or subscribers remains intact in the wires' operations. As a general rule, the initial wire service story about an event is written for use in newspapers. The story's various permutations—on the broadcast wire, as a cable bulletin, or on the abbreviated "pony" wire for smaller papers—are afterthoughts compared with the story's first manifestation on one of the continuously operated newspaper-oriented trunk wires. Cycled to conform to morning and afternoon newspaper deadlines and containing stories written by reporters using newspaper structure, language, and style, the A trunk wire is the conduit of the world's most important breaking news (as seen from the vantage point of American journalism), mixed with a modest dose of the wire's own analysis and enterprise.

The content of wire service reports is at once ever-changing and largely the same. Like any other news presentation, the wires' reports have a finite amount of time (or space) to work with and require a certain portion of that time or space to administer to or promote the report. Meanwhile, no two daily reports are even remotely similar in content, because the wires are mandated and structured to respond, within the strictures of journalism's news judgment, to the entire spectrum of possible news events that present themselves daily to the world.

This flexibility within continuity can be seen by examining two half-day cycles of AP's A wire. Transmitted by satellite (in this instance, to a thirty-inch dish attached to a high-speed dot-matrix printer at the Medill School of Journalism, Northwestern University), these A wire cycles for morning newspapers were selected randomly on January 30–31, 1989, and February 27–28, 1989. Table 11.2 shows the distribution of typical reports by number of items, lines of copy, and percentages of total lines. On a typical news day about 80 percent of total lines of copy would be devoted to reporting the news of the cycle, 5 percent would be devoted to informing editors of upcoming stories and the status of new leads ("digest-advisory assistance to editors") and the coverage of breaking stories, and about 15 percent would be devoted to mopping up breaking stories from the previous cycle and to trans-

Table 11.2

ANALYSIS OF AP NEWS REPORTS

| | January 30–31, 1989 | | February 27–28, 1989 | |
	Number of Items	*Lines of Copy*	*Number of Items*	*Lines of Copy*
Digest-advisory assistance to editors	5	161 (4.0%)	4	142 (4.2%)
A.M. reports and updates	86	3,234 (81.1)	72	2,649 (79.2)
Updates of previous P.M. cycle and A.M.-P.M. advances	15	596 (14.9)	7	556 (16.6)

mitting "enterprise" stories, sometimes investigative—longer stories initiated by the wire service or a member newspaper—scheduled for publication in the next few days ("advances"). This tidy package, of course, would quickly come unglued if there were an attempt on the president's life or if a jumbo jet with Americans aboard were to crash in the United States or anywhere.

The more common type of flexibility found on the A wire is reflected in the data in table 11.2, where these two A.M. cycles (both Monday-Tuesday cycles) on AP's A wire are examined in terms of their subject content. Using subject categories suggested by Ralph O. Nafziger in 1949 and applied in two instances to wire reports,[18] I tabulated the lines of copy devoted to each category. Variation between the reports, of course, measures the nature of the two news days. Some of the top stories on the January 30–31 report were the closing of the U.S. embassy in Kabul, Afghanistan; the beginning of the Oliver North trial; military maneuvers in Alaska; record-breaking cold in Alaska; pay raises for federal judges; exemptions for House and Senate members with campaign funds; and a Beirut car-bomb explosion. Some of the top stories on the February 27–28 report were the return of the president from a Far East trip; dissidents' criticism of the handling of a Bush banquet in China; a pledge by cabinet nominee John Tower to swear off alcohol; criticism by Michael Dukakis of a George Bush proposal to deal with urban problems; and investigation findings on damage to a Boeing 747 in Honolulu.

Two completely different news days generate somewhat different statistical profiles in table 11.3. The nuts-and-bolts school of reporting is evident in the overwhelming emphasis on spot news, especially involving government, the military, foreign affairs, crime, and accidents. These categories continue, as in the past, to constitute the wires' bread-and-butter coverage on the newspaper-oriented A wire.

Subject categories in content analysis, however, are tied too closely to the day's events to measure the changes that have gradually occurred in the wires' news reports over the past twenty-five years. AP's Walter Mears has explained that nothing in the news business has escaped the influence of television news coverage, not even the wire services. Comments Mears:

> In laying out a story, people who write for broadcast have a big edge on those of us who write for print. They get to say it first. By the time we can write it and get it printed, the surprise, or the shock, has worn off the information. It's news the next day, but it isn't new.
>
> That has a big impact on the way we handle a story. It has to be done with some touches that don't come across on the air. It needs

Table 11.3
CONTENT OF AP NEWS REPORTS

	January 30–31, 1989		February 27–28, 1989	
	Lines of Copy	*Percent of Total Lines*	*Lines of Copy*	*Percent of Total Lines*
GOVERNMENT, POLITICS, FOREIGN				
Politics	—	—	75	3.4
Nonmilitary government	474	16.8	154	7.0
State/local government	50	1.8	—	—
National defense	123	4.3	23	1.0
Foreign relations	46	1.6	175	8.0
Foreign news	531	18.8	474	21.6
Acts of war	233	8.2	111	5.1
Total	1,457	51.5	1,012	46.1
ECONOMICS AND BUSINESS				
Labor	—	—	—	—
Agriculture	—	—	48	2.2
Markets and stocks	—	—	—	—
General economic activity	113	4.0	149	6.8
Total	113	4.0	197	9.0
GENERAL NEWS				
Crime and vice	297	10.5	391	17.8
Accidents, fires, disasters	114	4.0	149	6.8
Safety and health	85	3.0	73	3.3
Religion and church	87	3.1	—	—
Education	96	3.4	—	—
Science and invention	63	2.2	39	1.8
Philanthropy	—	—	—	—
Books	—	—	31	1.4
Drama, stage, movies, TV	61	2.2	115	5.3
Music	55	1.9	—	—
Painting, graphic arts	—	—	14	0.6
Leisure activities	54	1.9	—	—
Total	912	32.2	812	37.0
SOCIETY, FAMILY, INDIVIDUALS				
Vital statistics	—	—	14	0.6
Personality sketches	—	—	—	—
Society	—	—	24	1.1
Personal achievement	—	—	—	—
Organizations, clubs	—	—	—	—
Civic entertainment	—	—	—	—
Obituaries	107	3.8	52	2.4
Items about people	18	0.6	28	1.3
Homemaking and fashion	—	—	—	—
Total	125	4.4	118	5.4
SPORTS	18	0.6	18	0.8
HUMAN INTEREST	103	3.7	20	0.9
WEATHER	100	3.6	18	0.8
GRAND TOTAL	2,828	100.0	2,195	100.0

analysis and explanation that used to be left for the follow-ups. That's become more difficult during my career because TV and radio reporting has improved so greatly.

But if you can work some of those touches of explanation together with the facts—and write it with some style—you can deliver copy that will stand up through all the hours it takes to put it into the newspaper. . . .

The kind of analytical touches I'm talking about aren't those you find in a column or an editorial. It's a matter of filling in background, having enough information in your head or readily at hand so as to be able to say that today's announcement fits with these things that happened before.

The same holds for color, which means nothing more than saying what it looked like, or what the candidate did before he confessed, or how many people were on the floor when the Senate passed the bill. There's nothing very deep or significant about items like that, but they let the reader into the event in a special way.[19]

Thus, when Mears is asked how the wires' news reports have changed in the past quarter-century, he lists more interpretation, analysis, enterprise, and explanation and more emphasis on good writing.[20]

These changes are dictated by television's growing ability—with minicams, videotape, communication satellites, and helicopters—to take the public to the scene of news, within a matter of minutes in most cases. In addition to having immediate access to news coverage by the various broadcast news networks, the public is treated on cable to the continuing live televising of congressional proceedings, presidential press conferences, business news, a growing parade of sports events, the national weather situation, and in many communities the meetings of numerous local boards, councils, and commissions. Both wire services are feeling the pinch of competition at both ends of their coverage spectrum. The wires' traditional spot news and bulletin coverage of breaking events is gradually being taken over by broadcasting and cable services. Meanwhile, the wires' efforts to capitalize on journalism's post–World War II surge in interpretive and enterprise reporting quickly bring the wires face to face with the numerous and flourishing supplemental wires.

As an extension of its many newspaper members, some of whom operate supplemental wires, the Associated Press has settled somewhere in the middle of the continuum between breaking news and analysis, avoiding direct competition at either end of the continuum and continuing to supply its newspaper members principally with the national and international reporting they must have to retain their credibility with their local readers. And in that role, Associated Press clearly sets the national and international agenda for the publishers, editors, and readers of two-thirds of the nation's daily newspapers. AP also at least indirectly influences the news decisions of broadcast newspeople around the country who would find it imprudent to ignore the voice of this venerable veteran reporter.

Meanwhile, the one daily newspaper editor in four who continues to rely on United Press International without benefit of AP's copy must be troubled by UPI's periodic shift in reporting emphasis. Like AP, UPI has had to cope with the growing presence of television news and the supplemental wires, but in addition UPI has had to search for an approach to news coverage that offers an alternative to AP's reports. In 1965, for example, UPI's Roger Tatarian sounded much like Walter Mears today when he announced that UPI's copy was becoming more devoted to interpretive, colorful, analytical, readable copy, calling it "journalism we're very proud to transmit."[21] In 1972, UPI president Mims Thomason announced, "We have, in effect, begun to deliver two news reports. While our basic task is the coverage of spot news, our second mission has been to inform the reader and listener about the background and meaning of the news."[22]

In December 1983, UPI editor Maxwell McCrohon, pointing to research showing that upscale readers wanted more international and national coverage, said he wanted "to begin to pull together teams of reporters on a national and international scale" to give "high-powered coverage to certain stories like the Middle East."[23] In November 1988, although it had announced that it would drastically reduce coverage in states and regions where subscribers were dwindling, UPI, under new management, reversed itself. "Our potential and current customers place the highest market value on state and regional coverage," said UPI president Paul Steinle, who added that providing such coverage would be possible by "streamlining some of UPI's news staffs in areas other than state and regional services" rather than by expanding staff.[24]

Clearly, although both wires search for new and unchallenged positions to occupy on the news spectrum, UPI's search is more frantic. Meanwhile, publishers' perceptions of the wires' news reports echo UPI's vacillation. In 1983 (before the bankruptcy and the parade of editors and managers), selected editors subscribing to UPI were asked to evaluate the UPI report under Ruhe and Geissler. Forty-nine percent said that UPI had improved in the latter half of 1983, 40 percent saw no change, and 8 percent said UPI had deteriorated.[25] In the spring of 1986, AP newspaper editors offered this evaluation of AP's service: 35 percent said that AP continued to get better and in the preceding year had improved its news coverage; 94 percent said AP was a good or excellent news service; 87 percent said that the quality of AP's reporting was consistently good or excellent.[26]

The Associated Press and the domestic newspaper business are so intimately entwined that the wire's future, at least in its present form, will rise or fall with the fortunes of its newspaper members. AP will deliver the news report its members want as long as its members are willing and able to pay for it. If the newspaper industry were to remain sluggish, or worse, if it were to experience further slippage in the news marketplace vis-à-vis television and cable, AP would face two alternatives: either ride the slide down with its newspaper members to a more compact and selective staff and news report or begin to move away from the newspaper industry by retooling its news-reporting apparatus to attract audiences on cable systems or through home computers. If AP is to preserve the bulk of its present volume, diversity, and depth of news report, the newspaper industry in this country must remain strong. The more superficial news report needed for direct home delivery would be little more than an investment scheme for AP's current members.

UPI, having built a large part of its reputation and revenue on the less-lucrative broadcasting and foreign markets, will benefit less than AP from a strengthening newspaper industry, but will be adversely affected by further deterioration in its relations with its already-small group of newspaper subscribers. Because UPI is neither the "essential wire" that AP is in the minds of American journalists nor an authentic, attractive supplemental wire, UPI seems to have one of two fates: (1) suspension of operations, as market forces continue to squeeze the lifeblood out of the wire or (2) relocation of its major news-reporting effort away from the United States, perhaps to Central and South American markets, where UPI has traditionally been a strong gatherer and distributor of news. Such relocation, however, would bring UPI into direct competition with two of the world's news powerhouses: Reuters and Agence France Presse, offering a fate at least as dubious as UPI's current situation.

At the end of 1989 in an excellent book-length description of UPI's downward spiral, ex-UPI staffers Gregory Gordon and Ronald E. Cohen glimpsed the wire's dismal future from a newsroom perspective. UPI's news staff, wrote Cohen and Gordon, "continued to fight, praying for a miracle. Yet, deep inside, the sad reality could not be ignored: their wire service could never again be what it once was. UPI's days of glory were gone forever. The old dream was over, the crusade lost."[27]

Wire services and their news reports are not yet anachronisms in American journalism, but as participants in the competitive, changing markets that offer news to a nation of consumers, AP and UPI cannot expect to survive for long on traditions and monopolies established decades ago by U.S. daily newspapers. Clearly these market forces cannot be ignored, but they should be deplored. Substantial changes in, or the loss of, either of these recorders of the day's news will undermine the search for truth in our free and open marketplace of ideas.

NOTES

1. John W. Kirk, "Historic Moments: The First News Message by Telegraph," *Scribner's* 11 (May 1892): 654–5.
2. Research for this section was conducted by the author for his two-volume history of the wire services, *The Nation's Newsbrokers* (Evanston, Ill.: Northwestern University Press, 1989, 1990). See also the author's 1965 doctoral dissertation, *The American Wire Services: A Study of Their Development as a Social Institution* (New York: Arno Press, 1979).
3. Contents of this section, except where specified in notes, are based on an examination of the news accounts about the wire services found in *Editor and Publisher, Broadcasting*, and *Fortune*.
4. "Wire Service Guild Strikes UPI," *Editor and Publisher* (March 23, 1974): 9–10.
5. "Beaton Puts UPI's Future in Hands of Advisory Board," *Editor and Publisher* (April 20, 1974): 26.
6. John Consoli, "AP Members Hit with 9.5% Special Rate Assessment," *Editor and Publisher* (November 6, 1982): 9.
7. The publisher, Don Becker of the *Detroit Free Press*, argued that the increase should come from broadcast members. "AP has charged reduced rates to broadcasters so it could compete with UPI," said Becker, who also criticized AP directors for being "too distant from the wire service business to ask [AP officials] some of the tough questions that need to be asked." Becker made these comments as a member of a group of Knight-Ridder newspaper executives visiting AP headquarters in the fall of 1982 to express their concern over the assessment hikes. Quoted in John Consoli, "Newspapers Protest AP Rate Assessment Hikes," *Editor and Publisher* (November 28, 1982): 8.
8. "Turnaround for UPI Seen If New Trends Continue," *Editor and Publisher* (April 17, 1982): 9.
9. John Consoli, "Why Not Give the New UPI Owners a Chance?" *Editor and Publisher* (August 9, 1986): 44.
10. John Consoli, "It's Up to the Union," *Editor and Publisher* (September 1, 1984): 7; and John Consoli, "UPI Gets a Reprieve," *Editor and Publisher* (September 22, 1984): 9.
11. Judith Roales, "Says UPI's Strategy Won't Win Back Subscribers" (letter to the editor), *Editor and Publisher* (December 10, 1988): 5. See also George Garneau, "UPI sues Clients Who It Contends Broke 'Open-Ended' Contracts," *Editor and Publisher* (October 15, 1988): 22.
12. John Morton, "UPI's New Strategy," *Washington Journalism Review* (January/February 1989): 10.
13. Leo C. Rosten, *The Washington Correspondents* (New York: Harcourt, Brace, 1937), 344.
14. Schwarzlose, *The American Wire Services*, 267.

15. John W. C. Johnstone, Edward J. Slawski, and William W. Bowman, *The News People: A Sociological Portrait of American Journalists and Their Work* (Urbana: University of Illinois Press, 1976), 224.
16. "UPI: A News Seller Tries to Sell Itself," *Business Week* (February 18, 1980): 70.
17. Walter Mears, telephone interview with the author, March 22, 1989.
18. Ralph O. Nafziger's categories are found in *Content of Selected U.S. Dailies*, Bulletin 16, Department of Agricultural Journalism, University of Wisconsin (October 1949). They were used by George Van Horn in "Analysis of AP News on Trunk and Wisconsin State Wires," *Journalism Quarterly* 29 (1952): 426–32; and by Scott M. Cutlip in "Content and Flow of AP News—From Trunk to TTS to Reader," *Journalism Quarterly* 31 (1954): 434–6.
19. John Chancellor and Walter R. Mears, *The News Business* (New York: Harper and Row, 1983), 47–8.
20. Walter Mears, telephone interview with the author, March 22, 1989.
21. Quoted in Tony Brenna, "Tatarian Gives UPI Aims on Reporting," *Editor and Publisher* (November 20, 1965): 13.
22. Quoted in "UPI Costs Rise to $57 Million," *Editor and Publisher* (April 22, 1972): 18.
23. Andrew Radolf, "McCrohon Maps Out Editorial Strategy for UPI," *Editor and Publisher* (December 17, 1983): 12.
24. George Garneau, "UPI Update," *Editor and Publisher* (November 12, 1988): 16.
25. "UPI Subscribers Rate the Service," *Editor and Publisher* (December 31, 1983): 29.
26. "Associated Press Gets High Grades from Its Membership," *Editor and Publisher* (April 19, 1986): 74.
27. Gregory Gordon and Ronald E. Cohen, *Down to the Wire: UPI's Fight for Survival* (New York: McGraw-Hill, 1990), 407.

Commentary

Walter Mears

My assignment is to write a commentary, but thirty-four years as a wire service man—more specifically an AP man—have taught me that before you comment, you deliver the facts. So I will start there.

By 1989, the AP served 1,485 of the 1,629 daily newspapers in the United States—almost 89 percent of the newspapers, representing more than 95 percent of newspaper circulation in this country. Many members place greater reliance, and in many cases exclusive reliance, on us. We have added staff to meet those new demands.

Yet there is more competition in the world of news than ever before. The supplemental news services, the networks, the cable news industry all are rivals for information and play. Others will have to assess the situation facing UPI, our historic rival. But I can testify that our competition is getting tougher to handle every day.

The AP has been described as the great engine of American journalism, and I think that description is truer today than ever. That truth would be more evident except for the fact that much of what we do reaches the reader or the viewer without our label on it. Newspapers and broadcasters who use our services send their own reporters out to match stories or features we deliver—and, of course, we do the same with some of what we see in print. Sometimes our copy is folded into staff stories; sometimes it is used without the logo. Although those practices make it more difficult to see the reach of the AP news report, it is there, almost everywhere.

Those two observations—more competition yet greater reach and usage—might seem to be in contradiction, if AP employees were content to conform to the stereotypes that long have been inaccurately affixed to us: We are not telegraphic reporters, stenographers, or nuts-and-bolts journeymen; some of the finest writing in the business is done under the AP logotype.

Our service is essential and secure in the back of the paper. We deliver the stock tables, the weather reports, the box scores and statistics no newspaper can do without. Those are a vital part of our product. Newspapers complain more over a late box score than over awkward phrasing in a front-page story. The latter is a flaw; the former holds up deadlines.

Competition for the display stories, the feature space, and the front pages is intense. In that competition we run head-on into the supplemental services, operated by the newspapers that are among our owners, delivered over AP circuits to hundreds of other newspapers. The reporter who writes a story on assignment from a newspaper editor knows that the story will wind up in print. The reporter who writes a story for the AP knows that the AP story must compete with a variety of other stories to make it into print. AP reporters also know that our exclusives become everybody's property as soon as we break them, and that our enterprise stories may well wind up as story ideas and assignments to be matched under other bylines.

There also is intense competition to be first, to break the major spot-news stories. In that arena, the most comparable and competitive reporters are the network and other broadcast correspondents. Like wire reporters, they have an outlet for the story whenever they can nail it down.

We not only compete with them, we serve their organizations. Television and radio stations, and the networks, represent a major part of our operations. In the broadcast field as with newspapers, wire service reporters face a two-way contest: we deliver stories instantly to our print and broadcast members, while we compete journalistically with the reporters those member organizations send out to cover stories. On the major spot-news stories, the coverage begins with us. Our bulletin mobilizes the rest of the industry, print and broadcast.

But then, nobody said it was going to be easy.

One of my concerns about the future is that we might be pushed further and further into the back pages of newspapers if editors turn increasingly to supplemental services for copy on major stories. Such a development would cost us the prominent display all reporters and writers seek. Our product would still be essential to the industry, but our work would be less likely to draw and hold the talented people who now enrich our ranks.

Ironically, the ultimate outcome would be a sort of sustaining, nuts-and-bolts news product in keeping with the cliché. In a sense, we are competing for our true identity. We intend to keep it.

Technology, as has been noted, has fundamentally changed the world of wire services. Copy now moves over our wires at twenty times the speed of the old all-caps wires I saw when I went to work in 1955. We are in the process of multiplying even that speed by nine.

The old-fashioned teletype machine is long gone. There is one at the Smithsonian. I also have one in my office and I turn it on periodically to hear the clatter that used to be the music of the newsroom. When I first went to work for the AP, we still received some of our copy via Morse code. Everything hums or buzzes nowadays.

The technological revolution has provided tools for major enhancements in our services—more specialized copy; faster photos, in color; a new and expanding graphics service, among other things. The technological revolution has also opened new business opportunities; we provide communications services far beyond those of the old AP.

All these changes pose another challenge for the editorial side. We can deliver so much copy so much faster that sheer volume becomes a problem. For example, we send out forty to fifty enterprise and feature stories a week as part of a special effort to broaden the menu of stories a newspaper can offer its readers. Twice a week we send out an editorial advisory describing all those stories and indexing them. Editors still have trouble finding them, and some editors still do not know they exist. Here is a more personal example: Since 1989, I have been writing three analytical columns a week. They are slugged with my name— which led one young editor to think I had died at age fifty-four and my column was an obituary. Nonetheless, I regularly encounter editors who say they would like to use the column and ask me how to find it.

We are working on solutions, concentrating on a computer program that would enable editors to get what they want without searching through everything we deliver.

All these examples illustrate how far we are from the era when editors would stand over teletypes, watching the bulletins come in and deciding which of competing stories was superior and should be printed. The copy flows silently into a computer these days. The story with the best slug line may be the one that gets used, simply because that is what shows in the computer directory.

Much of what I have been talking about, and most of what we in Washington and vicinity see, represents only a small fraction of the work of the AP. Local and regional coverage constitutes by far the greater share. That coverage is vital to our role in the industry. Tip O'Neill said that all politics is local, meaning that the issues closest to home are the ones that count most. The same is true of news service work. The stories closest to home are the most important daily fare. We cover the statehouse. When oil spills in Alaska, we are the first people there, often the only ones unless the story takes on a magnitude that attracts the networks and the specials.

Although competition at the local and regional levels may be less intense than it once was, we in the AP have another spur to speed and excellence. In every state, in every statehouse, the AP reporters work for the people who own their organization. The editors and publishers who make up the association that is the Associated Press always will guarantee our performance, because it is essential to their own newspapers.

Overseas, as many newspapers have reduced their foreign presence, our service has become more important to the industry. Our network of more than one hundred foreign correspondents, plus locally hired staffers and stringers, represents a resource that is unmatched in American journalism.

Finally, the suggestion has been made here that, if economic problems beset the newspaper industry, the AP might one day face shrinkage, reducing staff and services. Such a suggestion misreads the past as well as the future. Not that we have not had to temper our goals and sometimes reduce our staff levels in times of recession. We have had to cut expenses, but never at the cost of curbing our central, essential services.

The kind of decline that has been suggested is unrealistic for two reasons. First, one of the goals of AP managers is to find sources of revenue that will ease the share of our costs that are borne by our member newspapers. We are making steady progress in that direction through our services to other media, through such services as our AP–Dow Jones partnership overseas, and through our communications services. Second, were there to be long-term economic problems in the newspaper industry, while our ability to grow would be restrained our services to our members would become even more vital. The cost of AP service represents only a tiny fraction of the editorial budgets of most newspapers. We are a bargain. In hard economic times, we are an even greater bargain.

We are constantly changing, but as the editorial engine of an industry, the AP will be here, delivering, for a very long time to come.

Commentary

Kim Willenson

At least since the early 1960s, when I first joined UPI, newspeople have raised two questions about the future of American wire services: Is there really room in the market for two major agencies? and, What will happen to the news business if one of them dies? The first question implies that one of the wires will eventually fail because the industry cannot afford to support both. The second implies that the end of one wire service would be a disaster because competition is all that keeps the other on its toes. Richard Schwarzlose seemed to escalate these concerns by implying that the combination of broadcast news, cable TV, data bases, supplemental wires, and declining newspapers may destine *both* UPI and AP for extinction.

I disgree. The news industry will *never* be too poor to support news agencies: They are its lifeblood. If UPI or AP or both were to close, the reason would certainly *not* be that the market became too small; it would be that the agencies had failed to adapt to changes in demand and to find new clients. That they have already failed to adapt is well illustrated by the rise of newspaper-based supplemental services and by the booming financial health of Reuters, the British agency.

By the same token, the death of an agency would not be a disaster, either for the news business or for democracy in general. The republic survived perfectly well for more than a hundred years with no news agencies at all. A one-agency monopoly might, for a while, be pretty costly to the smarty-pants publishers and broadcasters who are now saving a few bucks by subscribing to only one service. But in truth, a gouging or visibly biased monopoly would only cause competition to be re-created in some other form. As more than one editor pointed out to me during my brief stint as a UPI executive, there are plenty of alternative sources from which to buy the news—not least, the supplementals and the foreign wires.

The argument that the news business cannot afford two wires just doesn't hold up. In fact the news industry is a cash cow. Newspapers, networks, and broadcast outlets, not to mention magazines, are the foundations of several first-order-of-magnitude personal and corporate fortunes in the English-speaking world alone. The names Annenberg, Bingham, Chandler, Cox, Gannett, Graham, Knight-Ridder, Maxwell, McClatchey, Murdoch, Newhouse, Paley, Patterson, Thompson, and Turner leap to mind. There has been no decent news property for which a top-dollar buyer could not be found in recent years. Is that a sign of decline? And there are many other huge media empires in Western Europe, Latin America, and Asia. For example, Asahi and Yomiuri, the two biggest news companies in Japan, between themselves control daily circulations totaling 17 million (35 million, counting morning and afternoon papers separately, as Western statisticians do). Each one also owns a national television network, a large magazine empire, and other enterprises including professional ball clubs.

With all that financial power around, it would be fairer to ask why the global media don't support *more* general news agencies, rather than whether one or more should die. In truth, they do. In addition to Reuters and the supplementals there is a fourth general wire, Agence France Presse (AFP), and there are a host of national agencies, including Deutsche Press Agentur (DPA) of West Germany, Agenzia Nazionale Stampa Associata (ANSA) of Italy, Efe of Spain, and Kyodo and Jiji Press of Japan. The foreign wire services cut sharply into American news agencies' potential revenues abroad, where the expenses are heaviest. Reuters and AFP are even trying to penetrate the U.S. market. While AFP has significant government backing (and therefore, like the cooperative AP, doesn't have to return a profit). Reuters is a private commercial entity, just like UPI. If the Brits can survive, why not the Americans?

The reasons boil down to a failure of vision in both the newsroom and the executive suite. UPI managements, over the years, didn't recognize editorial and commercial opportunities that might have secured the company's future—or might even have made it rich. UPI's competitors have used some of the opportunities to grow fat and sleek.

On the news side, Schwarzlose has documented the fact that the supplemental, newspaper-based wires helped to decimate UPI's client base. What he hasn't told us is why. In fact, the supplementals arose because sophisticated editors weren't getting enough satisfactory interpretive and enterprise reporting from the wires. They sent their own reporters out to produce their own exclusives and to put together stories that could put the news in focus. Gradually, starting in the late 1950s, they realized that they had a news product they could sell in competition with the wires.

Why didn't the wires do better *before* the supplementals came along? This is the first area of failed vision. Although the bulk of the revenues for both UPI and AP traditionally came from fifty or so major metropolitan dailies, the vast majority of wire service clients are small-town papers and broadcasters. Because they are service organizations, both agencies train their staff to treat client needs and requests as mandates from heaven. There is an unfortunate rough democracy in this attitude. To an agency editor taking a client phone call or studying how many clients use what stories, use by a small subscriber counts the same as use by a big one, despite the disproportion—as large as one to two hundred—in subscription fees.

I can't speak for the AP, but at UPI this system produced a tendency to edit the wire for the large number of small clients, rather than for the small number of large ones who paid the freight. Smaller dailies in general have smaller news holes and therefore want shorter stories. Local broadcasters want at most a few sentences giving the gist of the news. Both small dailies and local broadcasters prefer local and regional to national and international news. They prefer these emphases partly because they are what interests their readers most, and partly because local and regional coverage supplements the small clients' own reporters and saves the small clients out-of-pocket expense. But the pressures thus generated skew the wires' investment of resources toward state and local spot-news coverage and away from thoughtful stories of regional or national significance.

Other factors also contribute to this tendency. Editors faced with competing accounts of the same event are inclined to use the most dramatic copy. The version with the largest numbers (particularly of casualties), the most colorful nouns, the strongest verbs, and the most succinct lead is generally the one that gets printed. And because newspaper editors have differing political bents, there is a strong emphasis on "Dragnet" reporting—"Just the facts, sir or ma'am. Cover the breaking news and leave out the opinions, interpretations, and explanations."

All this is reinforced by the way UPI and AP measure their own performance. Each logs a sample of its clients by counting the number of newspapers using either its own or the competition's story of a given event and reports the results to its staff. With few exceptions, the little clients get the same weight as the big ones, so UPI and AP have tended to cut stories ever shorter, to hype them with hot leads and inflated numbers, and to neutralize them politically by leaving out interpretation and analysis. To illustrate, a standard scheduled lead was six hundred words when I joined UPI in 1963, five hundred words when I left it in 1974—and four hundred when I returned in 1987. But this reduction cut precisely against the needs of the big-league newspapers, which, in the quest to tell the news fully and understandably, were accustomed to printing thousands of words on major stories.

In 1962, when I worked on its city desk, the *Washington Post* was a heavy user of national and international wire stories from UPI, Reuters and AP. Commonly, half the front page stories in the *Washington Star* were from AP. Five years later, both were covering most of the news themselves, and the *Post* was offsetting some of the cost by syndicating its product jointly with the *Los Angeles Times*.

The growth of television as a primary medium for spot news and the rising public political consciousness of the civil rights and Vietnam eras generated a demand for new stories with more, rather than less, sophistication. The problem for the wires, particularly UPI, was that they didn't see the change early enough, and even when they saw it their response was half-hearted. Only in the mid-1960s, when the *New York Times*, the *Los Angeles Times* with the *Washington Post*, the *Chicago Daily News*, and several other papers began marketing supplemental services did UPI's managers recognize the danger.

They then began to tell the staff explicitly that in time some newspaper editors might feel comfortable with one major agency and one supplemental and that UPI was likely to be the one that got dropped. UPI managers did begin pushing to get more interpretive, analytic, and enterprise stories initiated by UPI on the wire. But the effort had mixed results. More enterprise stories did run, but the main news report continued to be filled with neutered, foreshortened, "Dragnet" reporting. The result was that big-league papers came to see UPI (and to a lesser extent, AP) mainly as a tip sheet and source of news briefs rather than the full-fledged news supplier of old.

To some extent, the trend among big papers to try to cover more of the news themselves may have been inevitable as they became richer and could afford to do more. In larger cities with competing papers, editors needed to distinguish their product from the competition. But in smaller cities (ironically, the very audience for which the wires thought they were editing), the supplementals also appealed strongly to smaller papers because the major agencies did not keep up with changing demands. Less emphasis on speed, and more on accuracy, thoughtfulness, thoroughness, and enterprise might have helped.

In any case, UPI's managers knew that newspapers were not going to be a reliable main source of revenue forever. They looked for other business opportunities but guessed wrong about which ones to get into. During the heyday of commercial newsreels, UPI and Movietone had been partners in a newsfilm operation. When the rise of television caused Movietone to drop out of the business, UPI set up a joint venture with the Independent Television Network of Britain called UPITN, to continue the business for TV. Despite considerable investment not only of money but of management time and attention, the subsidiary never became the large profit center the company had hoped, and UPI eventually sold out to its partner.

Meantime, in the mid-1960s, UPI executives missed two of the best prospects that came down the pike. One of those, created by the advent of commercial communications satellites, helped turn Reuters into the fat cat agency it is today. The newly available satellites sharply lowered the price of voice-grade transoceanic circuits. These circuits were useful not simply for telephone or telephoto transmissions; they could be subdivided into twenty or more teletype circuits. An odd circumstance gave the teletype circuits a huge potential value. The great postwar hunger for dollars had led the national telecommunications monopolies in many countries to set teletype tariffs at outrageously high levels. But the news agency franchise made it possible for UPI (and its competitors) to lease the large-capacity voice circuits, and then to market the unused time to other news enterprises at prices substantially below the monopoly tariffs.

UPI's managers in Asia at the time lobbied very hard to get the company to lease such a circuit. They proposed to resell part of the excess capacity and to use part to send a report on U.S. business for sale in Asia. UPI headquarters vetoed the idea, for reasons that I do not know. Instead, UPI chose to hire just a couple of teletype circuits and to try to defray their cost by carrying third-party newspaper traffic. This arrangement was called *NEAT* (for News Exchange Agreement Transmissions) and it was justified to suspicious telecommunications officials with claims that UPI was carrying the dispatches as part of its regular service. In much of Asia, at least, and, I suspect, elsewhere as well, the company stuck with old-fashioned, sixty-word-per-minute radio teletype communications until well into the 1970s.

Meantime, Reuters moved ahead. It leased broad-band circuits with worldwide reach. It set up a much more efficient third-party service, charging American newspapers and magazines two-thirds of the full telex rate to move their correspondents' copy from the field to the home office, thereby earning handsome profits and cementing its connections with leading publications.

Reuters also began transmitting a comprehensive business report, including fast and accurate market quotations. It branched out from the standard media customers and sold this service directly to traders, brokers and businessmen. In the 1970s, as computer technology evolved, the British news agency was able to offer an even more lucrative service under which a trader with a Reuters terminal acquired not only access to real-time market reports, but direct links to brokers elsewhere. With that, traders could order foreign exchange and some commodity trades over Reuters wires. That service made Reuters a financial giant—a worldwide organization that has 175,000 terminals, and plans to expand even further into direct electronic trading.

The other opportunity missed by UPI became, I believe, a substantial benefit to AP. In the mid-1960s, the New York UPI headquarters had some talks with Dow Jones about a joint-venture international financial wire. Why the discussions failed I do not know, but when they did, Dow Jones went to the competition and established what is now the AP–Dow Jones news service, with a significant overseas clientele. Afterward, UPI made a brief stab at setting up its own independent financial wire in Tokyo, but the company was unwilling to invest either in wire capacity or in editorial resources to create a product. The "wire" it produced with one part-time editor in New York and one full-time staffer in Tokyo consisted mainly of a handful of daily market reports and a few items from the U.S. domestic business service shoehorned into the information flow of already-overloaded international circuits. For obvious reasons, UPI's service was unable to attract clients, and it folded in a matter of months.

More than a decade has passed since the Scripps interests abandoned UPI. As UPI sank toward bankruptcy in the mid-1980s, its new owners put substantial pieces of the business up for sale. The newly cash-rich Reuters acquired UPI's international photo service as a way to help sell Reuters's news report to American clients who wouldn't subscribe to a service without pictures. UPI's photo archives were sold off to the Bettmann Archive, which now distributes them. The right to distribute UPI reports to data-base customers went to a third-party firm. Thus, instead of expanding into new areas or capitalizing on businesses it was already in, the company shrank. The bankruptcy period of 1985–86 decreased confidence among news subscribers that the agency could survive, thereby undercutting further the media base on which UPI relied.

The essential point here is not that news agencies are a dying breed, as Schwarzlose seems to argue. In the information age, the notion that large information-gathering organizations have no real future doesn't make much sense. But as is true of any other enterprise, to survive they need to expand and adapt to changing conditions. Reuters, and to a lesser extent AP, managed to do that. UPI's current management says it is moving in that direction.

12

The Supplemental News Services

Nathan Kingsley

Supplemental is one of those self-explanatory words describing something extra that extends or strengthens the whole. Over the course of the past two or three decades in the newspaper industry, however, supplemental news services that were once seen as an afterthought, a polish added to the traditional wire services, have assumed a different role. For many editors the supplemental news services are now the principal resource on many breaking stories, as well as the source of more traditional backgrounders and features on culture, entertainment, finance, and sports.

Little recognized outside the profession, these supplemental services have been a boon to those editors who are serious about journalists' obligation to create and sustain an informed electorate. "They have contributed spectacularly to providing the coverage essential for a free press," says Harry M. Rosenfeld, editor of the *Capital Newspapers* in Albany, New York, and onetime editor of the *Herald Tribune* News Service as well as a former assistant managing editor of the *Washington Post* during its Watergate coverage. "We cannot afford our own foreign correspondents or a full-time staffer in the nation's capital, but through these services we can afford to provide our readers with the best of American journalism," Rosenfeld explains.[1]

A significant force in the newspaper industry since their inception, these services have grown in popularity as advances in technology have helped them provide a smooth flow of polished reporting directly into the computers of client newspapers from where it can be fed with extraordinary speed into the printing process. Equally, the diminishing need for newspapers to subscribe to both AP and UPI, the two relatively expensive mainline news agencies, has increased the allure of the supplementals.

The most explosive period of growth for the supplementals came in the 1960s and 1970s, when many weekly newspapers converted to dailies and suburban sheets grew to a respectable size. "We came along at the right time," Rob Roy Buckingham, of the *New York Times* News

Service (NYTNS), told Jonathan Fenby, author of the Twentieth Century Fund's landmark study of press services. "We offered serious in-depth stories. The AP and UPI were not doing this kind of thing, but readers and editors were demanding it. What started happening in the United States was that papers found they could get more for their editorial dollar by taking a supplementary service, so they were ready to drop either the AP or UPI. And as smaller papers grew, instead of taking a second wire service as in the past, they found they could do well by taking a supplementary service in its place."[2]

Table 12.1
MAJOR SUPPLEMENTAL NEWS SERVICES AND
THEIR CLIENTS, 1989

News Service	Number of Clients
Los Angeles Times/Washington Post News Service	650
New York Times News Service	500
Scripps-Howard News Service	350
Knight-Ridder Tribune Information Services	270
Copley News Service	175
Christian Science Monitor News Service	118
Newhouse News Service	77

SOURCE: *Presstime* (May 1989).

The grim consequences of this development usually hit UPI. How-ever, UPI executives flatly reject comparison to a supplemental service, describing the agency as a full-service news wire. But its client list has been battered over the years from the supplemental challenge on one side and AP on the other. UPI's client rolls are estimated to number in the low hundreds, whereas AP has approximately 1,400 newspaper members.[3]

As UPI scrambles to find itself an economically viable role, it must fend off a mounting challenge from the supplementals. If a scaled-back UPI should try to evolve into a "super-supplemental," presenting a menu of more specialized coverage instead of its traditional file, UPI would find it impossible to match the supplementals' prices, because the supplementals sell a "by-product" of their parent paper's produc-tion, absorbing some immediate basic and heavy costs with which UPI must cope.

It is difficult to calculate the total usage of supplemental copy, be-cause many of the papers are multisubscribers. Table 12.1 gives a list of the major supplemental news services and their clients.

Dominating in volume, reach, and client list are the two majors in this field, the *Los Angeles Times/Washington Post* (LAT/WP) service and the *New York Times* News Service (NYTNS). Each claims to move about 125 stories daily for an average total of some 100,000 words. Knight-Ridder/*Tribune* News Wire (KRTN) says it moves about 200 stories daily; its news stories average 800 words and features average 1,400 words.

Blessed with a widely respected parent that is often considered as close as any to being a national American newspaper, NYTNS, after a brief debut in 1899, made its real start in 1917, a year that saw a sharp increase in American readers' level of interest in news both from Washington and from overseas. The Scripps-Howard News Service (SHNS) began operating the same year.

NYTNS offered its reportage of World War I to about a dozen leading U.S. newspapers by a relatively primitive process of supplying carbons to the New York bureaus of subscribers. About a decade later the NYTNS was incorporated into a package distributed by wire by the *Chicago Tribune* to papers west of the Mississippi, the *Times* reserving to itself eastern distribution rights.

World War II set off a greater, though still modest, growth in NYTNS subscribers, which accelerated after the end of that conflict. As Washington became the focus of world attention, service was extended to foreign papers with correspondents in the United States.

In the 1950s NYTNS began to serve medium-size newspapers; its major competition was limited to the *Herald Tribune* News Service (HTNS) and the Chicago *Daily News* Service, both of which subsequently vanished with their parent papers. NYTNS canceled its distribution arrangement with the *Chicago Tribune* in 1959 and set up its own wire network throughout the United States, Canada, Europe, the Far East, and Latin America. A little more than a decade later it added pictures from the *Times* staff, and in 1987 it leased its own satellite channel.

Keeping pace with modern technology, NYTNS began, in January 1989, a computer graphics service that daily provided subscribers with fifteen to twenty pieces of computer-to-computer art keyed to news service copy such as financial, science, health, and education reporting.

The *Los Angeles Times/Washington Post* News Service began operating in 1963 and a decade later came KRTN, originally launched under the initials KNT.

The appeal to subscribers, in economic terms, was always the offer of the full staff service of a major newspaper for less than the cost of one local reporter. Although information about subscription fees is tightly guarded, the fees range from $1,000 to several times that figure annually, depending on a combination of client circulation, prestige, and haggling capability.

According to the ANPA survey in 1989 the Eugene (Oregon) *Register-Guard* paid $7,800 to NYTNS and $12,700 to LAT/WP annually, in contrast to the $197,000 it paid annually for AP's full news, sports, photo, and graphic services. At the lower range of charges, according to ANPA, were the Spartanburg (South Carolina) *Herald Journal*, which paid KRTN $9,600 for news and graphic services, and the Victor Valley (California) *Daily Press*, which paid $1,440 for SHNS and $3,300 to NYTNS.[4]

Publishers' attitudes towards spending money for resources do not, of course, always coincide with those of their editors. Some years ago when I was managing editor of the *Herald Tribune* News Service, I visited a Canadian city in which both morning and afternoon newspapers were owned by the same man. The editors of both papers pleaded with me to present the case to the publisher to subscribe to HTNS. The publisher listened to my sales pitch, nodded, and then leaned back in his chair, flicked the ash off a large cigar, and said, "You know, Nat, I don't have the slightest doubt that taking the *Herald Tribune* News Service would make us better papers." Then he smiled and added, "But I don't have to have better papers."

For the parent paper, sponsoring a news service not only is an effective way of covering some of the cost of production but also reflects an element of pride and desire for broader recognition. "We showcase the parent papers," says LAT/WP editor and president John Payne.[5]

For client editors, subscription to a news service offers a rich range of coverage and expertise. For instance, Payne points out that on major stories the LAT/WP wire offers clients a choice of the main leads of both the *Los Angeles Times* and the *Washington Post* as well as *Newsday* and the *Baltimore Sun*.

Beyond the copy itself is the chance to draw on wide professional awareness. Says Joe Ritchie, national/foreign editor of the *Detroit Free Press*, speaking of access in NYTNS to the *Times* front-page advisory, "Generally we try to make sure we're covered on national and international stories that paper [features]. . . . We do recognize that there's a lot of expertise at Times Square and we want to give our own readers the benefit of that expertise."[6]

The parents of the supplementals relish this prestige and influence. Doug Gripp, then a senior executive of LAT/WP, told the ANPA, "It's an extension of what the papers do. It projects our logos worldwide."[7] Along similar lines, Albert Johnson, executive managing editor of the

Gary (Indiana) *Post-Tribune*, told the ANPA, "Some of it has to do with the corporations feeling a need to establish themselves as authoritative leaders in the industry."[8]

For the clients, the prestigious association with newspaper industry leaders is a factor, above and beyond the quality of the reporting they provide. As one editor of a small midwestern paper said on signing up as a client of HTNS, "Some of my readers will never get to New York but they know where it is and what it is."[9]

Is the cost worth it? Or can a paper get by with just the mainline wire services?

Several elements come into play, including the economics of the client paper and its need to be competitive—and the fact that the mainline agencies, AP in particular, have over the years increasingly faced up to the quality-versus-speed challenge of the supplementals and moved to meet it by offering more thoughtful, deeper, analytical pieces and more features. Nonetheless, the very nature of the wire services puts a premium on topicality and speed, which tends to push the analytical or feature coverage to a lower priority. As Fenby put it,

> What makes the greatest impact on subscribers and dominates the agencies' editorial activities is immediate coverage of significant events in terms that can be grasped straightaway by readers, listeners, and viewers—regardless of their prior knowledge of the subject involved. Agencies do not have time to deal in depth with any but the biggest events. Speed and simplicity are paramount; originality of thought ranks much lower on their scale of values, not because such values are disdained or distrusted in themselves, but because they conflict with three more highly valued elements in agency operations . . . to put out as many stories as possible . . . to appeal to as many subscribers as possible . . . producing more copy each day than would be possible if each story involved original thought and presentation.[10]

Volume alone makes the point. Most supplementals file a daily word count in the low tens of thousands and distribute between twenty and thirty stories a day. The major wire services produce millions of words and hundreds of stories a day.

Another difference is that the major wire services are available to any outlet able to pay, whereas some of the supplementals try to protect their own chains and the parent paper, withholding the service from potential or actual competitors.

It is clear the existence of the supplementals has led to a broader handling of the news and a greater resource for the editor who seeks

*Douglas Borgstedt (*Editor and Publisher*)*

depth of coverage. They provide the kind of background information knowledgeable print journalists recognize their electronic media competition cannot match, despite the latter's great advantage in immediacy.

For the client editor the supplementals offer a polished report, already edited, sometimes already reviewed by high-powered legal experts of the parent paper, pared to size by experienced desk editors, and bearing the names and datelines of star correspondents. They also provide an opportunity to hitch a ride on a major paper's exclusive reporting. Notable examples are, for subscribers to the LAT/WP news service, the *Washington Post*'s reports on the early stages of the Watergate scandal and, for NYTNS subscribers, the Pentagon Papers report.

Although many other services can be thought of in "supplemental" terms, such as Gannett News Service and Ottaway News Service, most of them are in business to serve their own groups or are supplied to outside clients through the larger supplementals. Foreign services, such as Agence France Presse, Reuters, and Deutsche Press Agentur, are sometimes handled as supplementals but operate as mainline major news services, despite strong pitches recently to move more heavily into the American market as secondary sources.

The strongest growth of the supplementals came during the 1980s. According to ANPA's 1989 survey, LAT/WP has the greatest distribution, with 650 newspaper clients worldwide having a total estimated circulation of 110 million. A decade ago the service had fewer than 200 subscribers. LAT/WP also sells an all-sports wire (begun in 1984) to 176 papers worldwide. NYTNS jumped from 285 newspaper subscribers in 1983 to 500 today. KRTN zoomed from 30 in 1978 to 270 today, and Scripps-Howard News Service from the 21 Scripps-Howard papers in the early 1980s to 350 subscribers today.[11]

These numbers, combined with the lamentable disappearance of several major afternoon newspapers, suggest that there is little room for further growth.

At a time when the field was considerably more open and the *Herald Tribune* News Service was fighting Chicago *Daily News* and NYTNS, the *Herald Tribune* editors discovered that the smaller papers were a lucrative source of income. Although each small paper paid a very modest fee, the HTNS costs were negligible. Long before fax and satellite transmissions existed or were considered commercially viable, HTNS had a desk editor edit out dated time elements in its wire stories, top them with a long-life or timeless lead, and reproduce them for a packet of stories mailed to smaller papers for fees that ranged from $15 to $20 weekly. When these fees were multiplied by several hundred clients who paid their own postage costs, the news service came out ahead.

Within the past two or three years the supplementals have again recognized this market and moved vigorously to exploit it. According to ANPA's 1989 report, NYTNS editor John Brewer says that the NYTNS has operated a pony wire for about a decade, and Dan K. Thomassen of SHNS says that "sixty to seventy percent of our growth in the last two years has been in the secondary markets."[12]

The supplementals have tried to tailor a package that meets the editorial requirements of the smaller papers at a price they can afford. In 1986 SHNS created a packet of shorter stories called "Design." KRTN has come up with a similar format called "Select," and LAT/WP offers a short form called "Basic Service," which consists of about fifty stories specially selected and edited for length.

One by-product of this market growth is an effect first noted in the larger papers but now more pronounced in those with obviously smaller news and features holes. Syndicate executives, who market the work of columnists, are complaining that they are having trouble placing new columns and seeing more cancellations because papers are using feature and analytical material provided by the supplementals.

For source material all the supplementals start with the parent company's staff. Some pick up stories from group member papers and other contributing papers. SHNS and KRTN use stories written specifically for their wire from some of the parent company reporters, and KRTN's editor Scott Bosley notes his reliance as well on material from the *Dallas Morning News, Boston Globe, Orange County Register*, and the *Seattle Times*. "In all," he says, "we distribute material from 40 sources to nearly 300 newspapers in the United States and around the world." NYTNS and LAT/WP, however, rely only on the copy originated for the parent and contributing papers.

THE WIRE AND ITS NEWS

The relationship between the wire's source material and the material of its news service has sometimes been troubling. During the 1950s, HTNS had a limited foreign staff and its editors scrambled to get their hands on good material. In those presatellite days when cable costs were a major expense, overseas bureaus were instructed to send timeless feature stories by mail, hard copy to the cable desk, and carbons to the HTNS desk.

The *Herald Tribune* cable editor's attitude toward news was simplistic: Anything that moved by wire had to be more valuable than anything that came through the mails. He would throw the mailed articles into the bottom drawer of his desk while editors at the HTNS desk, hungry to fill a nine-hour wire, would take the carbon, update it with any later wire developments, and send it to clients. Time after time the *Tribune*'s managing editor would come over to the HTNS desk to ask why AP was quoting a client paper with a story sourced to the *Herald Tribune* which he had never seen.

The whole resource issue—particularly the demand for features—is so circumscribed by staff limitations that supplementals on occasion have to overcome the prejudices and egos of the parent paper's staff and editors in purchasing outside material. Because of staff limitations, HTNS began to purchase free-lance material and in effect to syndicate copy from other publications or services. Both practices are dangerous. One valuable source for HTNS was the *London Observer* Foreign News Service (LOFNS), which offered fine content that required delicate editing. The LOFNS writers often put the lead near the end. A piece might start along the line of "I was strolling in the garden with the prime minister," and in the next-to-last paragraph the copy would read, "He turned to me and said, 'We declared war this morning.'"

The relationship between supplemental news services and their clients vary widely. Heath Meriwether, executive editor of the *Detroit Free Press*, commented to me:

For the *Free Press* our most important supplemental wires are
hardly supplemental. The Knight-Ridder/*Tribune* wire, to which
we are a major contributor, is probably our most important contributor for national and international news. And we use the *New
York Times* wire daily.

We edit and combine wire services heavily. Most major stories
draw on the supplementals instead of or in addition to the AP
and/or UPI.

We make heaviest use of the supplementals in our news sections
although we also use them frequently in such areas as lifestyles,
entertainment, and travel. They are probably used least in
business—our focus is strongly local, and we often staff important
national stories ourselves—and sports—tough deadlines make it
difficult to use the supplementals for breaking stories.

Meriwether's national/foreign editor, Joe Ritchie, adds that "in certain geographical regions we rely heavily on the Knight wire for stories
that provide a perspective the wires generally don't give." Among the
examples he cites are Latin America, where the *Miami Herald* reportage is valuable and "the *New York Times*, [which] helps our Soviet coverage and backs us up on Eastern Europe. . . . The *Times* and *Boston Globe*
have augmented our Middle East coverage." As another example of the
diversity provided by this particular supplemental, Ritchie points out
that the *Times* service includes the Cox news service, "which is useful
especially for its access to *Atlanta Journal and Constitution* staffers."

The flexibility of the supplemental, in effect extending the reach of
the client editor, is demonstrated in Ritchie's observation that "I can
easily call on editors in Miami, San Jose, and Philadelphia when I have
a question about a story or a request for an enterpriser or spot coverage . . . other papers' editors are indirectly accessible through the
Knight wire in Washington, and the filing editors in Boston and Chicago for the *Globe* and *Tribune* are also helpful."

The potential for "query rights for clients," a practice that HTNS
initiated among supplementals, was an innovation that paid off hand-
somely. With the *Herald Tribune* News Service, if a client editor's request turned up a story useful for the overall service there was no
charge. If the item was of interest only to the requesting client, the
HTNS would charge only for expenses, sometimes unconscionably
front-loaded.

Although the supplementals do not automatically emulate AP in
providing staff-written stories responsive to individual requests by
client editors, they do "make every effort to supply such coverage," as
Brewer says of the NYTNS operation. And although KRTN offers no

query rights as such, KRTN editor Bosley says that KRTN does allow clients to ask for a specific coverage story and the KRTN will "go find one."

Whatever their history, the role and influence of the supplemental services today has led some to question the appropriateness of the name *supplemental*. "Our role is really as the alternative to AP, which has emerged as the dominant news service of record," says Brewer.

"You really have to drop the term 'supplemental' these days," says Arnold Rosenfeld, formerly editor at three of the Cox leading papers in Dayton, Atlanta, and Austin, and now Cox News Service executive vice-president and editor in chief. Rosenfeld says there is a considerable difference between the early use of the supplementals as a source of material to combine with other files and today's situation, when editors "looking for the best stories" print the supplemental version intact.

KRTN serves about 230 clients including 20 in Canada and several overseas. Its total file approaches 5,500 stories monthly. The weekday file averages about 200 stories totaling 160,000 to 200,000 words. That size of file, says editor Bosley, led KRTN to approach the smaller markets with the "Select" service on the theory that the smaller-circulation dailies (under 100,000 or 50,000) were simply not staffed to "even look" at such a volume of material. KRTN came up with a daily service running about 35,000 words, averaging about 45 shorter, more tightly edited stories divided more or less evenly between hard news coverage and feature material. Whereas the main wire may carry several versions of a top story from Knight-Ridder/*Tribune* and the four contributing papers, the "Select" service limits its file to one story.

As with several other services, a mushrooming market for graphics has led KRTN to create and rapidly expand its graphics service. Although the effect of graphics on readership is still the subject of hot debate in the newspaper industry, the drive to improve the use of graphics has become so intense that "newspaper design has become a moving target," says one expert. "What looked modern three years ago now seems to have stepped out of the Stone Age."

Maintaining a strong graphics capability is an expensive and difficult recruiting and staffing problem for most medium-size and smaller papers. For supplementals to reach out into this market not only is a natural sales strategy but, as Bosley of KRTN points out, often leads to purchase of the wire for linked coverage.

All the "joint source" papers of KRTN file into Washington, where the news service desk fashions its wire for transmission to subscribers. The selection process goes beyond topical news play to features, "from food to chess," says Bosley, including daily features, columns, and every Wednesday a package of weekend pieces.

Acknowledging that for his parent papers the news service is a way of meeting coverage expenses, Bosley emphasizes that the rates charged are not designed to make the supplemental a "major profit center." Rather, as with the other supplementals, the service helps create a measure of pride in showcasing Knight-Ridder staff around the country and in helping to produce a variety of reporting and depth of coverage that is "healthy for journalism and therefore healthy for the country."

The fear among some students of journalism is that these services may take editing decisions out of the hands of local editors and shift this important function to unknown persons thousands of miles away, leading to homogenized coverage and news play judgments. Because so many papers rely so much on supplementals for cultural and commentary pieces, the fear extends to visions of some implicit "thought control" drifting foglike over a wide variety of audiences.

Executives of most supplementals respond vigorously that the opposite is true. The vast array of talent made available at economic prices provide local editors with a diversity to shape their papers in ways they could not otherwise afford. For example, consider editor Bill Breisky's *Cape Cod Times*. This paper has a modest circulation (approaching 60,000), but it consists of relatively well-informed readers interested in national and world affairs. His paper uses many of the principal supplemental services in reaching out as well to a summertime audience of vacationers with a similiar range of interests. This readership has easy access to other major urban newspapers and is not one to be satisfied with routine wire service coverage. Breisky and his colleagues tend to favor certain reporting that they have come to respect, such as NYTNS and LAT/WP on Soviet and Mideast affairs— matters of considerable interest to their audience. Despite heavy reliance on AP for main coverage, Breisky notes that, according to a survey a few years ago, the *Cape Cod Times* used 232 pieces from NYTNS and 230 from LAT/WP in the course of one month.

Breisky's paper also relies on the supplementals for some nontraditional support. Unable to match staffing of major New England teams by his wealthier urban competition, Breisky is able to draw on his supplementals for sports coverage, sometimes edging his competition in timeliness. The *Cape Cod-Times* tries to reach into the supplementals for the unusual, Breisky says, like a poem from the Baltimore *Sun* on Bette Davis, which was published with her obituary.

The threat to mainline agency competition is real. Some analysts believe that AP has already captured up to 90 percent of the mainline wire service market. But few editors view the supplementals' role in helping to create a near-monopoly position for the AP as a threat to their papers. More see the supplementals as a valuable resource that offers coverage more diverse than what they could expect from two more or less equal mainline agencies, and more affordable.

In surveying the torrent of incoming material in the newsroom from local stringers to the supplementals, some editors express a concern over other and distant hands exercising the editorial "gatekeeper" function, making decisions, often irrevocable because of time constraints, about what events will be covered and which version of them will be presented.

Whatever the merit of those fears, it is ultimately the judgment of the individual editor that determines the supplementals' value, and with it the judgment on journalism itself. More than a hundred and fifty years ago Thomas Carlyle observed, "Great is journalism. Is not every able editor a ruler of the world, being the persuader of it?"

NOTES

1. Personal conversation with the author.
2. Jonathan Fenby, *The International News Services: A Twentieth Century Fund Report* (New York: Schocken Books, 1986), 73.
3. Rolf Rykken, "Supplemental Wires Vie for Clients," *Presstime* (May 1989): 14.
4. Ibid., 16.
5. Personal conversation with the author.
6. Personal conversation with the author.
7. Rykken, "Supplemental Wires," 16.
8. Ibid., 18.
9. Personal conversation with the author.
10. Fenby, *International News Services,* 172–73.
11. Rykken, "Supplemental Wires," 16.
12. Ibid.

IV

Newsmagazines

13

Remaking *Time, Newsweek,* and *U.S. News and World Report*

Byron T. Scott and Ann Walton Sieber

The table was a large one, but the three were all crowded together at one corner of it. "No room! No room!" they cried out . . . . "I want a clean cup," interrupted the Hatter. "Let's all move one place on."
 . . . The Hatter was the only one who got any advantage from the change; and Alice was a good deal worse off than before. . . .
 —"A Mad Tea Party," from Lewis Carroll's *Alice's Adventures in Wonderland*, 1865.

In the fifties and sixties the newsweeklies were up there like kings . . . now they appear confused. They're thinking like monthlies and behaving like weeklies.
 —Magazine industry leader, in an understandably anonymous personal interview, 1989.

In the area of mass communications occupied by magazines, the nature of news has long been defined by three weeklies. In order of both circulation and revenue these magazines are *Time,* which was founded in 1923 and now has a total paid circulation of 4.3 million; *Newsweek,* which was established in 1945 and now has a paid circulation exceeding 3.1 million; and *U.S. News and World Report,* which was started in 1933 and now has a paid circulation approaching 2.3 million. In the elite club of only seventy-five American consumer magazines with paid circulations exceeding a million, *Time* ranks twelfth, *Newsweek* is nineteenth, and *U.S. News* (which downplays the ponderous tail of its logotype) is twenty-fourth.[1] In 1988, *Time* was the leading harvester of advertising revenue among the 156 members of the industry's Publishers Information Bureau (PIB); *Newsweek* was fifth.[2]

All the revenue-producing numbers associated with the three leading newsweeklies rank among the leading 1 to 2 percent of the estimated 18,000 to 20,000 magazines now published in this country. And yet, the March–April 1989 cover of *Columbia Journalism Review* depicted them as battling dinosaurs, with the cover line, "The Newsmags: Is the Species Doomed?"[3] How can three such powerful bastions of American journalism be in trouble, much less in danger of extinction?

The same facts that led the *Columbia Journalism Review* to see dinosaurs suggest other conclusions. In this chapter we contend that the Big Three newsmagazines will survive, although not in the forms known to past generations of American readers. Unlike the dinosaurs, these and other large-circulation consumer magazines will evolve rather than expire, and in doing so will be part of the modern redefining of the nature of news.

Newsmagazines occupy but one table, albeit in the forefront of the hall, in the "Mad Tea Party" under way. The results of their evolution will affect all media, heavily influencing patterns of information distribution into the twenty-first century. There is plenty of room at the table, but, like Alice's friends, the three major newsweeklies are struggling to find a better cup to offer their readers and advertisers.

BACKGROUND

If the three giant newsweeklies suffer from any dinosaurlike characteristic, it is their myopia. Assuredly at their current size and age, they are entrenched institutions. Lack of perspective is a well-documented institutional characteristic, whether the institution is a church, political party, university, or magazine. The world tends to change despite its institutions, which in turn live out life cycles in splendid isolation, ignorance, or defiance. Years before he claimed the Sunday magazine from the failed *New York Herald Tribune* and made it into the first successful modern city magazine, *New York*, Clay Felker wrote:

> At times the rise and fall of magazines has the fascination of classic Greek dramas, with fates seemingly pre-ordained and unsusceptible to the best efforts of intelligent men.
>
> There appears to be an almost inexorable life cycle of American magazines that follows the pattern of humans: a clamorous youth eager to be noticed; vigorous, productive, middle age marked by an easy-to-define editorial line; and a long slow decline, in which efforts at revival are sporadic and tragically doomed.[4]

Felker concluded that this phenomenon stems from the fact that magazines are edited by human beings, not by machines or corporations. Humans are a proud species and journalists an even prouder genus, fierce and competitive but often unable to see beyond the next deadline, the current issue, or this budget year. All of the three newsweeklies, *Time* in particular, have boasted phalanx-upon-phalanx of proud, fierce, and talented writers and editors, epitomized by Henry Robinson Luce. (With ironic prescience, Carroll has the Mad Hatter scold Alice, "If you knew Time as well as I do, you wouldn't talk about wasting it. It's him.")

Throughout the 1960s, when their combined weekly readership exceeded 47 million adults, the three major newsmagazines were central to the American definition of news. Sociologist Herbert Gans declared that the newsweeklies, along with the national TV networks, dictated who constituted the Knowns (who were almost continuously in the public consciousness) and segregated out the Unknowns (who only entered the news as victims of violence, voters, or statistical aggregates).[5] Like most critics of that era, Gans blamed the newsweeklies for encouraging international stereotypes (for example, South American countries are characterized by revolutions and volcanoes); fostering upper-middle-class values; and hiding fault lines in the national psyche, such as racism. As American media have diversified and diverged and as readership and viewership of national media have declined, such charges have become less common.

The current dilemma of newsmagazines continues to be encapsulated, as described by the *Columbia Journalism Review* and other oracles of modern publishing, in two words: "the numbers." Traditionally the fact-gatherers and storytellers have been schooled to ignore publishing economics in favor of "objectivity" and "editorial independence." Today's journalists have come to realize that the significance of certain numbers—circulation, advertising revenue, return on stockholder investment, for example—is that they vitally affect both the quantity of news ("the news hole") and the quality (editorial resources). Let us consider these numbers, beginning with circulation.

Circulation

In 1923, when Luce and Briton Hadden founded *Time*, there were fewer than 180 generally circulated magazines and only about 24 million households in the United States. In 1933, when *U.S. News* was born, there were still fewer than 200 national magazines and a total of 28.5 million homes. By 1937, *Newsweek* had become one of fewer than 250 general-circulation periodicals entering 37.5 million postwar homes.[6] The so-called golden age of magazines, as scholars and participants alike have come to regard the 1920–60 period, took place in a relatively small media universe dominated by some 1,700 daily newspapers and uncounted local radio stations. Now consumer magazines number in the thousands, and the racks of any larger grocery's "family reading center" have more than 300 titles.

During the years immediately following World War II, the three major newsweeklies shared equally in the general growth of all media. They continued to thrive even in the 1950s and 1960s, when the ability of television to reach millions with even mediocre shows killed many mass weekly magazines, including *Look, Collier's, American Weekly, Saturday Evening Post,* and even Luce's revered *Life* (the last two weeklies returned as monthlies several years later).

Table 13.1
CIRCULATION OF THE BIG THREE AND ALL MPA
MAGAZINES, 1970–90
(millions of copies)

Year	Time	Newsweek	U.S. News	All MPA members
1970	4.27	2.61	1.88	210.23
1975	4.39	2.92	2.11	207.78
1980	4.45	2.95	2.08	214.00
1985	4.69	3.06	2.07	244.12
1987	5.04	3.18	2.35	252.20
1988	4.74	3.31	2.36	256.27
1989	4.34	3.18	2.21	265.25
1990	4.09	3.21	2.31	259.25

SOURCE: Audit Bureau of Circulations statistics.

But in the 1970s, circulation stagnation set in on the Big Three, most noticeably on the flagship of Time Incorporated (table 13.1). In 1970, the total paid circulation of *Time* had reached 4.27 million, a penetration approaching 7 percent of 63.4 million American homes (204 million people). By 1988, its circulation had risen only about 470,000 (to 4.74 million) while the nation's population continued to grow at a far faster pace (240 million and just over 90 million households), so *Time's* market penetration dropped to 5 percent. In both 1988, 1989, and 1990, *Time* announced circulation cuts "to focus our demographics"—cuts that lopped thousands of subscribers from its lists. Its current guaranteed circulation to advertisers is 4 million.

During this same twenty-year period the circulations of the other two newsweeklies have been little better. While experiencing some circulation growth, the penetrations of *Newsweek* and *U.S. News* relative to the total population have shrunk. Between 1970 and 1990, the total paid circulation of *Newsweek* gained about 600,000 (from 2.61 to 3.21 million), with the largest gains coming between 1986 and 1988. *U.S. News* in the same period went up 430,000 from 1.88 to 2.31 million copies distributed, but with the largest growth in its history (300,000) coming in 1986 and 1987.

The average annual growth in circulation of the three largest news-weeklies has lagged behind the average for all Publishers Information Bureau member-magazines in every year since 1970 except for the 1986–8 period, when the aggressive circulation tactics of the smaller two attracted considerable media attention. After briefly crashing the 5 million barrier in 1987 in an expensive circulation war with its two competitors, *Time* actually circulated 250,000 fewer copies in 1988.

During a ten-year period when the 156 PIB magazines raised their aggregate circulation by 46 million (from 210 to 256 million), the three newsweeklies raised theirs a total of only 1.65 million. These statistics are not bad for a specialized magazine that focuses on some geo-graphic or socioeconomic substratum, but far too little for national periodicals of general circulation. The penetration of newsweeklies into the American home has slipped badly, despite TV promotions, gifts of plastic radios and calculators, and aggressive reporting and writing.

Advertising Revenue

Although the pattern is changing slowly, magazines typically earn 60 to 70 percent of their direct revenue from advertising sales. (Of course, in the thousands of controlled-circulation magazines, the contribu-tion is 100 percent.) According to a 1984 Price-Waterhouse survey, the pretax profit of MPA-member magazines averaged 11.29 percent; *Time*, the revenue leader for the year 1988 as well as many others, is estimated by one media publication to have cleared 41.48 percent before taxes last year.[7] Given numbers like these, the total circulation picture seems not so gloomy, but the apparent trends in this category can be deceptive.

Advertising in magazines simply costs more than ever before. A four-color, full-page advertisement in *Time* costs advertisers just over $120,000; the same ad in *Newsweek* runs about $100,000, and in *U.S. News* about $67,000. Of course, those are the costs before discounts, incentives, deals, and other inducements are introduced; much like the sticker price on a showroom automobile, the rate card or listing in the advertiser-oriented periodical, *Standard Rates and Data*, are only a beginning point for bargaining that may bring down published prices by 20 percent or more.

From an analytical viewpoint, the Standard Rates and Data Service (SRDS) rates tell less than another, calculated number, cost per thousand, or CPM (table 13.2). (The CPM formula is the one-page cost divided by the circulation and multiplied by 1,000.) The cost for reaching every one thousand readers in a magazine's audience is viewed as an index of competitiveness and audience quality. Nearly a quarter-century ago, general-circulation magazines came to realize that they could not match television for lowest CPM. More viewers look at the worst-rated network show than ever read *Look* or *Life* in their primes. A magazine's CPM tends to rise as the "quality" of its audience improves. "Quality" in a media audience is generally determined by age, income, education, residence, and other characteristics that suggest a predilection toward buying the advertised products.

Table 13.2
COST PER THOUSAND OF SELECTED MAGAZINES
DECEMBER 1990
(Based on the cost of a color page)

Magazine	Circulation (million)	Cost per Thousand
Better Homes and Gardens	8.0	$15.80
Family Circle	5.4	16.53
Good Housekeeping	5.2	21.93
Time	4.1	31.25
Newsweek	3.2	33.64
U.S. News	2.3	31.32

SOURCE: *Standard Rates and Data*, May 27, 1991.

Note: The depressed economy that created a more competitive magazine advertising market in 1990–91 only heightened the *Newsweek* cost-per-thousand advantage of so-called better demographics over its direct competitors and other such mass-circulation periodicals as women's magazines.

The CPMs of the newsmagazines have actually increased faster than their circulations, creating (prebargaining) more revenue per ad page. Although the prices look grossly different for the three news-magazines, the competition is decidedly tighter if measured by CPM. Clinging to the top is *Time*, with a color CPM of just over $27. But despite the difference in circulation, *Newsweek*, with a CPM of $32+, is not too far behind. This competitiveness is generally attributed to *Newsweek*'s ability to attract "DINK" (double income, no kids) and "PINK" (professional income, no kids) elements of the baby boomers in recent years. *U.S. News* has a CPM just exceeding $29, but has improved its demographics and thus its ad rates under the aggressive ownership of Mortimer B. Zuckerman, who bought the weekly in late 1984 and, to the horror of journalistic traditionalists, functions as owner-editor.

Of course, a potential advertiser is not limited to buying space to reach the entire mass circulation of *Time* or *Newsweek*. *Time* offers a potpourri of "split runs," including eleven regions of the United States, the fifty major markets, and special breakouts for business ("the largest business circulation of any magazine. . ." trumpets its SRDS listing), top management, college students, and the highest-income ZIP codes, among others. *Newsweek* offers a similar, slightly more limited selection, concentrating on geography. *U.S. News* offers advertising breakouts in California, major U.S. regions, and some twenty-six metropolitan areas. Of course, the CPM is considerably higher for these editions, although the number of readers reached is less.

The improved revenue picture for magazines in general has been created by a decidedly undemocratic strategy—focusing on desirable (to advertisers) demographic groups, thus "raising reader quality"— and newsweeklies are no exception. *Time*'s two recent circulation cuts were made with this goal in mind.

Although return on investment is what charms stockholders, there is evidence that the Big Three are losing sway in a related area: total ad pages (table 13.3). *Time* ran almost 1,000 fewer ad pages in 1988, when it led the industry in revenue, than in 1965. In 1965, described by PIB

Table 13.3
ADVERTISING PAGES OF THE BIG THREE AND ALL MPA
MAGAZINES, 1965–90
(thousands of pages)

Year	Time	Newsweek	U.S. News	All MPA Members
1965	3.43	2.77	2.60	82.67
1970	2.53	2.92	1.67	78.83
1975	2.42	2.63	1.65	80.73
1980	2.85	3.12	1.94	114.71
1985	2.70	2.71	1.78	152.57
1987	2.37	2.56	1.70	155.64
1988	2.50	2.48	1.87	166.72
1989	2.73	2.50	2.05	178.29
1990	2.73	2.30	2.01	171.69

SOURCE: Publishers Information Bureau.

as "the best [ad year] in the history of the magazine industry," the Luce flagship ran 3,430 advertising pages; in 1988, it ran 2,500.

Newsweek has actually surpassed its larger rival in total ad pages during eighteen of the past twenty years, although in 1988 it ran slightly fewer. Nevertheless, *Newsweek*, too, ran fewer ad pages in 1988 (2,480) than in 1965 (2,770), even though it has exceeded the 3,000-page level during half of the intervening years. By contrast, *U.S. News* is selling roughly 700 fewer ad pages than in the mid-1960s (1,870 in 1988, compared with 2,600 in 1965).

The slippage in ad pages among these three periodicals contrasts sharply with the growth of "non-news" PIB consumer magazines, which have more than doubled the number of ad pages sold, up from only 82,673 in 1965, when the Big Three had more than 10 percent of the market, to 166,718 in 1988.

These numbers suggest that not only are the three newsmagazines reaching a smaller proportion of American households, but they also have fewer editorial pages to work with by virtue of a long-standing diminution of advertising pages. Hence perhaps the most disturbing numbers affecting the Big Three are out of the control of even the brightest editors, writers, ad representatives, and circulation managers.

Trends to Note

The newsmagazines could argue that the nature of American media and of information consumers has changed dramatically since Vietnam (speaking in historical and economic terms—we tend to use our wars as benchmarks). The principal cause of the deteriorating numbers within the newsmagazines is, of course, other media. In his gloomy *Columbia Journalism Review* analysis, Bruce Porter noted the rapidly overcrowding field:

> Where once the newsmagazines stood alone in offering readers a colorful, well-written report of the week's events, larded with sufficient interpretation to put the news into clear perspective, in recent years this endeavor has drawn a heavy amount of competition from week-in-review sections of newspapers, as well as from television talk shows, magazine shows, and weekend insider programs about economics and Washington politics.[8]

Perhaps the most intense competition comes from within the species. Each year, more than three hundred new consumer magazines and uncounted business, trade, company, local, fraternal, and other periodicals are founded. There are now an estimated twenty thousand print publications calling themselves magazines in the United States alone. Regardless of their primary audience and focus, most have "news" as a principal component of their editorial formulas. The four largest-circulation U.S. magazines (*TV Guide, Reader's Digest, Modern Maturity,* and *Better Homes and Gardens*) are not newsmagazines, but they bring wanted information to clearly identified and characterized audiences that have a nonjournalistic definition of news.

To this situation add the explosion of other media, primarily electronic: the arch villain TV, with its wicked nephews cable and videotape, along with compact discs, videotext, and the reborn medium, fax. The litany is familiar and growing. At least print is seeking to survive against electronics by proliferation, if not by excellence.

So great is the media clutter that it has spawned at least one self-help book. Richard Saul Warman's *Information Anxiety* made a brief, impressive showing on best-seller lists in 1989. Warman defines "information anxiety" as "apprehension about the ever-widening gap between what we understand and what we think we should understand. It is the black hole between data and knowledge."[9] Warman advises readers to "minimize the time you spend reading or watching news that isn't germane to your life. . . . Bad news produces a sense of urgency . . . it preempts other events, the stories with heart and value." While leaving the operational definition of "germane to your life" to the information consumer, Warman advises overburdened consumers to avoid stories about problems and catastrophes. His philosophy is consistent with a growing public alienation with "bad news" and an interest in taking control of individual information consumption.

The changing nature of publishing, characterized by the dawning age of the megaconglomerate, has already struck profoundly at the newsweeklies. All three are owned by large corporations, but the largest has become mammoth. After months of courtroom and boardroom maneuvering—followed closely by platoons of stock analysts carrying cellular telephones, according to several accounts—the marriage of Time, Inc., with Warner Communications has taken place. What was originally a benign business deal for both, a proposed exchange of stocks resulting in merger, became a "leveraged buyout" of the bigger company (Warner) by the smaller, Time, Inc. The deal, consummated in late 1989, created the world's largest media conglomerate with revenue approaching $10 billion per year. By comparison, annual sales by West Germany's Bertelsmann A.G., until then the largest media-specific corporation, are "only" about $6 billion.[10]

Initial speculation about the result of the Time-Warner union centered on potential negative effects for competitors and on potential conflicts of interest (*Time* reviews of Warner movies, and so on). Less noted is the fact that the new megaconglomerate will no longer be dominated by print revenues. In 1988, Time, Inc.'s revenue totaled $4.5 billion, 59 percent of which was in magazines and books and 41 percent in cable TV and programming. Under the partnership, magazine revenue will amount to only about 18 percent. Warner Communications depends on broadcasting for 45 percent of its revenue and on all electronic media for more than 80 percent. Clearly, the largest portions of what media observers are beginning to call "the 8,000-pound gorilla" will be guided by the revenue and news standards associated with electronic communications and entertainment. (By comparison, publishing revenue supports 76 percent of Bertelsmann's enterprises.)

Media critics from A. J. Liebling to Ben Bagdikian have pointed to the dangers in mergers and "bottom-line journalism," but the Time-Warner merger is the largest demonstration to date that news also has become a commodity. As such, the news is increasingly governed by marketplace constraints. As Richard Wald, senior vice-president of ABC News, observed in 1987, "Where we are now is that the public good is served by private forbearance. And private forbearance is forthcoming as long as it can be afforded. . . . The managers of enterprise want to do good while doing well."[11]

One final trend to observe before moving on to the future of newsweeklies and their news products is the aforementioned activism of consumers and their often palpable desire to take control of their information consumption. This behavior has been accepted as a commercial fact more solidly than it has been documented by scholars; it has taken on the status of a given by strategists of the media. Increasingly, editors and publishers are equating reader selectivity with the nature of news itself. James Autry, editorial president of Meredith Corporation magazines, told a Center for Communication seminar, "The basic nature of the business is reporting problems, not solving them. So the news-oriented publications have become identified with problems, not solutions."[12]

Discontented readers, of course, do not hold public meetings to complain about journalism that fails to hold their interest—they merely stop buying the magazine. Among those calling for a conduit between readers and publications is Everette E. Dennis, head of the Freedom Forum Media Studies Center at Columbia University. The media are now obligated to establish formal, noncommercial feedback methods that elicit positive reader behavior rather than drive ad linage, he says. Speaking particularly of newsmagazines, Dennis admits, "Some newsmagazines once known for their heavy-breathing prose have cleaned up their act and are new exemplars of reporting. They are facing tough times, though, as competition for advertising dollars intensifies and as structural reorganization is brought on by an era of lean-and-mean management."[13]

THE PRESENT AS WINDOW TO THE FUTURE

Of what does "cleaning up the act" consist? All three major news-weeklies have undergone graphic redesigns since 1985. Like most modern magazines they now are what art directors call "cleaner products," that is, they have larger pictures, shorter stories, and more white space. Media critics have attacked aspects of these metamorphoses as substituting glitz for content. Assuredly a combination of these redesigns and the "soft" advertising climate for magazines in the late 1980s diminished both the number and length of stories in a typical issue. The average length of a newsweekly article, once thousands of words, is now fewer than 750. Although *Newsweek* and *Time* have recently attempted to publish essays of up to 1,500 words, *U.S. News* is less gray than ever before. Much of their prose and analysis has been reduced to charts and graphs in the new design category called "info-graphics." This trend, also increasingly popular in newspapers and traceable to the founding of Gannett's *USA Today*, is only slightly less evident in the other two newsmagazines.

Hundreds of column inches in *Folio*, the *New York Times* business section, and *Advertising Age* have been filled with the major and minor adjustments of personnel, advertising policies, and editorial philosophies. *Time* editors are quoted anonymously about the specter of Warner movies such as *Batman* influencing their story judgments, *Newsweek* writers complain about "glitz editing" that eliminates facts and analysis, and *U.S. News* staffers worry about conflict of interest resulting from the top editor's owning the bottom line. At this writing, it is impossible to prove whether any of these fears are justified. In the aggregate, these editorial perturbations are little different in kind or in number from those experienced by other consumer magazines during recent years. But as news giants, these three magazines are still considered newsmakers on a national scale. Their troubles have added mightily to the nightmares of journalists in all media. Only a few of the recent news stories really suggest the future of these publications.

EXAMINING THE BIG THREE: WHAT DOES IT ALL MEAN?

Despite a shared Monday cover date, all three news giants are, like all consumer magazines, on the newsstands considerably ahead of that day—in the case of weeklies, four to seven days ahead. On a typical Monday, May 13, 1989, there was no election or tragedy to dictate cover choices. *U.S. News*, selling at $1.95 per issue, featured the profiles of a rank of Russian soldiers illustrating the first of a series on Soviet military power titled, "How Serious a Threat?" *Newsweek*, charging a nickel more than *U.S. News* on the newsstand, opted for Candice Bergen, TV's "Murphy Brown," and a feature on "How Women Are Changing TV." Both issues had seventy-six pages, plus cover. *Time*, dominating in size and cover price at $2.25 and eighty-eight pages plus cover, featured a story about a middle-class black businessman, "Between two worlds . . . making it in white America—but they're paying a price."

Of course, covers are not the entire magazine. None of the three currently claims heavy newsstand sales. However, newsstands and free-distribution waiting-room copies are the primary sources of new subscribers. But covers also serve to draw in subscribers, and research has shown that covers are at the top of reader recall about any issues. When readers are asked why they do or do not renew subscriptions, they most frequently name cover articles when they cite specifics. The covers are the front windows to the editors' minds.

Those windows reveal the following:

- Features predominate over news in cover choices.
- Analytical pieces are aimed specifically at desirable (to advertisers) demographic groups.
- As often as possible, the magazine articles emphasize a "service" angle (that is, they explain a topic with the intent that readers will take some action on that information; personal finance leads the category, with health closely following).
- All three magazines frequently address the reader directly ("you . . .").
- *Time* favors the most traditional news and analysis features, while *Newsweek* favors features. *U.S. News*, long a traditional news publication, is now unabashedly a "service" publication, considerably more so than the other two.

We sampled the covers of the three magazines for a ten-year period, 1979 to 1988. One issue a month, usually the first cover date, was selected. Few changes of subject matter or approach are evident until 1986, a year in which *U.S. News* and *Newsweek* were making aggressive gains in circulation. Although the sample remains small, it appears that all three have tripled the number of covers devoted to topics of service to the reader.

Before the mid-1980s, the newsmagazines rarely used the first or second person on their covers. Now, "you" or "we" is commonplace. *U.S. News*, which advertises itself as "the newsmagazine with news you can use," is the leader in adopting this formerly inviolate journalistic shibboleth.

Communication scholars have referred to this effort to get readers involved as "mobilizing information." In previous studies, newsmagazines have been shown to do less of this "mobilization" than magazines of other types—at the level typical of newspapers. A study published in 1983 noted, "One important reason why MI [mobilizing information] is missing from news of controversy seems to be journalists' feeling that to report MI is to depart from objectivity."[14]

Never a bastion of objectivity, as the infamous parodies of Luce's "Time-speak" recall, all the newsmagazines have adopted strong viewpoints on any and all topics. Balance, in the sense of giving other viewpoints a fair hearing, has declined, although we do not have a good measure of that characteristic. Suffice it to say that the newsmagazines show greater evidence of appealing to specific, advertiser-desired demographic groups, a practice that introduces significant subjectivity.

Two observations seem appropriate here. First, in appealing to specific audiences, the newsmagazines are following the precedent of virtually all other magazines and, within the decade, of many metropolitan and suburban newspapers. Second, the objectivity of the newsmagazines has always been questionable. Previously, doubts about objectivity focused on the conservatism of a Luce or the liberalism of a Katharine Graham (the *Washington Post* Company owns *Newsweek*), not on marketing considerations.

Increasingly, communications scholars question the value and even the existence of what traditional journalists call objectivity. One sociologist has called it "a strategic ritual protecting newsmen from the risks of their trade."[15] James W. Carey, professor of communications at the University of Illinois and perhaps the most respected former dean of an American communications school, has referred to objectivity as part of "an inherited form of crypto-science. . . . I sense we are coming to the end of an era, to an end of our need for that sort of thing."[16]

What Carey suggests instead of objectivity appears to be what the newsweeklies are tending to provide on parallel paths. Whether it be the "service orientation" of *U.S. News*, the "baby-boom survival manual" of *Newsweek*, or the "older-generation explanation of the world" offered by *Time*, there is ample evidence that each is reaching an identifiable audience. Industrywide readership studies, such as the

Simmons Market Research study, confirm that audiences overlap little, and that reader behaviors are relatively distinctive.[17]

The technique of audience targeting is no more subtle in the newsmagazines than it is in any other consumer book. It is clear that many working editors are still uncomfortable with it and therefore occasionally clumsy. Recriminations are mixed with the embarrassment of an older generation of journalists, who insist that "news is news."

We believe that audience focus is justifiable because it facilitates more effective communication in a crowded, noisy marketplace. The news in newsmagazines apparently is in transition. The newsweeklies are trying, as Carey suggests, "to engage in a collaboration with their readers" that forms a trusting, continuing relationship.

By doing so, are newsmagazines collaborating against other segments of America? Of course. For nearly twenty years we have known, as Gans showed, that magazines in general and newsweeklies in particular are an "elitist medium" in the sense that they are not generally preferred by poorly educated, low-income, and disenfranchised persons in our society (although most of the last group do have individual magazines). The modern fallacy of magazines is that many of them still feel they can behave, as they did in the 1940s and 1950s, as true general media. That role has been usurped by others, primarily the electronic media, and it cannot be reclaimed without specific audience-oriented changes, probably in separate publications.

We asserted at the beginning of this chapter that newsmagazines will survive, but that is not the same thing as saying that *Time, Newsweek,* and *U.S. News* will survive. Sheltered as they are within larger corporations they may survive longer than economic realities dictate. *Time* is even more sheltered as the namesake of a corporation, but this is not an absolute hallmark of immortality. As Felker observed, all magazines die, as people do. The elixir of longevity is change. Much evidence suggests that both the newsmagazines and their definitions of news are changing in response to market pressures.

As observers within the journalistic or academic world, we may not approve of all that we see. Occasionally, an editor will foolishly purchase the ersatz diaries of Hitler, rock stars will be deified in preference to world leaders, and the world of the powerful will be explained in preference to the plight of the powerless. The newsmagazines will not ignore news, but they will treat it in ways contrary to our background, our experience, perhaps our older professional values.

As we attempt to form a twenty-first-century definition of news, the vast panoply of audiences and interests suggests that we adopt a simpler definition. Hence we nominate the definition of news attributed to the late Turner Catledge when he was managing editor of the *New York Times*: "My own definition of news is that it is something you didn't know before, had forgotten, or didn't understand."[18] By becoming increasingly attuned to audiences and their information needs, newsmagazines will find their "new cup" at the media tea party.

NOTES

1. Magazine Publishers Association Monthly Reports for 1988.
2. Publishers Information Bureau *Annual Report* (New York, 1988).
3. Bruce Porter, "The Newsweeklies: Is the Species Doomed?" *Columbia Journalism Review* (March–April 1989): 23–9.
4. Clay Felker, "Life Cycles in the Age of Magazines," *Antioch Review* (Spring 1969): 7.
5. Herbert W. Gans, *Deciding What's News: A Study of CBS Evening News, NBC Nightly News, Newsweek, and Time* (New York: Vintage, 1979), 12–15.
6. Magazine Publishers Association, *Advertising Bureau Report*, 1990.
7. Jeff Marcus, "Profit Profile: *Time*," *Magazine Week* (January 23, 1989).
8. Porter, "The Newsweeklies," 23.
9. Richard Saul Warman, *Information Anxiety* (New York: Doubleday, 1989), 34.
10. Ferdinand Protzman, "An Imposing Rival for Would-Be Time-Warner," *New York Times*, April 3, 1989.
11. Richard Wald, "A Ride on the Truth Machine" (New York: Gannett Center for Media Studies, 1987): 17.
12. Unpublished proceedings, 1985.
13. Everette E. Dennis, *The Changing Economics of News* (New York: Gannett Center for Media Studies, 1988).
14. James Lemert and Marguerite Ashman, "Extent of Mobilizing Information in Opinion and News Magazines," *Journalism Quarterly* (Winter 1983): 657.
15. Gaye Tuchman, "Objectivity as Strategic Ritual: An Examination of Newsmen's Notions of Objectivity," *American Journal of Sociology* 77 (1972): 660.
16. James Carey, speech at University of Missouri, April 1989.
17. *Simmons 1986 Study of Media and Markets, Multi-Media Audiences: Media Imperatives* (New York: *Simmons Market Research Bureau*, 1986).
18. Quoted in Bernard Roshco, *Newsmaking* (Chicago: University of Chicago Press, 1975), 9.

Commentary

David Gergen

It has been common in recent years to predict the demise of one or another of the three leading newsweeklies. Not only do I believe that prediction to be wrong; I think instead we should be asking, Are there going to be four newsweeklies instead of three?

Demography favors the newsweeklies. For a long time, the newsweeklies have made their greatest penetration among readers in their forties and fifties. It is not surprising that readership lagged during the past twenty years as the baby boomers entered their twenties and thirties. Now that the baby boomers are entering their forties, the potential readership for the newsweeklies is rising. Of course there are many indications that baby boomers are not serious readers, but I expect those habits will change as they assume greater responsibility for the nation's future.

I also believe that as other news media target narrow audiences, there will be an increasing need for a common information base, which the newsmagazines have traditionally provided.

It is also likely that as network television viewing declines, some advertisers are going to look to the newsmagazines as a way to reach national audiences. This may be especially true of foreign companies, particularly the Japanese, who have already sharply increased their national advertising. The automobile companies still find the newsweeklies a good place to advertise when they have special national deals they want to tell people about.

The newsweeklies have an important informational role to play. Our whole economy is becoming internationalized and people need to understand international affairs. Most newspapers in the United States do not deal well with international affairs. That is why the larger papers, like the *Wall Street Journal* and the *New York Times*, are winning a national audience. They fill a need for international reporting, and I think the newsmagazines have a similar role to play.

There are some obvious challenges facing the newsmagazines. All the different news media have shifted somewhat in what they do. Traditionally, local TV news broadcasts covered strictly local news, the network evening news presented the first national and international headlines, the daily newspapers published the first full news stories, and the newsmagazines provided the interpretation and analysis.

Now the local news stations have increasingly moved into national news. One of the reasons that the network news shows are losing audience share is that many people have seen the national news by the time the network news goes on the air. When Larry Grossman became president of NBC News he told me that his greatest challenge was figuring out how to make the news fresh when so many people had already seen the national and international news stories that the network provided to local stations. That problem has since gotten worse for the networks, as their affiliates frequently send their own reporters to cover international events.

And of course the network news broadcasts—as well as the daily newspapers—have moved more and more to provide the interpretation that the newsweeklies used to do. In response to this, the newsweeklies can no longer simply provide a snapshot of the week's events. They have to provide some wider, often more historical perspective. In effect, they ought to provide the depth that the monthly magazines have captured for a long time. If the newsweeklies move to this broader perspective they can address the news in a way that people will welcome.

It is still possible at the end of the week for a magazine to provide some fresh understanding of how the world works if it has some really bright, interesting, well-educated people who can write well. *The Economist* is an example of what we in this country ought to be thinking about. A growing number of Americans reads *The Economist* because it is both original and incisive.

I doubt that an American version of *The Economist* would appeal to a mass audience, but newsweeklies like *U.S. News* ought to be moving in that direction—toward providing the fresh perspective that *The Economist* provides. Other publications as well—magazines like the *New Republic*, the *New Perspectives Quarterly*, and the *National Interest* —offer pieces that are refreshing and provocative. The newsmagazines have to strive to do the same thing.

Television news clearly helps to build newsmagazine readership on significant stories. When there is saturation coverage of a major event by television—the *Challenger* shuttle disaster is an obvious example— the newsstand sales for newsmagazines will skyrocket the following week. People want to read more about what they have been hearing and watching on television.

There are some notable exceptions, of course. When President Reagan met with Mikhail Gorbachev for the first time at the Geneva summit in 1985, television coverage was massive. One would have assumed this would have led to booming magazine newsstand sales but when all three newsmagazines put the Reagan-Gorbachev summit on the cover it was the worst seller of the year. All of us in journalism clearly have our work cut out in persuading our readers and viewers to pay more attention to the forces sweeping the world.

Commentary

Thomas Griffith

America's weekly newsmagazines have been pictured as dinosaurs struggling to survive in a hostile world, but the death watch over the newsweeklies is premature. Unlike the dinosaurs, newsmagazines have shown themselves to be surprisingly adaptable.

When Henry Luce set out to create *Time* magazine in the 1920s, it was his Calvinistic belief that every citizen had a duty to be well informed. *Time* would make them so. This ambition is rather different from the superficial broadcasting slogan, "Give us 22 minutes and we'll give you the world," which permits all kinds of froth to parade as news. Devoting just two hours a week to reading *Time* would give earnest readers the facts they needed to be alert, responsible citizens. The goal *Time* set for itself was to be "curt, clear, and complete."

In the beginning *Time* cribbed much of its material from newspapers—it did not have its own correspondents—but it also covered wider fields of interest that newspapers neglected. *Time* offered sections on art, music, books, education, religion, medicine, the press itself, and science. Apart from the brevity of the writing, *Time*'s innovation was to tell the news through people—a device that marked the real beginning of personality and celebrity journalism, which has had some hazardous side effects.

Luce wanted a magazine that appeared to have been written by one person (a formulation I never liked) and read by one person who would be able to understand everything in it. That reader would read it from cover to cover. For example, because it was assumed that women were not interested in business, and not well informed about it, whenever *Time* used a word like *parity* or *debenture*, it always put in a footnote to explain the term.

Luce's fond dream of the well-informed cover-to-cover reader, who enjoyed testing his or her comprehension in *Time*'s current events quizzes, faded as the pages of the magazine fattened with advertising. Sometime in the 1940s it became clear that many readers were skipping around, not reading everything. This realization prompted editors in each section to concentrate more on readers especially interested in a subject, thus increasing the breadth and sophistication of the writing. This notion did not really trouble Luce; he did not want to lose the general reader, but had always believed in stretching the reader's mind a little.

In compressing the news, Luce found it necessary to make editorial judgments on what mattered and what did not, and he concluded that objectivity was impossible. Making sprightly, and sometimes impish, judgments was one thing, but before long Luce discovered in himself a Calvinistic duty to tell readers what they should think. This determination was not a problem so long as Luce was biased only in favor of God, country, and Yale, but when he included the Republican Party and Chiang Kai-shek's China in his partisanship, the magazine made a number of enemies. It took *Time* years to live down this side of its reputation. *Newsweek*, in contrast, although it had a much smaller budget for news coverage, was more open to a variety of opinions: its less didactic openness was its greatest strength in the years when *Time* dominated the newsmagazine world.

Today *Time* and *Newsweek* are in many respects much alike. What *Time* calls its People page, *Newsweek* labels Newsmakers. Both now practice a kind of undogmatic, skeptical, mainstream opinionizing. This similarity gives both magazines an identity problem, but one more troubling to *Newsweek* as the number-two newsweekly. The third newsmagazine, *U.S. News and World Report*, concentrates on politics, world affairs, and business, usually disdaining culture as frivolous and irrelevant. Editorially there is room for everybody, but economics is another matter. The newsweekly form may survive, but not everyone in it.

The newsmagazines are no longer in competition just with one another. The problem is that all forms of journalism are not content to do what they do best; they want to do what everyone else does. Television, for example, is unexcelled at showing news in action—wars, riots, fires—and bringing the camera up close to people in the news who can speak for themselves. But television also insists on doing what it is not so good at—presenting instant analysis of events by glib commentators voice-activated by the sight of a camera's red light. Too often this amounts to speech before thought, and judgments before there is adequate information.

And newspapers are no longer content to give readers the fullest account of what has happened each day. The Sunday *New York Times*, with its long analyses and personality pieces, has itself become a stretched-out newsmagazine, although much heavier to carry. Perhaps such borrowing is only fair, because newsmagazines began as parasites of newspapers. But this convergence of different forms of journalism, all unwilling to do just what they do best, partly explains the news glut of today. Even when there is little news to report, such news as there is will be repeated hourly on the radio, seen in full color on television, extensively reported in the newspapers, and then analyzed and condensed in the newsmagazines. The newsweeklies come last in that food chain.

They are also being buffeted from another direction. They find it hard to serve the needs of a new generation that does not follow the news closely, does not read newspapers regularly, feels no duty to be well informed, and finds other distractions more compelling. The newsweeklies do try to follow this generation in its new curiosities. Where *Time* once had sections titled "Animals," "Aviation," and "Miscellany," it now has sections called "Behavior," "Living," and "Travel." *Newsweek* lumps these all under the vogue title "Lifestyles." But chasing after lifestyles does not quite fit the basic premise of newsmagazines. On occasion *Newsweek* in particular has wandered from its moorings, emphasizing trivia and shortchanging serious news and cultural coverage.

Newsmagazines have always had something to worry about—the cost of paper, circulation, or advertising, or the effect of inflation on pricing—but acknowledging problems facing the magazines is not the same as predicting their demise. What newsweeklies now suffer from most, aside from the news glut, is a trendiness glut. Trendiness profits other publications more—those that do not feel the burden that the newsweeklies do to say something serious about serious matters. But trendiness, by definition, is ephemeral. I do not expect most of the trendy magazines to be around, as the newsmagazine form has been, for nearly seventy years.

14

Foreign News: How *Newsweek* Has Changed

Milan J. Kubic

The first story I wrote for *Newsweek* from the Latin American beat, in the spring of 1963, was about a thriving industry in Belem, then an isolated Brazilian town on the equator. As Belem's mayor proudly told me, the whole town was servicing and selling into the interior used cars that were smuggled to Brazil on boats from as far away as Florida. It was an amusing little tale that had no news peg, no major significance, and no natural U.S. audience except for used-car dealers. I mention it only because the story ran four columns—more than a page—in *Newsweek*, a play that would be unthinkable today.

In those balmy years of my first overseas assignment, *Newsweek* lavished attention on foreign news, including stories from south of the Rio Grande. The magazine had not only a regular international news section but also a separate subsection titled "The Americas," and stories not much more earthshaking than the Belem smugglers would occasionally command a two-page spread.

At the end of an era of domestic tranquillity and just before the age of package tours and cut-rate air travel, reportage from abroad was still something of a journalistic feather in the cap. For the publisher, foreign coverage was offered as a touch of the exotic, wafting among ads for Camel and Budweiser; for the editor, it was a measure of reporting strength; and for the staff, a dangled image of Ernest Hemingway or C. L. Sulzberger. Opening a new overseas bureau, which is what I did in Brazil, was an all-around cause for celebration.

But major changes were just down the road. Even before I left Washington for Rio de Janeiro, the civil rights movement was picking up steam in the South, and in Vietnam, the ranks of American "advisers" were swelling into the thousands. The Belem smugglers—and a lot of other people whose doings I covered—were rapidly slipping beyond my readers' scope of attention.

The full truth struck me on the night in late 1963 when I arrived, after a daylong trip, at a godforsaken village in the north of Brazil to be told by two somber Peace Corps volunteers that John F. Kennedy had been assassinated. Suddenly, my journalistic fare of military *golpes*, features about the Alliance for Progress and pursuits of leftist guerrillas in out-of-way places lost pertinence. I still remember how, shortly after the Watts riots, I almost lost patience with an official in Quito who griped that the American media ignored his country. "Why on earth should the old lady in Duluth be interested in Ecuador," I finally could not resist asking, "when she has so many troubles at home?"

My editors must have pondered the same question, because from the mid-1960s on, the foreign coverage of *Newsweek* would increasingly focus on the drama in Vietnam. Moreover, when the war story was slow, the foreign bureaus would collectively lose space to the civil rights story and other dramatic domestic news. By the time I left Rio, in May 1967, "The Americas" section had been scrapped, and my last adventure yarn about "The Unknown Amazon" was destined for oblivion. Such marginal use as the magazine made of the story marked the end of an era. Robert Christopher, *Newsweek*'s innovative foreign editor, included my space-devouring jungle trek in an early mockup of what was to become part of the magazine's answer to the changing winds in publishing. *Newsweek International*, as Christopher's mutation was called, was an idea whose time was coming, even though it did not go fully on-stream until a few years later.

Christopher, a former foreign correspondent with an exceptionally well-organized mind, was inspired by two surveys that had crossed his desk at the end of the 1960s. One was his own tally showing that, week in and week out, his international news section was cut by three to five columns—one page or more—in order to beef up other departments in the magazine. The space cuts resulted in underemployment of some of *Newsweek*'s foreign correspondents precisely at a time when the magazine was building up its network of overseas bureaus.

The other survey that caught Christopher's eye showed that eight out of ten *Newsweek* readers abroad were not, as it was widely assumed, expatriate or vacationing Americans, but English-speaking foreigners who wanted to know more about the state of the world. After considerably more research, Christopher concluded there was a market overseas for stories that were being increasingly squeezed out of *Newsweek*'s domestic editions. By the end of 1972, he won a green light from the *Washington Post-Newsweek* company to launch Atlantic and Pacific editions of the magazine, which were printed, respectively, in Switzerland and in Hong Kong.

When it first took its bow in December 1972, *Newsweek International* typically left out a page or so of domestic U.S. news and substituted a couple of stories from Europe and Asia for which there was no space in the domestic editions. But as time went on, *Newsweek International* acquired its own editing and writing staff in New York as well as regional reporters abroad, and the weekly change-over rose up to 40 percent of the contents of the magazine. The overseas magazine included a regular back-page interview about foreign events and, with increasing frequency, a different cover story for each regional edition.

At first glance, *Newsweek International* looked like a poor cousin of its slick and sassy domestic counterpart: it was printed on a distinctly inferior paper, it had fewer ads, and the photo reproductions—mostly in black and white—were gray and not very clear. In the United States, where *Newsweek International* was not sold at all, it remained virtually unknown. But overseas, Christopher proved that American journalism had a substantial export market. Crammed with news from all over the globe, *Newsweek International* sold beyond expectations.

Six years after it first came out, *Newsweek International* added a Latin American edition, and another six years later, a slightly shorter version became part of the *Bulletin*, Australia's big newsmagazine. Three years ago, yet another version of *Newsweek International*—translated from cover to cover into Japanese—went on sale in Tokyo. Since then, the annual ad revenue of the venture has surpassed $55 million, and circulation has hit 800,000 copies. The prestige of the magazine is high, and its editorial demands keep the foreign bureaus busy. Had it not been for Christopher's invention (which was later copied by *Time*) the ranks of *Newsweek*'s foreign staff, I suspect, would have been thinned considerably years ago.

With minor changes, the stock in trade of *Newsweek International* has remained hard news. But the "main" magazine, as the domestic editions were called by some staffers in the New York headquarters of *Newsweek*, frequently varied its formula in response to the changing tastes and interests of the American public. In the late 1960s and early 1970s the editors gave big play to *Newsweek*'s superstar Arnaud de Borchgrave, an adventurer at heart and a globe-trotter par excellence, who was beyond doubt the most enterprising foreign correspondent of my generation. De Borchgrave's exploits, which included extensive combat coverage in Vietnam, would fill a book. Those I witnessed as *Newsweek* bureau chief in Beirut included his exclusive interview with Gamal Abdel Nasser—the first given by the Egyptian strongman after the traumatic Arab defeat in the Six Day War—unprecedented twin roundtables with Israeli and Palestinian intellectuals, and gripping reportage from the Intercontinental Hotel in Amman, where de Borchgrave and other journalists were held hostage by Palestinian fedayeen.

Doonesbury, *by Garry Trudeau. This 1977 Doonesbury follows a September 13 memo from Executive Producer Av Westin to his staff to increase the "content, the pace and the impact of the 'ABC Evening News.'... The whip-arounds have to be produced... so that one correspondent leads to another or picks up from another. We are now electronically wiping from one area to another. This requires extra video pad ... so that we may wipe into and wipe out of each spot." (Copyright © 1977 G. B. Trudeau. Reprinted with permission of Universal Press Syndicate. All rights reserved.)*

A professional with guts and panache, de Borchgrave unfailingly materialized in the eye of any international crisis and, before deadlines, delivered copy that almost invariably received *Newsweek* cover treatment. During the Jordanian-Palestinian showdown in September 1970, for instance, de Borchgrave's reporting gave the magazine four Middle East covers in a row. Three years later, de Borchgrave topped his Middle East exploits by flying to Libya, crossing the desert by car, and joining a front-line Egyptian unit just before it conquered an important Israeli position. Once again, de Borchgrave's exclusives made several *Newsweek* covers, but the time for heroic foreign coverage was fast running out. According to readership polls, the disheartening experience in Vietnam had soured most Americans on all foreign news, and their focus shifted to the multitude of domestic problems.

For those of us abroad, the pressure of stateside news meant more work. Keeping abreast of the news was no longer enough; editors demanded more creativity, more special angles to intrigue the lukewarm audience. Foreign developments still commanded substantial space, provided they affected the American reader. When I was based in Vienna and in Bonn in the mid-1970s, my longest stories dealt with the falling value of the U.S. dollar in Europe. Strong pictures also were in great demand, and a so-so tale with dramatic illustrations sometimes got better reception than a good tale with poor art. The editors were so intent on "socially relevant" yarns that during one particularly slow period, I despairingly proposed a piece on a German

Shoe, *by Jeff MacNelly. In 1991, Jeff MacNelly several times had his characters reflect on the growing ubiquitousness of CNN as a "visual wire service" in other newsrooms as well as in many government offices around the world. (Reprinted with permission of Tribune Media Services)*

chain of whorehouses. To my surprise, the story ran; moreover, *Time* published the same tale the same week that *Newsweek* did.

The growing tendency to entertain the reader caused a shift in *Newsweek*'s cover subjects from news stories to instantly recognizable celebrities. One of the best examples of the new trend was the editors' decision not to change covers in July 1976, when Israeli commandos staged a spectacular raid on the Entebbe airport and rescued 103 hostages. The swashbuckling operation took place right on deadline, but made such breathtaking reading that *Time*—whose timetable was similar to *Newsweek*'s—made a last-minute switch and put the commandos on its cover. *Newsweek* stayed with the smiling face of Princess Grace of Monaco, although it did run a sizable Entebbe story inside the magazine. The choice of cover raised eyebrows in the publishing industry and, among the foreign staff of *Newsweek*, it triggered much griping. The last word, however, belonged to the circulation department, which triumphantly announced that the Princess Grace cover sold, as I recall, more than 350,000 copies on the newsstands. It was *Newsweek*'s best-selling issue of the year and the only one to sell more copies on the stands than *Time* did the same week.

The growing impact of television has increased the importance of once-snubbed "soft" news and trendy features. By the end of the 1980s, the tube had not only lured many big advertising bucks away from the newsweeklies, but it had also wrought deep changes in the reading habits of our audience. The college-educated, aware, and preferably affluent readers whom both *Newsweek* and *Time* wanted as subscribers saw so much history-in-the-making on the morning and evening TV news that they had little need (or patience) to read similar stuff in the magazines. To make the media scene still more compli- cated, in September 1982, *USA Today* brashly set out to preempt the newsweeklies by running daily "cover" stories and by heavily exploit- ing nationwide fashion and lifestyle stories that used to be the monop- oly of *Time* and *Newsweek*.

Scrambling to meet the new challenges, *Newsweek* adopted a new look that affected all departments in the magazine, including foreign coverage. The size of the international section remained the same— about twenty-one columns, or seven pages, each week—but the text was cut an average 20 percent. The saved space went for larger pic- tures, longer headlines, charts, graphs, and blown-up excerpts from the article. Altogether, the new graphics gave readers so much simple, schematic information at a glance that they scarcely needed to read the main body of the story.

At the same time, the editors strove for more sophisticated coverage. They emphasized "big impact" exclusives, one of which—*Newsweek*'s cover on Hitler's bogus diaries—was a memorable fiasco. But the for- eign bureaus also produced a wealth of imaginative reporting that frequently used the news event only as a takeoff for novel inquiry or analysis. Thus the British-Argentine war over the Falklands inspired a *Newsweek* cover about the future of big warships, the TWA hijack in Beirut led to a ten-point program to combat terrorism, and the Sabra and Shatilla massacre—which took place before the eyes of Israeli troops in Lebanon—sparked a special takeout on the changing ethics of the Israeli society.

From the mid-1980s on, however, even this demanding formula was judged inadequate. For reasons that remain obscure, it became part of conventional wisdom in the publishing industry that eventually the American public and advertisers would support no more than two newsweeklies. Because *Time* had exceptionally strong resources, the publishing dogma ordained that either *Newsweek* or *U.S. News and World Report* would go out of business. The response of *Newsweek* was to undertake its biggest personality change in thirty years. The magazine did not give up its franchise to cover foreign news—indeed, *Newsweek* has three bureaus covering Latin America, where I used to roam alone, and its staff abroad is as high as ever, twenty persons. But with few exceptions, hard news—both domestic and foreign—has become strikingly absent from *Newsweek* covers.

The face that the magazine presents each week is inspired much more by the readers' needs and fancies than by the events of the preceding seven days. By the new standards, Lyme disease is more captivating than a massive challenge to communism played out in the streets of Beijing; John Le Carré's new novel rates more attention than the first-ever resignation in disgrace of the Speaker of the House of Representatives. *Newsweek*'s competitors also skimp on their coverage of hard news. The first rough draft of history, the newsmagazine specialty, seems to sell best—and perhaps only—as an adjunct to the latest health tips and advice for new parents. The obsession with useful news should give all of us pause. Granted, the old lady in Duluth does not have to know about the Belem smugglers. But the pendulum has swung too far, and the fault lies more with the American audience than with the newsweeklies themselves.

V

Performance

15

How News Media Cover Disasters: The Case of Yellowstone

Conrad Smith

In less than twenty-four hours starting on September 6, 1988, a single forest fire swept through 267 square miles of Montana's wilderness, burning more in that amount of time than all the fires in recorded history have done in Yellowstone National Park, two hundred miles away. The national media did not notice. A few days later, a wildfire in California's Sierra Nevada foothills destroyed a hundred expensive homes—more property than was burned during the entire summer by a dozen major wildfires in and near Yellowstone National Park. The national media noticed, but just barely. Reporters were busy that week covering the Yellowstone fires.

"We Could Have Stopped This," said the headline in *Time* on September 5, quoting front-line fire fighters who did not like environmental restrictions that kept them from driving bulldozers at will through Yellowstone's pristine backcountry. "Part of our national heritage is under threat and on fire tonight," said CBS's Dan Rather on September 7, describing wildfires that "menace one of the nation's most scenic sights." "Old Faithful Will Never Be the Same," said the *Chicago Tribune* on September 8, implying the geyser itself had been damaged. "This is what's left of Yellowstone tonight," said NBC correspondent Roger O'Neil on September 9, as his audience saw scene after scene of charred moonscape suggesting that all of Yellowstone was reduced to cinders. "Sea of Fire Engulfs Once-Splendid Park," said the *Milwaukee Journal* headline on September 11. "A Legacy in Ashes," said the cover of Denver's *Rocky Mountain News* Sunday magazine on September 18.

The press treated the forest fires in Yellowstone as a major disaster. But nobody died in the park, and there were few reports of injuries. No major buildings were destroyed. Official reviews after the fires identified no significant blunders in how the fires were fought. None of the park's thermal features or other major attractions, such as

Yellowstone Falls, was affected by the fires. Wildfire scientists consistently said that fires on the 1988 scale have occurred periodically in Yellowstone for millennia and are a natural part of the biological process. So why did these fires get so much media play?

How this story was covered is more than an academic curiosity. At stake are fundamental issues about how public lands should be administered. Is it appropriate, for example, to have privately operated ice cream stands, a pizza parlor, and a golf course in Yosemite National Park? Does the nation's need for oil justify drilling in Alaska's Arctic National Wildlife Refuge? Should the lightning-caused fires that shaped Yellowstone's backcountry be allowed to burn, as they did before Europeans arrived? Should our national parks be administered as "vignettes of primitive America," as suggested by the 1963 Leopold Report,[1] or as commercial amusement parks, as suggested by some of the comments made by James Watt when he was Ronald Reagan's secretary of the interior?

Public opinion about these questions was influenced by how the media covered the Yellowstone fires. Although the issues themselves are beyond the scope of this chapter, I do attempt to analyze how reporters failed in their efforts to cover this story, and to explore the implications of that failure for media consumers, journalists, and journalism educators. I begin by describing how I examined media coverage of the fires. Then I show how the fires became news, describe some of the errors made by journalists who covered the fires, and attempt to explain why these errors occurred. I conclude with some speculation about how news will be covered in the future.

METHOD

The print media analysis for this study is based on 112 newspaper and newsmagazine stories about the fires published during the peak coverage period, August 24 through September 16, 1988. After locating addresses for 178 of the 198 sources named in the articles, I sent to each source a copy of an article mentioning that person, along with a questionnaire about the accuracy of the information in the article. I also sent a more general questionnaire to eighty-nine newspaper and newsmagazine reporters who covered the fires. Respondents were promised they would not be identified if they were quoted. A total of 146 people who were cited as news sources and sixty-eight of the reporters responded. The returned questionnaires contained more than twenty thousand words of comments about how the fires were covered.

The television analysis is based on all 1988 evening network TV stories about the fires, which I obtained on videotape from the Vanderbilt Television News Archive. After getting initial reactions to these stories from five journalists who covered the fires, I obtained formal evaluations from four groups of experts: (1) five incident commanders who supervised Yellowstone fire-fighting efforts, (2) four wildfire behavior experts who analyzed the fires as they burned, (3) three wildfire ecologists who have published scientific papers on the subject, and (4) three experts on wildfire management policy, two of whom participated in the fire management policy review requested by the secretaries of agriculture and interior to investigate how the Yellowstone fires were fought.

To supplement these efforts, I interviewed reporters, photographers, editors, producers, news sources, ecologists, fire policy experts, and Yellowstone Park personnel who dealt with reporters. I also spent several hundred hours in aircraft and rental cars and on foot examining the burned areas in Yellowstone.

THE YELLOWSTONE FIRE AS NEWS

According to hundreds of scientific papers, Yellowstone National Park and much of the western United States have been ecologically dependent on fire at least since the last ice age. Without periodic wildfires, the health of forests and the variety of wildlife decline. With this ecological fact in mind, Yellowstone authorities in 1972 adopted a policy that attempted to reinstate fire's biological role by allowing some lightning-caused fires to burn themselves out when they did not threaten people, structures, or endangered species. Fires caused by humans would continue to be fought. Similar policies were in effect at Yosemite and in other national parks. On July 21, 1988, when wildfires began to threaten tourist areas, Yellowstone's natural-burn policy was abandoned.

The Yellowstone fires became national news on July 24 after three thousand people were evacuated from a visitor facility near Yellowstone Lake. During this first news period, reporters described these fires as part of a larger story about wildfires that were burning throughout the West. Television accounts talked of acres (not trees) "consumed," "scorched," and "destroyed." On August 5, NBC's Tom Brokaw brought the initial phase to a close. "The danger from fires in Yellowstone National Park is over," he said, "and officials plan to reopen the big Grant Village tourist center there tomorrow."

Then the unexpected happened. In the high winds of August 20, which became known as "Black Saturday," the various fires burned through 250 square miles of Yellowstone and nearby national forests. Just about everyone who ordinarily interprets wildfires was caught off guard. Weather predictions based on a century of records were wrong. No summer had ever been so dry. Scientifically based predictions about what would burn were incorrect. Young, healthy trees that were not supposed to burn did. The public belief that wildfires can be put out proved false. The most experienced fire fighters in America had difficulty slowing the fires' advance.

The national press returned in force, and the other wildfires burning throughout the West were largely forgotten. The forest fires in Yellowstone became front-page news, and the lead in television newscasts. By early September, these fires were fought by nearly ten thousand people at a cost of three million dollars a day.

Yellowstone's abandoned natural-burn policy became so controversial that a Republican senator from Wyoming called for the resignation of the Republican administration's National Park Service director. A local newspaper called editorially for the resignations of the National Park Service director, Yellowstone's superintendent, and President Reagan's interior secretary. In the ensuing media firestorm, important issues were lost to the drama of flames and the spectacle of politics.

FACTS AND PERSPECTIVE

The media coverage of the fires was characterized by surprising factual errors. For example, an ABC television story on August 30 contained an interview with a Yellowstone tourist who was identified as "Stanley Mott, Director, National Park Service."[2] The real director's name was William Penn Mott. Stories in the *New York Times* in August and early September said that the natural-burn policy, which had been abandoned late in July, was still in effect.[3] Another *New York Times* story, on September 22, said that it had been National Park Service policy never to suppress natural fires and that it was Forest Service policy always to suppress them.[4] In fact, each agency had been using a mix of both approaches.

Among news sources named in the 112 newspaper and newsmagazine stories about the fires, 9 percent of those who responded to my survey said they were misidentified and 10 percent said their names had been misspelled. Sources quoted by the *Chicago Tribune*,

Washington Post, and *USA Today* said comments attributed to them were fabricated. According to one source, a *Chicago Tribune* article published on September 8 contained more errors than facts.

But people who had served as sources for newspaper and newsmagazine articles tended to discount such mistakes.[5] "Most errors were not on the 'factual' side, but in interpreting the event," wrote a Forest Service spokesman who has been quoted in the *Denver Post.* "News accounts don't lie," wrote the superintendent of a National Forest near Yellowstone who was quoted in a United Press International story, "they just don't tell all the truths." "This particular *Washington Post* story was accurate—as far as it went," wrote Wyoming governor Mike Sullivan. "My overall impression, however, [from] news coverage of the fires in total, particularly during August and early September, was that Yellowstone National Park was totally consumed and destroyed by fire. That was not the case, as large areas within the fire perimeter suffered little or no damage."[6]

"The problems were of emphasis, not factual error, for the most part," said a reporter for the *Billings* (Montana) *Gazette.* The mistake was "slowness in putting the story in a context that gave it meaning," said a reporter for an Idaho newspaper published near the park. "Not errors in fact, exactly," said a reporter from Texas, "but a lack of perspective that gave readers and viewers no sense of the fires' ultimate impact." "Not until the end of the fires," said a Minnesota reporter, "was there any perspective about the environmental effects of the fire—and those effects weren't entirely negative. The errors in reporting this story were on analysis."

Reporters and news sources consistently complained that stories tended to overplay the damage caused by the fires instead of covering the related issues. A *Washington Post* reporter, for example, described the coverage as "a weird combination of ambulance-chasing and reports from the trenches." "The subject matter is complex," said another Washington-based reporter. "Is fire bad or good? Such subtleties do not lend themselves to the quick hit-and-run journalism practiced at most newspapers and virtually all broadcast outlets." "Wildfire is not a simple subject," wrote a *USA Today* source who lives near the park. "Causes, effects, nature's role, political pressure/concerns, and short-term vs. long-term considerations are not easily understood by the average reporter and cannot be accurately reported in a 60-second sound bite or a story that makes interesting, brief newspaper reading."

Consider these examples:

• August 22, Roger O'Neil, NBC: "In towns like West Yellowstone, where merchants depend on tourists for their economic survival,

there's increasing criticism of park policy of letting fires caused by nature burn themselves out."
- August 25, Brian Rooney, ABC: "The Park Service lets the fires burn themselves out. It's painful to watch."
- September 7, Bob McNamara, CBS, from Cooke City, Montana: "But what still angers many is a Park Service policy to let park fires burn themselves out."
- September 7, Jim Carrier, *Denver Post*, in "Anger Grows as Town Awaits Death by Fire," quoting a man whose summer home near Cooke City was threatened: "When they had a chance to put those things out they could have stomped them out, and they didn't. The Interior Department has wanted this land for years and years, and they finally found a way to get it."

What's wrong here? To begin with, Yellowstone's natural-burn policy had been abandoned a month before the earliest of these stories. More than 98 percent of what burned did so after that, while the fires were being fought. Another problem is that neither of the specific fires alluded to in these stories was subject to Yellowstone's natural-burn policy. The only fire that threatened the town of West Yellowstone was started by humans, would not have been allowed to burn under any policy, and was fought from the day it started. The fire that threatened Cooke City on September 7 started outside Yellowstone on land managed by the U.S. Forest Service. The Forest Service is administered by the Department of Agriculture, the National Park Service is administered by the Department of Interior.

"The media bought a lot of myths about the fire," wrote James Habeck, who is a University of Montana professor with a research specialty in fire ecology and who was cited as a source in the *Christian Science Monitor*.

> One myth is that fire fighters can put out fires in a dry season (they do not—rain does). Another myth is that 'let-burn' policy caused the cataclysmic fires. In fact they were bound to happen and the park policy made almost no difference. The two worst fires were human-caused, started outside the park, and were fought from the beginning. The media rarely got beyond these myths.[7]

Media scholar Gaye Tuchman has said that journalists create news stories by transforming real events into a socially constructed "reality" that meets the organizational needs of "news work." Some sources and facts are discarded, she observed, because of shared notions among journalists about what constitutes news.[8] This process, according to sociologist David Altheide, often distorts events by removing them from the context in which they occurred. "Journalists," he said, "look for angles, interest, and entertainment value."[9] In Yellowstone, this transformation of events into news became a triumph of combustion over substance.

GONZO FLAME VIDEO

"By showing gonzo flame video, everyone leaves the impression that everything in Yellowstone is burning," wrote Larry Warren, who reported the fires for KUTV in Salt Lake City.[10] Roger O'Neil, the NBC correspondent who did the most reports from Yellowstone, said that editors' desires for the "best stuff" are a constant in the back of any national reporter's mind.[11] Bob Tewes, who shot fire video for ABC, said the pressure for "today's flames" was so intense that dramatic fire footage shot after the 4:30 P.M. daily network deadline was acceptable for the morning news shows the next day but generally considered too old for the next evening's newscast.[12]

"The most sensational story seems to get the time, not the most accurate or informative," said Denny Bungarz, an incident fire commander who was called "the hero of Old Faithful" by the *Billings* (Montana) *Gazette*.[13] "The networks seemed intent on giving people the images they expected to see—troops on the fireline, fire fighters marching in columns, air tankers in action, and lots of wildlife," said MacArthur fellow Stephen Pyne, who wrote a book on the cultural history of American wildfires.[14]

"I've often felt," wrote Forest Service wildfire analyst David A. Thomas, "that reporters didn't dig beyond the common clichés associated with forest fires—scorched earth, epic events, devastation and destruction, etc.—and the result is a one-sided, one-dimensional view of fire. The coverage associated with Yellowstone was piecemeal, and the public got only a splintered view of what was going on."[15]

James K. Brown of the Intermountain Research Center in Missoula, Montana, who has published many scientific papers on wildfire, wrote:

> It seemed to me that a single theme that carried through practically all of the stories made an accurate ecological understanding of the fires very difficult. The theme was that fire fighters battled to stop wildfires that threatened to destroy lives, property, and resources. Loaded words and phrases such as "acres consumed," "acres destroyed," "disaster," "a shame," etc., were used to

describe the fires. . . . The fires did burn over the landscape, but they did not destroy it.[16]

A merchant from a town near Yellowstone National Park who was featured in a network story about the fires said that national television reporters came not to seek information, but to cast playlets they had already written.[17] A district fire manager who was a news source for the *Denver Post* wrote that "reporters were trying to create conflict, not report facts." Each of the four reporters who approached him, he said, was seeking confirmation of a preconceived story.

The correspondents for each of the networks who reported the most stories from Yellowstone conceded afterwards that coverage was exaggerated, but suggested there were good reasons for this. ABC's Gary Shepard said the exaggerated information came directly from the officials, and that reporters often did not have the time to explain that although fire had swept through an area, the fire did not burn everything. CBS's Bob McNamara said he had to rely on inept public relations people who could not take reporters to reliable sources. NBC's Roger O'Neil said that as the fires got bigger, so did the amount of misinformation.

SCIENCE AND JOURNALISM

Sharon Dunwoody and other media scholars have persuasively demonstrated that communication between journalists and scientists is often poor.[18] Scientific literacy is not particularly widespread, either among reporters or media consumers. For example, one recent study shows that about half of adult Americans do not know that the earth revolves around the sun. Reporters who did not have the technical expertise to understand a science story about the biological role of fire in shaping the Yellowstone landscape are unlikely to communicate that knowledge effectively in their stories.

A reporter who covered the Yellowstone fires for an Ohio newspaper wrote that stories like this "require scientific expertise and technical education on subjects most journalists can't even spell." Six of the sixty-eight print reporters who covered the fires and responded to my survey had pursued academic majors or minors in subjects related to science or ecology in college. Sixteen of them said that their regular beats included coverage of the environment, natural resources, or science. None of the television correspondents who covered the fires was regularly assigned to a science or ecology beat.

In theory, any reporter can cover any story by consulting appropriate experts to make up for gaps in the reporter's knowledge. In practice, finding good information sources is often difficult. Reporters must know who the experts are, how to contact them, and what questions to ask. Deadline pressures encourage journalists to interview the most accessible sources rather than those with the most expertise, and to tell the story the way it has always been told instead of looking for the ways in which each news event is different. Some reporters in Yellowstone—Diane Dumanoski of the *Boston Globe* and Brian Rooney of ABC, for example—regularly went beyond the standard fire clichés, but many others did not. "If you ask local bartenders and senators about fire policy," wrote the president of an environmental organization who was a source for the *New York Times*, "you are not going to produce coverage reflecting good science—particularly in thirty-five-second segments."

At least two misconceptions interfered with good science reporting from Yellowstone: (1) that all fires are pretty much the same and that fire is always bad, and (2) that nature is static—that the current state of any landscape, such as Yellowstone National Park, is pretty much fixed and can be preserved as it is. Until a few decades ago, even among respected geologists, the notion of continental drift was taboo. The notion that green forests in today's Yellowstone were shaped by cataclysmic, stand-replacing fires in past centuries was initially alien to most reporters and media consumers.

NEWS SOURCES

Three-fourths of the print journalists who covered the fires and virtually all the television journalists in Yellowstone were general assignment reporters. Media scholar Herbert Gans has observed that general assignment reporters are like tourists who "seek out what is memorable and perceive what clashes with the things they take for granted,"[19] such as wilderness fire suppression techniques that clash with urban fire-fighting methods. Gans also concluded that reporters tend to rely on sources who are easily available and eager to provide information; people who, in Gaye Tuchman's words, often "have an axe to grind."[20] Because of the way general assignment reporters deal with sources in local stories that have become national news, Gans said, "the result almost always is a national story which, by local standards, is inaccurate and exaggerated."[21] This was certainly true of the fires in Yellowstone.

Many of the country's top wildfire experts were in the Yellowstone area while the fires were burning, but few reporters sought them out.

Richard Rothermel, who pioneered the computer modeling of wild-fire behavior, was approached by no network TV reporters and by fewer than a dozen of the hundreds of print reporters in the park. Stephen Pyne, who wrote the best-known history of wildfires, was interviewed by about half a dozen print reporters and by CBS's "Nightwatch," which he said was interested in drama and scandal rather than objective fire information.[22]

Local residents outnumbered scientists two to one in television sound bites, and three to one as sources named in print stories. Both print and television journalists also interviewed more tourists than scientists. When reporters did interview scientists, they usually talked to those who were most accessible, not those who had the most specialized expertise. When they talked to fire fighters, reporters often talked with grunts on the front lines instead of the supervisors who understood the larger picture. One fire information officer compared this practice to asking the janitor at the stock exchange about the day's trading.

"On the whole, the network reporting was very disappointing," wrote Duke University ecologist Norman L. Christensen, the only university scientist to appear in any of the network sound bites.

> None of the networks attempted to place this event in any context or synthesize the information. All closed with a superficial happy ending. At the risk of sounding self-serving, I am amazed no advantage was taken of the hundreds of experts on various aspects of the policy, technology, ecology, and economics of wilderness management of fire.[23]

The mood of much of the reporting was disaster-as-usual. Little attention was paid to the policy implications of the story, or to the differences between these fires and urban fires.

Treating the Yellowstone fires as a routine disaster story made reporters' jobs easier. Because disaster victims are assumed to be impartial, journalists could ignore the usual rules about journalistic balance, even if the "victims" had strong opinions but little knowledge—even if the "victims" made totally unfounded charges that fire fighters and the National Park Service were botching the job. Thinking of the story as routine also eliminated the time-consuming job of seeking appropriate experts. If this was a standard fire story, there was no need to talk to anyone except the land managers (the National Park Service), the "victims," and the fire fighters. Treating the fires as a science story would have made reporters' work much more demanding.

THE URBAN FIRE MODEL

Most of us take it for granted that fire is bad. In the urban setting in which most journalists function, that perspective is appropriate. Urban fires destroy property and are usually extinguished in a matter of hours. If a fire is big, authorities simply call in more equipment. Reporters who imported this urban fire model to Yellowstone looked for what reporters always seek in fire stories: victims, damage, and what causes the fires. In the absence of deaths or serious injuries, "victims" became inconvenienced tourists and angry local residents, many of whom earned their living from tourist-dependent businesses. In the absence of major structural damage, burned trees (or destroyed acres) became substitutes.

It was understandable but inappropriate that reporters brought these unconscious urban values to Yellowstone. Consider, for example, the differences between the Yellowstone fires and one of the largest urban fires in recent memory—the gas-fed Marina District fire in San Francisco that followed the 1989 earthquake. A single mile-wide fire front in Yellowstone gave off about fifty times as much energy as the Marina District fire at its peak, had essentially unlimited supplies of fuel, and often occurred in rugged terrain, miles from the nearest road, where it was difficult or impossible to bring heavy fire-fighting equipment. At any given time in Yellowstone, there were a number of fire fronts like this. It was as though several hundred fires burned at the same time in San Francisco, each of which was as big as the one in the Marina District and each of which had to be fought with helicopters ferrying water a bucket at a time from San Francisco Bay.[24] Forest fires are controlled by fuel, terrain, and weather, not by urban fire-fighting techniques.

OTHER MISCONCEPTIONS

Some people who lived near Yellowstone had their own misconceptions about wildfires. In stories about what caused the Yellowstone fires, accusations and rumors voiced by angry local residents received prominent play. This situation is not surprising, because reporters rubbed elbows with these people every day at the restaurants where they ate and the motels where they slept. Many local people believed, for example, that the fires were spreading because of the park's initial natural-burn policy. In fact, scientists not associated with the National Park Service who were consulted for this study said that forests and grasslands of the same order of magnitude would have burned in 1988 no matter what the fire management policy was.

Some area residents also believed that the National Park Service did not allow fire fighters to put the fires out. Incident commanders from outside the National Park Service assured me that they had, indeed, been allowed to put the fires out.

Another point of contention was the use of bulldozers to build firebreaks in the backcountry. Although bulldozers were generally not used here because of the permanent scars they would have left, many local residents believed that more bulldozed firebreaks would have brought the fires under control. Because wind-borne embers regularly started new fires in front of existing fires at a distance a thousand times the width of a bulldozer, it seems unlikely that firebreaks would have stopped the flames.

JOURNALISM AND PUBLIC ISSUES

It would be comforting to believe that the excesses and oversights of the Yellowstone coverage are an exception to the way the media normally cover catastrophes, but the literature suggests otherwise. Sociological studies of how the press deals with natural and industrial disasters indicate that coverage tends to focus on immediate events rather than the context in which they occur, and suggests that these stories often perpetuate myths about disasters instead of presenting objective accounts of what actually happened. Other studies suggest the mass media often do a poor job of covering environmental issues. Stories about delays in construction of the Tellico Dam in Tennessee, for example, focused on the endangered snail darter fish rather than on the related environmental issues.

It is only fair to mention that some media organizations did a good job in Yellowstone. For example, while other publications continued to sensationalize the fires, the *Los Angeles Times* published a particularly levelheaded editorial on September 13, saying "The unwarranted criticism of the Park Service, the U.S. Forest Service, and environmental experts has reached a level of misinformed hysteria that is racing out of control as the fires have done." Bob Secter and Tamara Jones of the *Los Angeles Times* wrote perceptive articles about issues related to the fires, a subject often overlooked by other media organizations.

Although some headlines and editorials in the *Billings* (Montana) *Gazette* were shrill and sensational, the stories themselves, especially those by Robert Ekey, were usually evenhanded and fair. The *Bozeman*

(Montana) *Daily Chronicle* and *Casper* (Wyoming) *Star Tribune* also did a generally good job of covering the story, as did some television stations in the region, such as KUTV in Salt Lake City. Many of the *Washington Post* stories also were well done. There were other individual reporters who did good reporting despite the pack journalism atmosphere in which the story was covered. And it is important to remember that journalists in Yellowstone were working under difficult conditions in which solid information was hard to come by, and even as basic a reporting tool as a working telephone was often difficult to find.

That some reporters and news organizations did a good job does not change the fact that coverage as a whole was flawed. "The media blew it," said *Washington Post* reporter T. R. Reid, who covered the fires in 1988 and wrote about them again in a July 23, 1989, commentary. "Much of the coverage," said a source for the *Los Angeles Times,* "would lead you to believe that the involved media personnel were auditioning for the *National Enquirer.*"

Media scholar James W. Carey has said that "the most frequent, punishing, and uncharitable accusation made of daily journalism" is that it lacks sufficient background and context.[25] News, he argues, is a curriculum that must be examined collectively—first, the breaking stories, then the subsequent analyses, then the magazine stories that go into more depth, and, finally, the books that are eventually published. This standard presumably would not apply to media consumers who stop seeking information after the breaking stories, but who nonetheless form opinions on the basis of that information.

Journalism ethicists Stephen Klaidman and Tom L. Beauchamp, on the other hand, believe that even one well-reported story can serve the information needs of the public. Klaidman and Beauchamp have proposed a "reasonable reader" standard that would require a story or series of stories to contain enough information that a reader or viewer with no specialized knowledge would understand what happened and the implications of what happened. An important part of this standard is "substantial completeness," the requirement that a news account "satisfy the needs of an intelligent nonspecialist who wants to evaluate the situation."[26]

The lesson of the Yellowstone fires for media consumers is not to place too much faith in breaking news stories except for the most general and most literal account of events. Breaking stories about the 1989 earthquake near San Francisco, for example, gave us a general idea about how much of the Nimitz freeway had collapsed, but little information about why some sections collapsed and others did not. Stories in 1988 about the Yellowstone fires gave us a good idea of what the most dramatic flames looked like and how many people were evacuated on a given day, but rarely provided good information about the scientific context in which the fires burned or the policy under which they were being suppressed.

The Yellowstone coverage provides several lessons for journalists and journalism educators: (1) Reporters must constantly be on their guard to avoid treating each story as interchangeable with others that deal with similar subject matter. News suffers when reporters assume that all fire stories, or all accident stories, or all election stories, are the same. (2) Accuracy in the literal sense of correctly spelled names is meaningless if the reporter misses the essence of the story. (3) Reporters who are outside their normal beats, either geographically or conceptually, must be particularly sensitive to their need to rely on others for the expertise they lack. Perhaps the greatest conceit in journalism is that any reporter can quickly become an expert on any subject.

IMPLICATIONS FOR THE FUTURE

It is clear that coverage of the Yellowstone fires is a poor model of how journalism should be practiced. Why did these mistakes occur? Is it reasonable to expect comprehensive reporting of public issues in breaking news stories? Has the changing structure of print and television news influenced the way this and other stories are being covered? Is the reporting described in this chapter part of a pattern that can provide insights into where journalism is headed in the future?

In this context, several trends in daily journalism are worth noting. *USA Today*, with its ten-inch stories and attention-getting graphics, is an example of publishers' efforts to make print media more visually attractive—a trend driven partly by television—that has brought shorter stories, more photographs, more color, and better graphic design to newsmagazines as well as newspapers. This trend is likely to continue. In some cases, the graphics augment coverage. The *San Jose* (California) *Mercury News*, for example, was awarded a Pulitzer prize in 1990 for earthquake coverage that made excellent use of maps and diagrams. In other cases, however, the drive for better design has been at the expense of comprehensive reporting.

There is a similar trend in broadcast news. Plans by the television networks to expand national newscasts to a full hour were doomed in the 1970s when local stations discovered that they could make a profit with local news as well as meet the public-service demands of the

Federal Communications Commission. Instead of yielding that half-hour, they expanded their own newscasts. Critics charged that the subsequent profit-driven lust for viewers has encouraged shorter, easier-to-digest stories and flashier presentation in lieu of good journalism.

These shorter print and television stories seem a logical response to market research that suggests that media consumers have a limited attention span. The market research that fuels these trends is itself more likely to occur as upper-level media managers get further from news and more concerned with the business side of journalism. This distancing of managers from news seems particularly likely to happen at media outlets that are part of a national group with bottom-line quotas for return on invested capital.

The realities of media economics may also influence the professional values of journalists. If journalists are rewarded and recognized more for timeliness than for thoroughness, and if editors and producers are rewarded and recognized more for the audience appeal of their news presentations than for news content, it seems reasonable to expect that these news values will become increasingly accepted among journalists. Journalists and would-be journalists who are uncomfortable with these values will be more likely to pursue other lines of work.

Another trend is the changing technology that allows television and print media to report the news more quickly. In television, electronic cameras and satellite transmission allowed viewers to see instantaneous pictures of Yellowstone flames that would have taken hours or days to reach the public a decade ago. Computerized typesetting and lap-top word processors that can transmit text through telephone lines have had a less dramatic but equally substantial influence on newspapers. New portable photographic technology allowed color negatives of walls of flame to be transmitted by telephone directly from Yellowstone-area motels to photo editors hundreds of miles away. This ability to cover news instantaneously introduces pressures to beat the competition by providing more raw data at the expense of time-consuming interpretation and verification of those data.

Some of the best reporting on the Yellowstone fires was in specialized magazines targeted toward small but specific audiences. The January 1989 *Audubon* and November 1989 *BioScience,* for example, contain thorough and thoughtful accounts about the fires and some of the related issues. If there is a trend here, it may be that the national news media are increasingly catering to a mass audience, the majority of which is thought to have little interest in a story like the Yellowstone fires beyond the flames and political drama. At the same time, media aimed at audiences with specific interests or in particular geographic areas may be doing a better job than before of meeting the needs of their readers and viewers.

News consumers hungry for comprehensive information about public issues probably will continue to be able to find it, although perhaps less often than before in the traditional national news media. People who have the interest to pursue the "news curriculum" described by James Carey may be better served than before by better local print and television coverage and by a larger number of news accounts in the specialized media. But this opportunity for the most motivated of news consumers may come at the expense of even less information about public issues for most Americans.

CONCLUSION

Yellowstone National Park was not destroyed in 1988, although some Americans concluded, after following the news accounts of the fires, that it had been. The "let it burn" policy of the National Park Service was not what caused so much to burn, despite media suggestions to the contrary. The fires of August and September 1988 could not have been put out with heavy equipment such as bulldozers, contrary to the well-publicized comments of some front-line fire fighters and area residents. Fires like these do not ordinarily damage forests in the biological sense or cause animals to flee in terror, as suggested by network TV anchors and the Disney movie *Bambi*.

The news-consuming public was poorly served, especially at the height of the hype when the fires were on the front pages and in the leads of television newscasts. The groups of experts convened for this study rated network news accounts during this peak period as significantly less accurate than stories broadcast earlier and later. The errors in the Yellowstone coverage occurred largely because journalists relied on urban reporting models of routine fires and disasters that simply did not apply to the 1988 wildfires—reporting models that made journalists' jobs easier by allowing them to fit this atypical story into the daily routine of journalism. As long as reporters cope with the pressures of newswork by invoking standard stories, these kinds of mistakes will continue. Caveat emptor.

NOTES

1. Named after Berkeley zoology professor A. Starker Leopold, who chaired the Kennedy administration's Advisory Board on Wildlife Management. This report is the philosophic foundation for how national parks are managed. The complete text of the Leopold Report is in the *Sierra Club Bulletin* (March 1963): 4–11.
2. The actual network graphic, superimposed over the tourist, said "Stanley Mott" on the first line and "Director Natl Park Service" on the second line.
3. Jim Robbins, "Fires in Yellowstone: Renewal and Criticism," *New York Times*, August 10, 1988; Jim Robbins, "Ideas and Trends: In Yellowstone, Determination to Leave the Flames Alone," *New York Times*, August 14, 1988; and David S. Wilson, "U.S. Forest Fires Worst Since 1919," *New York Times*, September 1, 1988.
4. Timothy Egan, "Ethic of Protecting Land Fueled Yellowstone Fires," *New York Times*, September 22, 1988.
5. Sources and reporters are not named here because they were promised that only compiled data and quotations that did not identify individuals would be published.
6. Sullivan's office gave the author permission to use this quotation from the survey of news sources.
7. James Habeck gave the author permission to use this quotation from the survey of news sources.
8. Gaye Tuchman, *Making News: A Study in the Social Construction of Reality* (New York: Free Press, 1978).
9. David L. Altheide, *Creating Reality: How TV News Distorts Reality* (Beverly Hills, Calif.: Sage, 1976), 176.
10. Personal correspondence with Larry Warren after he viewed the author's videotapes of all 1988 evening network TV stories about the fires.
11. Personal correspondence with Roger O'Neil after he viewed the author's videotapes of coverage.
12. Personal interview in Gardiner, Montana, April 1989.
13. Written comment from Denny Bungarz, one of the group of incident fire commanders who evaluated network television coverage. The article describing him as the "hero of Old Faithful" is on the front page of the September 19, 1988, *Billings* (Montana) *Gazette*.
14. Personal correspondence with Stephen Pyne after he viewed the author's videotape of the 1988 network coverage. Pyne is author of *Fire in America: A Cultural History of Wildfire and Rural Fire* (Princeton, N.J.: Princeton University Press, 1982).
15. Written comment from David Thomas, one of the group of experts who evaluated wildfire behavior as portrayed in network television coverage.
16. Written comment from James K. Brown, one of the group of experts who evaluated ecological issues in network television coverage.
17. Telephone conversation with Ralph Glidden, October 1988. Glidden was featured in a September 8, 1988, NBC story about the fires.
18. See, for example, Sharon Dunwoody and Michael Ryan, "Scientific Barriers to the Popularization of Science in the Mass Media," *Journal of Communication* (1985): 26–42; Sharon Dunwoody and Byron T. Scott, "Scientists as Mass Media Sources," *Journalism Quarterly* (1982): 52–59; Susan Cray Borman, "Communication Accuracy in Magazine Science Reporting," *Journalism Quarterly* (1978): 345–46; Robert B. McCall, "Science and the Press: Like Oil and Water?" *American Psychologist* 43, no. 2 (February 1988): 87–94; Dorothy Nelkin, "The Culture of Science Journalism," *Society* (September–October 1987): 17–25; Robert Gordon Shepard and Erich Goode, "Sci-

entists in the Popular Press," *New Scientist* (November 24, 1987): 482–84.

19. Herbert W. Gans, *Deciding What's News: A Study of CBS Evening News, NBC Nightly News, Newsweek, and Time* (New York: Vintage, 1979), 140.

20. Tuchman, *Making News*, 93.

21. Gans, *Deciding What's News*, 141.

22. Telephone conversation, March 1989.

23. Written comment from Norman Christensen, one of the group of experts who evaluated ecological issues in network television coverage for this study.

24. The author is indebted to the San Francisco Fire Department for providing information about the Marina District fire and to Richard Rothermel for his help in calculating the energy released by that fire and by the 1988 Yellowstone fires. Denny Bungarz and Fred Roach also contributed to the example by comparing the wildfire suppression techniques used in Yellowstone with those used on urban fires.

25. James W. Carey, "Why and How? The Dark Continent of American Journalism," in Robert Karl Manoff and Michael Schudson, eds., *Reading The News* (New York: Pantheon, 1986), 150.

26. Stephen Klaidman and Tom L. Beauchamp, *The Virtuous Journalist* (New York: Oxford University Press, 1987), 35.

Epilogue

Peter Braestrup

As the preceding chapters in this volume make clear, the highly competitive business of informing the American public has been dramatically transformed during the past two decades, and the future of news is, within the trade, a matter of intense speculation. Outside the trade, this future is a matter of some importance to everyone who believes that the health of democracy in America depends on an informed, interested citizenry.

There is nothing to indicate that either broadcast or print news organizations are moribund. Technology has given television journalism greater immediacy (satellite transmission, videotape, live broadcasts of the dismantling of the Berlin Wall, Scud attacks from Iraq, or a putsch in Moscow); the computer and the satellite have given newspapers and magazines more efficient ways to publish. Technology has brought cable television, including cable news, with its multiplicity of channels, into more than half of U.S. homes; it has permitted the development of electronic data banks and the proliferation of specialized newsletters and magazines. Overall, technology has opened up access to a wide range of information (and entertainment) that was inaccessible to most Americans in the past.

American journalists are not an endangered species, although their pay and perquisites vary with the size and prosperity of their employers. From Bangor, Maine, to San Diego, 1,643 daily newspapers employ, by one estimate, a total of 56,000 editors, reporters, photographers, and other newspeople (no reliable estimates exist for the nation's 7,500 weekly newspapers). Feeding news to the dailies and other media are the robust Associated Press and an ailing United Press International, with some 2,400 newspeople between them. Drawing on the wire services and the dailies, as well as their own reporters, are the three major newsweeklies—*Time, Newsweek, U.S. News and World Report*—with combined news staffs still totaling 600 people, despite some cutbacks.

On the local broadcast side are commercial radio stations with an estimated 11,400 full-time announcers, producers, reporters, and technicians, and television stations with 18,400 people in news operations. Despite staff reductions begun during the 1980s, each of the major television networks—ABC, CBS, NBC—deploys perhaps 1,000 anchors, producers, film editors, camera operators, reporters, and technicians; Cable News Network, the round-the-clock star of the Gulf War, claims a worldwide news staff of 1,500.

Yet, as has been noted, certain unhappy trends are apparent. The audience for news is growing slowly, and relative to population growth, may not be growing at all. Roughly two-thirds of all households tune into some kind of TV news program (local, morning, evening, late night) in the course of the day. But only one-fourth of the nation's 92 million television households tune in to the network evening oracles (Dan Rather, Tom Brokaw, Peter Jennings) each night; no anchorman attracts more than 5 percent of the households as often as four nights per week. These network news programs have been steadily losing audience share to entertainment shows on cable and on independent TV stations. The circulation of the other "national" news outlets—*Time, Newsweek, U.S. News*—has remained flat, at around 10 million for almost a decade, despite radical changes in design and content intended to make the magazines more appealing to a new generation reared on television. And one-third of all American adults now get along without a daily newspaper.

With the *Wall Street Journal* and the Associated Press, the nation's big-city newspapers constitute the bulwark of the American news system (table 6.2). Television news, with its fleeting sound bites and devotion to drama, is dispensable. These newspapers are not. They provide the most comprehensive coverage of local, state, national, and foreign news available to the people who live in their metropolitan areas; almost all are fatter and more sophisticated than they were two decades ago. Survivors since 1945 of Darwinian struggles for readers and advertising that have made most American cities one-newspaper towns, these papers might seem to be invulnerable. Yet they are acutely sensitive to local economic downturns. And their editors and publishers see limits to growth and various threats to their well-being— from vigorous new local-interest dailies in the suburbs, from the continuing plight of the central cities, from cable TV, from the proposals of telephone companies to sell electronic classified advertising, and from rises in the price of newsprint (which almost doubled between 1978 and 1988).

Across the United States, the health of these big metropolitan newspapers, their smaller brethren, and the newsweeklies, and even, indirectly, the television news organizations will be affected during the 1990s by several factors beyond their control but, in some cases, not outside their influence.

The first, fundamental factor is the eventual success or failure of current local and state efforts to raise the quality of public education and the level of literacy—reversing the "rising tide of mediocrity" deplored in *A Nation at Risk*, published by the National Commission on Excellence in Education in 1983. These efforts have gained considerable political support from state governors, the blessings of the White House, financial help from corporate America, and mixed reactions from teachers unions, taxpayer groups, and spokespeople for minorities. Mediocrity in education, of course, demands less from teachers, administrators, parents, students, politicians, and taxpayers; it raises no painful issues of "standards" versus "equality"; its glaring failures can be blamed variously on television, family breakdown, poverty, racism, and drugs. But plainly the oft-cited horror stories— 1 million functionally illiterate youths receiving high-school diplomas each year, college freshmen unable to give the dates of the Civil War, seventeen-year-olds unable to locate France or Germany on a map of Europe—have direct relevance to the future audience for news, as well as to the future of U.S. society.

The second underlying factor which may heavily influence both the content of the news and its audience is the continuing diversity of American public life. The expansion, dynamism, and increasing complexity of both government and nongovernment activity have fostered the growth of special publications and even cable TV channels for various kinds of news—news about defense, the environment, law, housing, science, religion, international business—inasmuch as no single newspaper or magazine can now chronicle all significant events in all such fields. Even the *New York Times*, for example, no longer attempts, as a matter of strategy, to be the "newspaper of record"; for lack of space and personnel, it no longer serves as a daily monitor of Congress or of the politics of Britain or even of the statehouse at Albany. Instead, it has deliberately become something akin to a daily newsmagazine, covering the same big stories of the day as network television and then choosing and examining, often brilliantly, events or situations at home and abroad that seem to have some unusual interest or importance. Health, crime, social change, "lifestyles," the arts—all get more attention. In ranging more widely in their daily choices of "news," the *Times* and other serious newspapers have turned over much of the press's traditional institution-watching role to specialized magazines (*Congressional Quarterly*, *National Journal*), to special-interest newsletters, to local weeklies, and even to expensive data banks.

It is not difficult to imagine an America in the year 2000 where the audience for news is fragmented far more than it is now. If we assume no upward surge in American literacy, the major television networks, the major newspapers, and the newsweeklies will attempt to hold their audiences by increasing their focus on people of general interest (presidents, a few foreign leaders, TV stars), compelling drama (war, sports, disaster, human tragedy), transient controversy (abortion, AIDS), and personal guidance (health, finance, fashion). As this process continues, print journalism will become even more like television, with some honorable exceptions. Stories will become shorter, as they have during the past two decades. The attention span of the major news media, already diminishing, will become even more abbreviated. As time goes on, information about the daily course of public affairs in every sphere will become the domain of various specialized media serving small, interested elites. The gap will grow between the information "haves" and "have-nots." It is likely that one effect on the general public will be a further decline in civic consciousness and voter participation.

World events will, inevitably, also shape the future of news in the United States. The brief 1991 Gulf conflict attracted—and disappointed—a record media horde at great expense for a ground war that lasted only 100 hours. It did not reverse the decline in foreign news, especially on television. The apparent end of the cold war is no small blessing, but it removes a forty-year-old framework for news from abroad and seems to encourage a certain isolationism among American news executives (without the Red menace, why should anyone care about Angola?). Some pundits still suggest that the diminishing Soviet-American rivalry overseas will prompt journalists to focus on planetary matters: human rights, global warming, hunger. (*Time* declared in 1989 that it would campaign in favor of worldwide environmental protection.) Some skepticism is warranted. Old habits die hard. American news media will cover dramas involving U.S. allies (e.g., Israel), threats to U.S. interests (the Gulf, the Philippines), the unpredictable sequels to the cold war. Much of the world, as always, will be left in obscurity, hungry or not, and, for reasons of cost, fewer American journalists will be stationed overseas.

Barring war or grave economic trouble, domestic news themes will probably be shaped in considerable measure during the 1990s, even more than in the past, by the words and deeds of whomever is in the White House. There is, at this writing, much hand wringing in Congress over the environment, the national debt, the lack of U.S. competitiveness, the seemingly intractable plight of the urban underclass; at the same time there is little consensus or even clarity of debate on what to do about such difficulties. The rise of special interest groups, the weakening of the major political parties, and the diffusion of power in Congress have all led, among other things, to incoherence in both politics and the news media, and to increasing dependence by the media, led by television, on the president as the prime source of a national news agenda. Thus, as during the 1980s, press "themes" are likely to be highly cyclical—the homeless one week and El Salvador the next. But who knows? Who would have predicted "the sixties" in 1960, or "the eighties" in 1980?

The future of news rests in the final analysis with that eclectic mix of people who produce "the news," and, no less, with the tastes of the people who buy (or don't buy) their products. Journalists have shown themselves in the past to be resilient, shrewd, and sometimes even courageous in their determination to survive the vicissitudes of the marketplace while providing the American people with the vital benefits of a constitutionally protected "free press." Whether the journalists will continue to do so, and whether a new generation of American consumer/citizens will support the journalists' best efforts, remains to be seen. A disquieting new age is upon us.

BACKGROUND BOOKS

Douglas Gomery

TELEVISION

The study of television news came of age in the 1980s with a spate of impressive books examining the influence and inner workings of TV journalism, past and present.

The best of these is John P. Robinson and Mark R. Levy's *The Main Source* (Sage, 1986), which takes a comprehensive look at how TV journalists communicate and how viewers respond to what they see on the screen. "The good news . . . is that the public is far better informed about the news than most previous studies have suggested," Robinson and Levy conclude. "The bad news is that public information levels are far lower than most news workers may assume as they prepare their stories."

Shanto Iyengar and Donald R. Kinderin, in their *News That Matters: Television and American Opinion* (University of Chicago Press, 1987), theorize that network news influences its audience in two fundamental ways. First, it helps set the political agenda: "Those problems that receive prominent attention on the national news become the problems the viewing public regards as the nation's most important." Second, TV news "primes" its audiences, setting up "the standards that people use to make political evaluations."

Kathleen Hall Jamieson and Karlyn Kohrs Campbell take yet a third tack to analyze how TV news affects viewers in *The Interplay of Influence: Mass Media and their Publics in News, Advertising, and Politics* (Wadsworth, updated edition, 1988). Here two classically trained rhetoricians look at TV news as a form of discourse and try to help readers develop skills to make better use of the information on television.

Many critics believe that TV news would be improved if its practitioners more generally represented the full range of the national audience—in other words, more women and blacks should be hired as TV news reporters. Marlene Sanders and Marcia Rock's *Waiting for*

Prime Time: The Women of Television News (University of Illinois Press, 1988) offers a curious combination of a first-person memoir by Sanders, a veteran correspondent for ABC, and third-person analysis by Rock, of New York University's School of Journalism. Also see Liz Trotta, *Fighting for Air: In the Trenches with Television News* (New York: Simon and Schuster, 1991).

One important aspect of TV news that should never be ignored is the role of network "anchors" who have increasingly come to assume the aura of moral and intellectual authority so vital to the success of the more serious news shows. Barbara Matusow's *The Evening Stars: The Making of the Network News Anchor* (Houghton Mifflin, 1983) is the first complete history of the species, from John Cameron Swayse to Dan Rather, Tom Brokaw, and Peter Jennings. The immense power, wealth, and fame of these TV personalities, Matusow argues, leave them dangerously isolated from the real world they seek to interpret and describe.

Throughout the 1970s the three major networks accounted for the bulk of TV news coverage. In the 1980s, at least in the literary world, one network—CBS—garnered all the attention. Of all the books about CBS that have been published, Peter J. Boyer's *Who Killed CBS? The Undoing of America's Number One News Network* (Random House, 1988) is the best researched single-volume account of the fall of the House of Edward R. Murrow. Boyer, who formerly covered TV for the *New York Times*, seems to have talked to everyone involved. His tale of power-grabbing can be called pathos or black humor, depending upon one's point of view. Central to Boyer's story is the role of Van Gordon Sauter, the CBS veteran who held a series of important CBS positions, landing in the early 1980s as head of CBS News. Boyer lays out in detail how Sauter almost destroyed the most important TV news organization before departing for California to write screenplays.

Fair Play: CBS, General Westmoreland, and How a Television Documentary Went Wrong (Harper and Row, 1988) by Burton Benjamin, a former vice-president and producer at CBS, is the result of a request to Benjamin by CBS management to do an internal investigation of a documentary on Vietnam after William Westmoreland filed a $120 million libel suit against the network. Benjamin found the CBS broadcast to be unbalanced but argued that critics should focus on the truth of the documentary's assertions rather than on the extent to which the producers did not meet the hoary CBS News standards of fairness, accuracy, and balance. Benjamin's book reveals much about the internal workings of CBS News that have made the network the butt of many criticisms and the subject of so many books.

For historical interest, one of the best of these books about CBS is by David Schoenbrun, who died in May 1988 after a brilliant career as a correspondent. His *On and Off the Air: An Informal History of CBS News* (Dutton, 1989) attempts to be encyclopedic, but Schoenbrun is at his best when he writes about his twenty years as the CBS man in Paris. As one of "Murrow's boys," he helped make CBS the top news network. He laments that in the 1980s no correspondent covered any beat long enough to learn the ropes. The rules of current network economics prohibit anyone from remaining twenty years in Paris; indeed, in 1989 all three networks closed their Paris bureaus.

Les Midgley, author of *How Many Words Do You Want? An Insider's Stories of Print and Television Journalism* (Birch Lane, 1989), was one of the founders of "CBS Evening News." His book is more than a simple defense of the past; it is a description of the process of newsmaking television-style. The enormous pressure of deadlines, he says, offers those who labor in TV news no time to dig out complex stories or to reflect on the significance of events.

Peter McCabe, *Bad News at Black Rock* (Arbor House, 1987), Bill Leonard, *In the Storm of the Eye* (G. P. Putnam's Sons, 1987), and Ed Joyce, *Prime Times, Bad Times* (Doubleday, 1988), provide more insider views of CBS, with the authors often defending their own roles as the "good guys" in a process gone bad. The shared conclusion is that they were not responsible for the decline of CBS—someone else was.

For background on the rise of CBS as a network with news as well as entertainment functions, see Lewis Paper's *Empire: William S. Paley and the Making of CBS* (St. Martin's, 1987) and Robert Slater's *This . . . Is CBS: A Chronicle of 60 Years* (Prentice Hall, 1989). Both survey the history of the one-time "Tiffany network," from its creation by William Paley in the late 1920s to the takeover by Lawrence Tisch in the mid-1980s.

Paley's favorite newsman, in the glory days of the 1950s, was, of course, Edward R. Murrow. There have been two major biographies of Murrow in recent years: Ann M. Sperber, *Murrow: His Life and Times* (Freundlich Books, 1986), and Joseph E. Persico, *Edward R. Murrow* (McGraw-Hill, 1988). Both are filled with dazzling detail, but Persico's book is better organized.

While there are many versions of events at CBS, the only comprehensive inside account of NBC News has just been provided by one who went from writer of the "Camel News Caravan" to executive producer of "The Huntley-Brinkley Report" to president Reuven Frank, *Out of Thin Air: The Brief Wonderful Life of Network News* (Simon and Schuster, 1991).

Edward Bliss, Jr., in *Now the News: The Story of Broadcast Journalism* (Columbia University Press, 1991), offers a six-hundred page examination of the rise of news, first on radio and then on television. Bliss, who worked for two decades at CBS News and then taught journalism at American University in Washington, D.C., has penned the account all future historians will need to read first.

TV news can certainly make a story out of the strangest events. Tom Rose, in *Freeing the Whales: How the Media Created the World's Greatest Non-Event* (Birch, Lane, 1989), shows how even in October 1988, as a presidential campaign was grinding to an end and Ronald Reagan was glowing in the final hours of his presidency, the nation was fixed on the rescue of two whales trapped in the ice in Alaska. "Network news producers love animal stories," says Rose. "They give the network anchors a chance to display their warm, human side." This was a perfect made-for-television story, with little real effect on public understanding of the complexities of an ever-changing world.

In any discussion of the television news, the subject that interests most people is the role of television in political campaigns. A good place to begin is Sig Mickelson's *From Whistle Stop to Sound Bite: Four Decades of Politics and Television* (Praeger, 1989). Here is a personal history by a former CBS executive turned professor, who has watched TV political coverage from the beginning. Indeed, in the early 1950s he was directing CBS's coverage of the 1952 and 1956 campaigns. His conclusions hardly offer much hope for the future; for example, Mickelson reminds us how the great expectations held out for political debates were dimmed as candidates took control of the media machinery.

Leonard Reinsch's *Getting Elected: From Radio and Roosevelt to Television and Reagan* (Hippocrene, 1988) provides historical background on politicians' use of the media, from the fireside chats of FDR to the media orchestration of Michael Deaver and James Baker. For the campaigns and the presidency during the 1980s in particular see Bob Schieffer and Gary Paul Gates's *The Acting Presidency* (Dutton, 1989). This book is really a description of Ronald Reagan as a "disengaged" and "hands-off" president. One of the most interesting accounts in the book is the famous preelection clash between candidate George Bush and CBS's Dan Rather, where Bush-as-wimp set up Rather, the reporter-as-tough-guy.

Doris A. Graber's *Mass Media and American Politics* (Congressional Quarterly Press, 1988) is the third edition of a basic text examining the issues of press freedom, the media's influence on attitudes and behavior, elections in the TV age, crisis reporting, and foreign affairs reporting. A companion volume, *Media Technology and the Vote* (Westview, 1988), edited by Joel Swerdlow, is a collection of papers from a 1988 Annenberg Washington Program conference. Although the papers may be somewhat dated, the bibliography is excellent. The two books are useful guides to the controversy over television's effect on elections—a controversy that is likely to be with us well into the next century.

Brian Lamb's *America's Town Hall* (Acropolis, 1989) is the in-house history of C-SPAN, the cable TV network that offers the American public an unedited and intimate view of the U.S. Senate and House of Representatives in action.

Presidential Debates: The Challenge of Creating an Informed Electorate (Oxford, 1988) by Kathleen Hall Jamieson and David Birdsell focuses on more than broadcasting. The authors examine the elections before the first television debate and then move to the role and influence of the debates, first on radio and then on television. Their pessimistic conclusions make for gloomy reading on the current state of the coverage of presidential debating.

Robert E. Denton's *The Primetime Presidency of Ronald Reagan: The Era of the Television Presidency* (Praeger, 1988) goes beyond the 1980s to deal with the political effects of television in its broadest dimension. Denton, too, is not optimistic. Indeed, it is difficult to find an analyst who thinks that TV coverage of politics and government does not need reform, for underlying all these analyses is an assumption that TV plays the most powerful of roles in American elections—*too* powerful a role.

PRINT

Although TV news is in the forefront of attention at the moment, print news has a far longer history and, as conceded even by people who study TV news closely, the newspaper still has the greatest effect when it comes to informing and influencing the American people.

What is the current state of the newspaper business? This is what Ellis Cose's *The Press* (Morrow, 1989) seeks to answer by looking at the personalities and trends that have revolutionized the newspaper industry during the past twenty-five years. Cose profiles five corporations that account for a quarter of the 60 million newspapers sold each day: the *New York Times* Company, the *Washington Post* Corporation, Gannett, Times-Mirror, and Knight-Ridder. This is a book for the uninitiated because, unfortunately, it contains little new information for insiders or those who follow the industry closely. Indeed, those who have read Harrison Salisbury's *Without Fear or Favor* (Times Books, 1980), Robert Woodward and Carl Bernstein's Watergate tales published in *All the President's Men* (Simon and Schuster, 1974), Gay Talese's *The Kingdom and the Power* (World Publishing, 1969), and David Halberstam's *The Powers That Be* (Alfred A. Knopf, 1979) will recognize many of the anecdotes that make up the bulk of *The Press*. Peter Prichard's *The Making of McPaper* (Andrews, McMeel and Parker, 1987) tells more about Gannett, and Joseph Goulden's rancorous biography of Abe Rosenthal, *Fit to Print: A. M. Rosenthal and His Times* (Lyle Stuart, 1988), gives the reader more about how the *New York Times* works.

William A. Rusher's *The Coming Battle for the Media: Curbing the Power of the Media Elite* (Morrow, 1988) surveys the news business from a conservative perspective, arguing that the liberals who run the editorial offices around the nation are injecting a liberal bias into the news. Surely it is no surprise to learn that many reporters tend to be liberal in their outlook, but a liberal outlook does not necessarily lead to bias. Rusher does not understand that all news reporters challenge the status quo because it is their job to be skeptical.

Not all editorial decisions, liberal or conservative, are made in local newsrooms. Newspapers and broadcasters both have long depended on copy from the wire services. Too little has been written about these stalwarts of news coverage, but two recent books prove extremely helpful. Jonathan Fenby's *International News Services* (Schocken, 1986) lays out the workings of four international news services that offer the majority of reports around the world: Reuters, Agence France Presse, Associated Press, and United Press International. Fenby, a former correspondent for Reuters, provides an exhaustive account of how the "Big Four" function in the modern world. Their influence remains considerable.

Richard A. Schwarzlose's *The Nation's Newsbrokers* (Northwestern University Press, 1989) examines the creation of the wire services.

Some of the best books about print journalism grow out of the larger-than-life careers of those who have built and directed the great media enterprises. The most controversial of this genre is Al Neuharth's *Confessions of an S.O.B.* (Doubleday, 1989). The founder of *USA Today*, a self-described conniver and backstabber, is one of the most successful executives in the contemporary newspaper business. *Business Week* was right on the mark: "There's no point in reading this book for its management advice—unless you're likely to be surprised or improved by exhortations to have fun at your job or to learn from your mistakes. As an autobiography *Confessions of an S.O.B.* has its compelling moments. How could it not? Neuharth's rise from impoverished South Dakota farm boy is nothing short of extraordinary."

Succeeding against the Odds (Warner Books, 1989), the autobiography of John H. Johnson, the publisher of *Jet* and *Ebony*, is another Horatio Alger–style narrative of a publishing success.

David Leon Chandler's *The Binghams of Louisville* (Crown, 1987) offers the opposite side of the same coin. Here is the sad tale of the Louisville family that for years ran the *Courier-Journal*. After a bitter intrafamily quarrel, the Binghams sold out to the Gannett chain in 1986, another example of a newspaper dynasty's giving way to the trend of chain ownership.

But the biographical model is simply one way to write history. More and more scholars are studying the social influence and importance of newspapers in America's history. Louis Liebovich in *The Press and the Origins of the Cold War, 1944–1947* (Greenwood, 1988) focuses on four major news organizations—the *New York Herald Tribune, Chicago Tribune, San Francisco Chronicle,* and *Time* magazine—and describes how they dealt, fairly unsuccessfully, with the major foreign policy issues of the post–World War II era.

Sally M. Miller's *Ethnic Press in the United States: A Historical Analysis and Handbook* (Greenwood, 1987) is a collection of articles that examine the role of some 1,300 foreign-language newspapers that served the United States in the years before World War I. The volume covers twenty-seven immigrant groups, from Germans and Danes, to Portuguese and Ukrainians. We forget that these papers could be found in every American city well into the twentieth century. They played an important role in maintaining ethnic pride and cohesion among major urban populations.

A Place in the News: From the Women's Pages to the Front Pages (Dodd, Mead, 1988) is a history of the rising role of women in contemporary journalism, written by a *Los Angeles Times* staffer, Kay Mills. Women's struggle for acceptance and influence in newsrooms and broadcast studios is a story of hard-fought marginal victories and, for some people, immense power and wealth.

A useful companion volume is *Women of the World: The Great Foreign Correspondents* (Houghton Mifflin, 1988) by Julia Edwards, which offers biographies of a dozen or so female foreign correspondents who worked from the middle of the nineteenth century to the recent past.

Mitchell Stephens's *A History of News: From the Drum to the Satellite* (Viking, 1988) is a credible attempt at an impossible task—to write a single-volume history of news from the beginning of time. He describes the separation of the reporting, editing, and publishing functions and the continuing changes wrought by new technologies. The book is a pleasure to read but ultimately unsatisfactory, for no one book can adequately cover this vast subject.

Michael and Edwin Emery, in *The Press and America: An Interpretive History*, 6th edition (Prentice Hall, 1988), limit their history to the United States, but the volume still comes to almost 800 pages. This is a classic college text that provides a vast fund of information about the development of American journalism.

Contemporary social scientists also offer their view of the news media. Carolyn Martindale's *The White Press and Black America* (Greenwood, 1986) is the most comprehensive study available of press coverage of black Americans between 1950 and 1980. This is a carefully researched analysis of past deficiencies in press coverage with some provocative suggestions for how it could be improved.

One of the best ways to evaluate the effects of news coverage is to focus on a single event. For example, Lee Wilkins, in *Shared Vulnerability: The Media and American Perceptions of the Bhopal Disaster* (Greenwood, 1987), chronicles the media's coverage of the 1984 chemical spill in Bhopal, India. David E. Morrison and Howard Tumber in their *Journalists at War: The Dynamics of News Reporting During the Falklands Conflict* (Sage, 1988) offer an in-depth look at the 1982 confrontation between Argentina and Britain over the Falkland Islands (or Malvinas). This content analysis seeks to understand how journalists might improve their coverage of such conflicts in the future.

The social science that matters the most, at least to practitioners in the industry, is economics. With news media profits reaching into the millions, we see the rise of applied management analysis. Jim Willis in *Surviving in the Newspaper Business: Newspaper Management in Turbulent Times* (Praeger, 1988) offers a concise overview of who does what in today's news business. Jon G. Udell's *The Growth and Outlook for U.S. Newspapers and Newsprint Consumption* (ANPA, 1988) is a useful summary of basic information about the newspaper business, compiled for the American Newspaper Publishers Association.

The best of the recent books on newspaper economics, however, is *Press Concentration and Monopoly: New Perspectives on Newspaper Ownership and Operation* (Ablex, 1988), edited by Robert C. Picard and his associates. This first-rate study of the contemporary economics of the newspaper business offers no definitive conclusions but provides a vast fund of useful information about the dangers of media consolidation.

Ben H. Bagdikian, author of *The Media Monopoly*, revised edition (Beacon, 1987), required no such mountain of data. He has long been concerned about the purchase of independent newspapers by large chains and now finds that the pace of newspaper consolidation has exceeded his grimmest expectations, posing serious implications for the future. His greatest concern is that "a handful of corporations [will] control most of what the average American sees and hears."

Peter J. S. Dunnett's *World Newspaper Industry* (Methuen, 1988) is a survey of the newspaper industry worldwide. American readers who rejoice in the reality of the U.S. press may be startled to learn that the capital of France has a dozen newspapers, whereas the capital of the United States has but two. The United States may be one of the most literate nations of the world, but it does not lead in newspaper readership.

No compilation of books about print journalism can adequately cover the burgeoning literature in this field. So, for further study, Richard A. Schwarzlose's *Newspapers: A Reference Guide* (Greenwood, 1987) is recommended. This book begins with a historical survey of the development of the American newspaper industry and then considers the relationship of newspapers and society and legal, technological, and economic issues. It ends with listings of major research collections.

For an engrossing look at contemporary journalism, there are many books that discuss the way newspapers, newsmagazines, and television report on and shape the political process. In *Behind the Front Page: A Candid Look at How News Is Made* (Simon and Schuster, 1987), David S. Broder, the highly respected political reporter of the *Washington Post*, analyzes how news is made in Washington, by looking at the major news sources.

Broder is more optimistic than some of his colleagues that the system is working. Consider three examples:

Lewis W. Wolfson's *The Untapped Power of the Press: Explaining Government to the People* (Greenwood, 1985) is a plea for more systematic, thorough reporting of governmental issues by journalists. The examples of poor reporting are from Washington, but could be found in almost any state capital.

Elie Abel's book, *Leaking: Who Does It? Who Benefits? At What Cost?* (Unwin Hyman, 1987), is a Twentieth Century Fund report about a way of life in Washington. The author describes from his own experience how leaking works and what should be done about its excesses.

Mark Hertsgaard's *On Bended Knee: The Press and the Reagan Presidency* (Farrar, Straus and Giroux, 1988) argues that the public relations teams of President Reagan "reduced the press and especially television to virtual accessories to the White House propaganda apparatus." This harsh critique may be overdrawn, but Hertsgaard's evidence is disturbing.

ABOUT THE AUTHORS

William B. Blankenburg is a professor of journalism and mass communications and codirector of the Frank Thayer Center for the Study of Media Law and Management at the University of Wisconsin–Madison. He received his B.A. degree from South Dakota State University and a master's degree and Ph.D. from Stanford University.

Leo Bogart, adjunct professor of marketing, New York University, was for many years executive vice-president and general manager of the Newspaper Advertising Bureau. He holds a Ph.D. degree in sociology from the University of Chicago and is a fellow of the American Psychological Association. A former president of both the American and World Associations of Public Opinion Research, he is the author of *Press and Public* (1981, 1989), *Premises for Propaganda* (1976), *Polls and the Awareness of Public Opinion* (1972, 1986), *Strategy in Advertising* (1967, 1984, 1990), and *The Age of Television* (1956, 1958, 1973).

Peter Braestrup is senior editor at the Library of Congress. He received his B.A. degree from Yale University and was a Nieman fellow at Harvard in 1959–60. He was a journalist for twenty years with *Time*, the *New York Times*, and the *Washington Post*, and was the founding editor of the *Wilson Quarterly.*

Raymond L. Carroll is associate professor of television and film at the University of Alabama. He received a B.S. degree and a master's degree in speech communication from Indiana State University, and a Ph.D. in communication arts from the University of Wisconsin–Madison.

Barbara Cohen is vice-president and Washington bureau chief of CBS News. She received a B.A. degree in English literature from Swarthmore College and a master's degree from the Columbia University Graduate School of Journalism. She joined the *Washington Star* in 1968, becoming national editor and managing editor. She was news director of National Public Radio from 1979 to 1983. Before joining CBS News, she was executive producer of the NBC News program "Meet the Press."

Philip S. Cook is former director of the Media Studies Project of the Woodrow Wilson International Center for Scholars. He received a B.A. degree in American history from Williams College. He has been a newspaper reporter (*Hartford Courant, New York Herald Tribune*), *Newsweek* correspondent, and managing editor of *Issues in Science and Technology*. He is coeditor (with Douglas Gomery and Lawrence W. Lichty) of *American Media: The Wilson Quarterly Reader* (1989) and editor of *Liberty of Expression* (1990).

James Devitt is a graduate student in communications at the University of Pennsylvania. He received his B.A. degree in rhetoric from the University of California at Berkeley. He has been a reporter for the *Daily Californian* in Berkeley and a stringer for the Associated Press and United Press International.

Robert M. Entman is associate professor of communications studies, journalism, and political science at Northwestern University. He received his B.A. degree in political science from Duke University and Ph.D. in political science from Yale University. He is the author of *Democracy without Citizens: Media and the Decay of American Politics* (1989) and coauthor (with David L. Paletz) of *Media Power Politics* (1981).

Jean Folkerts is associate professor of journalism at the George Washington University, Washington, D.C. She received a B.S. degree in journalism and a master's degree in journalism and mass communications from Kansas State University, and a Ph.D. in American studies from the University of Kansas. She is coauthor (with Dwight Teeter) of *Voices of the Nation: A History of Mass Media in the United States* (1989).

David Gergen is editor at large for *U.S. News and World Report*. He received a B.A. degree from Yale University and a law degree from Harvard Law School. Before entering journalism as editor of *U.S. News*, Gergen worked for eight years in the White House under Presidents Nixon, Ford, and Reagan. He has been a fellow at the American Enterprise Institute in Washington and at the John F. Kennedy School at Harvard. He is a regular commentator on National Public Radio and the "MacNeil/Lehrer NewsHour."

Douglas Gomery is professor of radio, TV, film at the University of Maryland at College Park, and senior researcher, Media Studies Project of the Woodrow Wilson Center. He received a B.A. degree in economics from Lehigh University and an M.A. degree in economics and a Ph.D. degree in communication arts from the University of Wisconsin–Madison. His books include *Film History: Theory and Practice* (1985), *The Hollywood Studio System* (1986), *American Media: The Wilson*

Quarterly Reader (1989), *Movie History: A Survey* (1991), and *Shared Pleasures* (1992).

Thomas Griffith is the former editor of *Life* magazine. He received a B.A. degree in journalism from the University of Washington and was a Nieman fellow at Harvard in 1942–43. He joined *Time* in 1943 as a writer and served as foreign editor, assistant managing editor, and senior staff editor of all Time, Inc., publications. He is the author of *The Waist-High Culture* (1959), and *How True: A Skeptic's Guide to Believing the Press* (1974), and has been a columnist for the *Atlantic Monthly*, a special writer for *Fortune*, and media critic for *Time*.

Richard Harwood is the ombudsman of the *Washington Post*. He received a B.A. degree from Vanderbilt University and was a Nieman Fellow at Harvard University in 1955–56 and a Carnegie Fellow in Journalism at Columbia University in 1965–66. He joined the *Washington Post* in 1966 and served as national correspondent, Vietnam correspondent, national editor, assistant managing editor for national affairs, and deputy managing editor, and twice as ombudsman. His books include *Lyndon*; *Of the Press, by the Press, for the Press (And Others Too)*; *Fall of a President*; *Guyana Massacre*; *The Pursuit of the Presidency: 1980*; *The Wounded Generation: America After Vietnam*; and *Challengers*.

Nathan Kingsley is public and congressional affairs adviser in the Bureau of Human Rights and Humanitarian Affairs at the Department of State. He received his B.S. degree from City College of New York and a master's degree in political science from Columbia University. He has been a radio and television correspondent, managing editor of the *Herald Tribune* News Service and the *International Herald Tribune*, director of news for Radio Free Europe, a senior editor at *U.S. News and World Report*, and chief of correspondents at the *Washington Times*.

Milan J. Kubic is a former guest scholar with the Media Studies Project of the Woodrow Wilson Center. A native of Czechoslovakia, he received his B.A. in journalism from Northwestern University. He was a foreign correspondent for *Newsweek* for twenty-six years, serving in Rio de Janeiro, Beirut, Vienna, Bonn, and Jerusalem.

Mark R. Levy is professor and associate dean in the College of Journalism at the University of Maryland. He received a B.A. degree in political science from Johns Hopkins University, a master's degree in politics from Rutgers University, and a Ph.D. in sociology from Columbia University. Prior to his academic career, he worked as a newspaper reporter, a writer, editor, and associate producer for NBC News in New York, and as associate national affairs editor of *Newsweek*. His eight books include *The Main Source: Learning from Television News* (1986), and *The VCR Age: Home Video and Mass Communication* (1989).

Lawrence W. Lichty is director of the Media Studies Project of the Woodrow Wilson Center and professor of radio, television, film at Northwestern University. He received his A.B. degree from the University of Southern California and Ph.D. degree from Ohio State University. He is the coauthor (with Malachi C. Topping) of *American Broadcasting* (1975) and (with James G. Webster) of *Ratings Analysis: Theory and Practice* (1991). He has been the director of audience research at National Public Radio, was director of media research for the 1983 PBS series "Vietnam: A Television History," and was historical consultant for "Making Sense of the Sixties" (PBS, 1991).

Walter Mears is vice-president of and a columnist for the Associated Press. He joined the Boston bureau of the Associated Press during the summer of 1955 before receiving his B.A. degree from Middlebury College. He has served with the Washington bureau since 1961 and as bureau chief from 1977 to 1983. He won the Pulitzer prize for national reporting in 1977 for coverage of the 1976 presidential election. He is the author (with John Chancellor) of *The News Business* (1983).

Richard Richter is executive producer of news and public affairs at WETA in Washington, D.C. He is currently in charge of "Washington Week in Review" and produced PBS's coverage of the congressional debate authorizing the use of force in the Gulf War. Richard Richter worked for more than twenty years at ABC and CBS news, and is best known for his work on ABC's "Closeup" series.

Thomas B. Rosenstiel is a media writer in the Washington bureau of the *Los Angeles Times*. He received a B.A. degree in English literature from Oberlin College and a master's degree in journalism from Columbia University. He has been a reporter for Jack Anderson's *Washington Merry-Go-Round* column; business editor of the Palo Alto, California, *Peninsula Times Tribune*; and a business writer for the *Los Angeles Times*.

Richard A. Schwarzlose is associate dean and a professor at the Medill School of Journalism at Northwestern University. Born in Chicago, he received a Ph.D. in communications from the University of Illinois and held various reporting and editing positions, including telegraph editor, with the *Champaign-Urbana* (Illinois) *News-Gazette*. He is the author of *Newspapers: A Reference Guide*, a book-length bibliographic essay (1987), and *The Nation's Newsbrokers*, a two-volume history of the American wire services (1989, 1990).

Byron T. Scott is Meredith Professor of Magazine Journalism, chairman of the editorial department, and director of the service journalism program at the University of Missouri School of Journalism. He received a B.A. degree and master's degree in political science from the University of Miami, and a Ph.D. in political science from Ohio State University.

Ann Walton Sieber is a master's degree candidate at the University of Missouri School of Journalism. She received a B.A. degree from Saint John's College, Annapolis, Maryland.

Conrad Smith is an assistant professor in the School of Journalism at Ohio State University. He received a B.A. in physics, a master's degree in cinema from Ohio State, and a Ph.D. in communications from Temple University.

Kim Willenson is the publisher of *The Daily Japan Digest*, a newsletter on Japanese-American affairs. He received a B.S. degree from the University of Wisconsin–Madison, and a master's degree in journalism from the Columbia University School of Journalism. He was a reporter for the *Wisconsin State Journal* and the *Washington Post*, and a correspondent for United Press International in Tokyo, Bangkok, Saigon, and Washington, D.C. He served as a writer and correspondent for *Newsweek* from 1974 to 1987, when he returned to UPI for one year as international managing editor. He is the author of *The Bad War* (1987).

INDEX

ABC: anchors for, 18, 21; coverage of disasters, 226, 228, 230, 231; documentaries on, 37–43; economics, general, 5–6; management of, 20, 22–23, 200; revenues of, 3; talk shows on, 74. *See also specific programs and journalists*
"ABC Evening News," 18
Abel, Elie, 254
advertising: computers and, 114; magazines and, 195–98, 206; mail services offering, 113–14; newspapers and, 87–89, 92, 95, 101, 102, 103, 111–17, 119; Standard Advertising Units, 89, 106; total market coverage, 113–14; TV, revenues of broadcast, 6–11; TV, revenues of cable, 10; TV, revenues of local, 16; TV documentaries and, 40; TV news programs, promotion of, 21–23, 28, 31
affiliates: anchors, salaries of, 8; elections, coverage of Super Tuesday, 53–67; networks, relations with, 3, 13, 35–36, 45–51, 54–67; wire services and, 148, 152, 155
African Americans: anchors, of local TV news, 63; print media, coverage of, 253; TV, coverage of, 37–38, 60, 131; newspapers, 131
afternoon newspapers, 92, 129
age factors: magazines, 206; newspapers and, 90, 92, 98, 100, 117
Agence France Presse, 156, 164, 182
"Agronsky and Company," 74–75
Altheide, David, 229
American Newspaper Publishers Association, 111, 117, 119, 179–83
American Society of Newspaper Editors, 6
Anastos, Ernie, 8
anchors, 18, 21–22, 24–25, 247: African Americans as, 63; historical perspective on, 18–21, 24–25; local TV and, 8, 15, 63; on-location work by, 24–25; salaries of, 8, 16, 22, 124; star status of, 8, 15–26, 71, 124–25, 247; women as, 63, 125, 246–47. *See also specific anchors*
Apple, R. W., 78
Arbitron, 15–16
Arledge, Roone, 20, 24
Associated Press (AP), 146–51, 155–70, 173, 176, 242; supplementals and, 178, 185–186, 188
Atlanta Journal, 155
attitudes: disasters, reporters and, 232–34, 236; newspaper readers, 92–99. *See also* public opinion
audience. *See* ratings
Autry, James, 200
awards and prizes: documentaries receiving, 39, 41; education, journalism fellowships for, 106; newspaper reporters receiving, 133, 236

Bagdikian, Ben H., 253
Baker, W. W., 134
Barnes, Fred, 76
Beaton, Roderick, 152
Beauchamp, Tom L., 235
Becker, Don, 165
Benjamin, Burton, 247
Bertelsmann A.G., 199
Birdsell, David, 250
black newspapers. *See* African Americans
Blankenburg, William, 140–41
Blethen, Frank A., 117
Bliss, Edward, Jr., 249
Boca Raton News, 112–13
Bogart, Leo, 106, 117, 119
Bosley, Scott, 184, 186–87
Boston Globe, 231
Boyer, Peter J., 247
Bradlee, Benjamin C., 81
Brazil, 213–14
Breisky, Bill, 187
Brian, Earl, 154
Brinkley, David, 18, 20, 24, 74, 80
broadcast journalism, 241–42: wire services and, 146, 147, 149, 162. *See also* television

Broder, David, 75, 78, 80, 254
Brokaw, Tom, 18, 21–23
Brown, James K., 229–30
Buchanan, Bruce, 129
Buchanan, Patrick, 75, 81
Buckingham, Rob Roy, 177–78
Bungarz, Denny, 229
Burke, David, 22–23
Burns, Kathleen, 128
Bush, George, 22, 57, 59–60, 62, 105
Bush administration, 23, 74, 160; CBS coverage of, 23
business acquisitions and mergers, TV networks and, 3, 40

Cable News Network. *See* CNN
cable television, 4, 28–31, 241; advertising revenues of, 10; CNBC, 6, 20, 28, 31; C-SPAN, 5, 28, 30–31, 67, 250; economics of, general, 31, 34–35; ESPN, 6; local TV, competition with, 13; newspapers, modeled after, 119. *See also* CNN
Campbell, Karlyn Kohrs, 246
Capital Cities, 40, 134. *See also* ABC
"Capital Gang," 75–76, 81
Capital Newspapers, 177
Carey, James W., 203–4, 235
Carlyle, Thomas, 188
Carrier, Jim, 228
Carroll, Raymond L., 13, 38
Carter, Hodding, 78
Carter, Jimmy, 104
Carter administration, 17
Cashau, George, 117
Catledge, Turner, 205
CBS, 80, 247–49: affiliates of, 54–67; anchors for, 18, 21; Bush administration, coverage of, 23; disasters, coverage of, 228, 232; election coverage by, 54, 55–60, 64; Gulf War, coverage of, 34; management decisions, 5–6, 17, 23, 28, 247–48; revenues, 3, 6
"CBS Evening News," 18–19, 28, 248
"CBS Morning News," 125
celebrities. *See* personalities
Center for Communication, 200
Chancellor, John, 18–19
Chandler, David Leon, 252

Chicago Daily News, 174
Chicago Tribune, 6, 77, 128, 133, 135, 138, 140, 179, 223, 226–27, 252
Christensen, Norman L., 232
Christian Science Monitor, 228
Christopher, Richard, 214–15
"Closeup," 39, 40–41
Cohen, Ronald E., 164
Columbia Journalism Review, 138, 192–193, 198
Corry, John, 41–42
Cose, Ellis, 250
Cronkite, Walter, 18, 20–22
Chung, Connie, 8
Clark, Ruth, 116
Clift, Eleanor, 79
CNBC, 6, 20, 28, 31
CNN, 5, 8, 28–31, 34, 67, 97, 217; election campaigns, coverage of, 27–28; Gulf War, coverage of, 11–12, 17, 27, 28, 34, 35; "News Hound," 15; political talk shows on, 75–76, 81; satellite use by, 46; videotapes, by amateurs, 15
CNN Headline News, 28, 30, 46
computers and computer science: magazines and, 241; newspapers and, 89, 102, 114, 117, 241; wire services and, 148–49, 150–51, 176, 179
Congress, U.S., 16; Tower, John, nomination hearings of, 74, 79
content analysis: magazines and, 199–202; newspapers and, 89, 95–100, 108, 112–17, 119, 129–30; TV election coverage and, 55–63; wire services and, 159–64, 173–74, 180–82
CONUS, 31, 46
conventions, political: CNN coverage of, 28; TV coverage of, general, 9, 20–21, 47
cost factors: local TV news and, 50; magazine, advertising rates of, 196–97; magazines, prices for, 202; newsprint, 112, 117; wire services, subscription fees of, 147, 179–80
court cases. *See* litigation
crime and criminals: TV coverage of, 14–15

C-SPAN, 5, 28, 30–31, 67, 250
"Current Affair, A," 4, 26–28, 101, 125

"D.C.—A Divided City," 43
de Borchgrave, Arnaud, 215–16
demographic factors, 243: age factors, 90, 92, 98, 100, 117, 206; educational attainment, 243; literacy, 243–44; magazine readership, 196–97, 203–4, 206. *See also* minorities
de Montmollin, Phil, 112
Dennis, Everette E., 200–201
Denton, Robert E., 250
Denver Post, 227–28, 230
Des Moines Register, 133–34
Detroit Free Press, 133, 180, 184–85
direct mail advertising, 113–14
disasters, 223–40, 253; ABC coverage of, 226, 228, 230–31; CBS coverage of, 228, 232; magazine coverage of, 223–24; NBC coverage of, 227–28, 229–30; newspaper coverage of, 223–40; reporters attitudes toward, 232–34, 236; sound bites, use of, 227–28, 232; TV coverage of, 227–40
Dishon, Colleen, 140
documentaries, 34, 36–43, 247
Dole, Robert, 57, 62
Donahue, Phil, 4–5
Donaldson, Sam, 20, 42, 80, 124
Dow Jones, 176
Dukakis, Michael, 57, 59, 62, 64, 160
Duke, Paul, 79
Dumanoski, Diane, 231
Dunnett, Peter J. S., 254
Dunwoody, Sharon, 230, 239

Ebert, Roger, 125
economic factors: academic fellowships and, 106; cable TV and, 31, 34–35; magazines and, 199–200; newspapers and, 85–90, 106–7, 112, 117, 119, 122–24, 139, 149, 253; TV, general, 5–7, 31; TV networks, business acquisitions and mergers involving, 3, 40; TV political talk shows and, 75–76; wire services and, 146–57, 180. *See also* advertising; cost factors; wages and salaries

Economist, The, 207
Editor and Publisher Yearbooks, 155
education: newspaper journalists and, 106, 108, 121–22
educational attainment, 243; literacy, 243–44
Edwards, Douglas, 18
Edwards, Julia, 252
Ekey, Robert, 234–35
elections: CBS coverage of, 54–60, 64; CNN coverage of, 27–28; content analysis, TV coverage of, 55–63; conventions, coverage of, 9, 20–21, 28, 47; C-SPAN coverage of, 30; TV coverage of, general, 9, 20–21, 41, 53–67, 80, 249–50; sound bites and, 57–58, 62–63, 249; wire services and, 145. *See also* Super Tuesday
Emery, Edwin, 253
Emery, Michael, 253
employment and unemployment, 121–23, 241–42; labor-management relations, 9, 123–24, 152–53; newspapers, owned by employees, 134. *See also* wages and salaries
entertainment television, 2, 3–4, 28, 34; game shows as, 19, 48; "infotainment," 4–5, 26–27, 31
"Entertainment Tonight," 4, 26–28, 101
ESPN, 6
Ethnic Press in the United States: A Historical Analysis and Handbook, 252
E. W. Scripps Company, 147, 152–53

"Face the Nation," 74–75, 78, 81
Falkland Islands, 218, 253
Fallows, James, 79
Felker, Clay, 192–93, 204
Fenby, Jonathan, 178, 181, 251
Fico, Frederick, 130, 132
Fielding, John, 41
Financial News Network, 154
Florida News Network, 46
foreign countries, 244, 253: Brazil, 213–14; Israel, 215, 217; Japan, 23–24, 206, 215; magazines, coverage of, 213–19; South Africa, 41. *See also* war
"48 Hours," 36, 42

Fox Television, 4, 125; ratings of, 10; video technology, use of, 14
Frady, Marshall, 41
Frank, Reuven, 248
Frankel, Max, 140
Frank N. Magid Associates, 15, 62
Friedman, Steve, 4

game shows, 19, 48
Gannett Corporation, 134, 251–52
Gans, Herbert, 193, 204, 231
Gates, Gary Paul, 249
Geissler, William, 153
Gelatt, Rod, 121–22
gender factors: newspapers and, 94, 96, 108. *See also* women
General Electric, 17, 21, 23
Gephardt, Richard, 57, 60, 80
Gergen, David, 76
Germond, Jack, 76, 125
Goldenson, Leonard, 37, 39
Gorbachev, Mikhail, 11, 207–8
Gordon, Gregory, 164
Gore, Albert, 57, 59
Graber, Doris A., 249
Graham, Katharine, 203
Greider, William, 79–81
Grossman, Larry, 207
group ownership, 134–36
Group W, 46
Gulf War, 11–12, 14, 21, 23, 28, 32, 244; CBS coverage of, 34; CNN coverage of, 11–12, 27–28, 34–35; C-SPAN coverage of, 30; local TV coverage of, 11–12; ratings and, 19, 21, 35

Hale, James H., 134
"Hard Copy," 4, 26
Harris Group, 129, 135
Hart, Gary, 60
Hart, John, 19
Hart, Mary, 26–27
Hartford Courant, 115
Harvard University, 106
Hearst, Randolph, 147
Hearst Corporation, 85
Herald-Tribune News Service, 177, 180–81, 184–85
Hertsgaard, Mark, 254
Hill, Pamela, 37, 39

Hispanic Americans, 60, 131
historical perspectives: magazines, general, 138–39, 191–98, 201–5, 209–10, 213–19; newspapers, general, 87–89, 96–98, 100, 102, 104–7, 111–13, 118, 121, 127, 236–37, 250–54; newspapers, relation to wire services, 148–49, 151–52, 155; *New York Times,* special sections in, 138–39; TV, anchors, 18–21, 24–25; TV, general, 5–8, 246–50; wire services, 145–69, 171–73, 177–80. *See also* technological innovations
History of the News: From the Drum to the Satellite, A, 252
Hoge, James, 124
Hoge, Warren, 78
Horrock, Nicholas, 75, 77
human interest stories, 27, 116. *See also* "Infotainment"
Hunt, Albert, 76
Huntley, Chet, 18, 20, 24
"Huntley-Brinkley Report, The," 18, 248

Independent Television Network, 175
"Infotainment," 4–5, 26–27, 31
Intermountain Research Center, 229–30
International News Service, 147, 157
International News Services, 251
international perspectives. *See* foreign countries; *specific countries*
Isham, Chris, 41
Israel, 215, 217
Iyengar, Shanto, 246

Jackson, Jesse, 57–60
Jamieson, Kathleen Hall, 246, 250
Janowski, Gene, 6
Japan: Bush, trip to, 23; magazines and, 206, 215
Jennings, Peter, 18–21, 23, 42
Jews, 39
Johnson, Albert, 180–81
Johnson, John H., 252
Joyce, Ed, 248

Kalikov, Peter, 123
Kansas City Star, 133–34

Katz, Jon, 125
Kelly, Grace, 217
Kennedy, Allyson, 78
Kennedy, John F., 40, 104–5
Kinderin, Donald R., 246
King, Martin Luther, Jr., 58
Klaidman, Stephen, 235
Knight-Ridder, 112, 165
Knight-Ridder/*Tribune* News Wire, 179, 183–87
Kondracke, Morton, 73, 76
Koppel, Ted, 20, 23, 42–43
Kramer, Larry, 77

labor-management relations, 9; newspapers and, 123–24; strikes, 9, 123; wire services and, 152–53
Lacy, Stephen, 129–30, 132
Lamb, Brian, 250
Lanker, Brian, 133
lead-in programming, 48
legal issues: First Amendment, rights under, 106; litigation, 106, 123, 154, 158, 176; profanity as, 37, 39; regulation, of TV, 17, 20
Leonard, Bill, 248
Leser, Larry, 153
Levy, Mark R., 246
Lewis, Anthony, 81–82
Liebovish, Louis, 252
literacy, 243–44
litigation, 158; newspapers and, 106, 123; wire services, bankruptcy of, 154, 176
local news, general: newspapers, coverage of, 89, 93, 108, 115–16, 127, 135, 229, 234–35; newspapers, wire services, and, 130–31, 156
local TV stations: advertising revenues of, 16; African American anchors on, 63; anchors, general, 8, 15, 63; cable TV, competition with, 13; competition among, 13–14; Congress, coverage of, 16; cost of, 50; elections, coverage of Super Tuesday, 53–67; Gulf War, coverage of, 11–12; location work by, 68; networks, relations and competition with, 5, 11–15, 39, 45–51, 53, 64–66, 207; ratings

of, 13, 15–16; satellite telecommunications, use of, 13, 45–47, 64–65; surveys conducted by, 64; time slots and, 48–49; videotapes, use of, 15. *See also* affiliates; syndicates
London Observer Foreign News Service, 184
Los Angeles Herald Examiner, 85
Los Angeles Times, 76, 78, 90, 92, 94, 107–8, 127, 234, 252; wire services and, 157, 174, 178–80, 182–84, 187
Luce, Henry Robinson, 193, 203, 209–10
Lynch, Jones, and Ryan, 156–57

McCabe, Peter, 248
McClure, Jessica, 27
"McLaughlin Group," 73, 75–76, 78–81, 125
McNamara, Bob, 228, 230
"MacNeil/Lehrer NewsHour," 67
magazines, 191–219, 241, 242: advertising in, 195–98, 206; age factors related to, 206; computer use by, 241; content analysis of, 199–202; demographic factors related to readership, 196–97, 203–4, 206; disasters, coverage of, 223–24; economics of, general, 199–200; foreign countries, coverage of, 213–19; historical perspectives on, 138–39, 191–98, 201–5, 209–10, 213–19; Japan and, 206, 215; newspapers incorporating, 137–41, 205–6, 210–11; politics of management of, 210; scope of, 94; TV and, 207–8. *See also specific magazines*
magazine format, 38
management and managers: ABC and, 20, 22–23, 200; CBS and, 5–6, 17, 23, 28, 247–48; labor, relations with, 9, 123–24, 152–53; NBC and, 17, 20, 23, 207; network TV, general, 15–23, 35; newspapers, general, 112–13, 123–24; 135–36, 253; wire services, 152–53, 176
marketing research done by newspapers, 113, 115, 116. *See also* advertising

market shares: local TV and, 15; TV,
    vs. other media, 3. *See also* ratings
Martindale, Carolyn, 253
Matthews, Christopher, 73, 77, 80
Matusow, Barbara, 79, 247
Maxwell, Robert, 85
Mears, Walter R., 158, 160, 162
Media News Corporation, 152–53
"Meet the Press," 74, 81
Meredith Corporation, 200
Meriwether, Heath, 184–85
Mickelson, Sig, 249
Midgely, Les, 248
Miller, Sally M., 252
Mills, Kay, 252
Milwaukee Journal, 135
minorities: African Americans as,
    37–38, 60, 63, 131, 253; Hispanic
    Americans, 60, 131; newspapers
    and, 94, 108, 252; TV news and,
    65; racism, 63
Moffett, E. Albert, 47
Morrison, David E., 253
Morse, Samuel F. B., 145
Morton, John, 156–57
Mott, William Penn, 226
Movietone, 174–75
Murdoch, Rupert, 123–25
Murrow, Edward R., 39, 247–48

Nafziger, Ralph O., 160, 166
National Enquirer, 4, 235
National Journal, 74–75
National Labor Relations Board, 123
NBC, 248: affiliates, relations with 13;
    anchors for, 18, 21; CNBC, 6, 20,
    28, 31; coverage of disasters,
    227–28, 229–30; documentaries
    on, 42; management of, 17, 20,
    23, 207; revenues of, 3; talk shows
    on, 75
"NBC Nightly News," 4, 18–19, 26, 48
Nelson, Jack, 76, 125
networks, 11, 24, 34–35, 206–7, 241–42;
    advertising revenues of, 6–8, 10;
    audiences of, 8–9, 21, 242; busi-
    ness acquisitions and mergers, 3,
    40; economic factors, general, 3,
    5–7, 31; elections, coverage by, 53–
    67; entertainment within news
    programming on, 4; local stations,

relations and competition with, 5,
    11–15, 39, 45–51, 53, 64–66, 207;
    management of, 15–23, 35; news-
    papers, substitution by, 66; ratings
    and, 21, 34, 48; satellites, network
    to local station feeds, 13, 45–47,
    64–65; time slots, 48–49. *See also*
    affiliates; *specific networks*
Neuharth, Al, 251
Newman, Edwin, 74
New Republic, 76
News and Information Weekly Ser-
    vice, 46
News Exchange Agreement Transmis-
    sions, 175
"News Hound," 15
Newspaper Advertising Bureau, 92–
    101
Newspaper Advisory Board, 152
Newspaper Guild, 123
newspapers, 85–141; advertising in,
    87–89, 92, 95, 101–3, 111–17,
    119; afternoon editions of, 129;
    age factors related to, 90, 92, 98,
    100, 117; attitudes of readers,
    92–99; awards for, 133, 236;
    books on, 250–54; celebrities, re-
    porters as, 121–26; computer use
    by, 89, 102, 114, 117, 241; content
    analysis of, 89, 95–100, 108, 112–
    17, 119, 129–30; coverage of di-
    sasters, 223–40; economics of,
    general, 85–90, 106–7, 112, 117,
    119, 122–24, 139, 149, 253; edu-
    cation of journalists, 106, 108,
    121–22; gender factors and, 94,
    96, 108; historical perspectives
    on, 87–89, 96–98, 100, 102, 104–
    7, 111–13, 118, 121, 127, 236–37,
    250–54; local news, coverage of,
    89, 93, 108, 115–16, 127, 135,
    156, 229, 234–35; magazines in-
    corporated in, 137–41, 205–6,
    210–11; litigation involving, 106,
    123; magazines, included in,
    137–41, 205–6, 210–11; manage-
    ment of, general, 112–13, 123–
    24, 135–36, 253; market research
    for, 113, 115, 116; minorities
    and, 94, 108, 252; op-ed pages of,
    96–97; ownership of, 134–35,

253; politics of, 127–28; professional associations, 6, 111, 117, 119, 179–83; regionalism and, 127–36; specialists, use of, 108, 115–16; sports, coverage of, 96; suburban, 102, 118, 128; Sunday editions of, 87–88, 90, 92, 101, 111, 117, 134, 137, 210–11; syndicates and, 77, 98–99, 112; technological innovations and, general, 89, 102, 107, 124; telephone services and, 113, 117, 119; time spent reading, 100, 111; TV and, general, 93, 101; TV political talk shows and, 73–82; wire services and, general, 148–49, 151–52, 155–58; wire services and, historical perspectives, 148–49, 151–52, 155; women and, 94, 108, 252. *See also specific newspapers*
Newspapers: A Reference Guide, 254
News That Matters: Television and American Opinion, 246
"News 12 Long Island," 28, 30
Newsweek, 138, 139, 191, 193–98, 201; TV, relations with, 8–9, 76, 79, 201–5, 210–11, 213–19
Newsweek International, 214–15
newsweeklies. *See* magazines
Newton, Gregory D., 48
New York, 192
New York Daily News, 118, 124, 139
New York Herald-Tribune, 118, 192, 252
New York Post, 118, 123
New York Review of Books, 79
New York Times, 6, 27, 41–42, 78, 88, 107–8, 113, 115, 129, 137–41, 226, 231, 243, 251; magazines and, 205–6, 210–11; wire services and, 157–58, 174, 177–79, 183
New York Times News Service, 178–80, 183–84, 185, 187
New York Times vs. Sullivan, 106
Nielsen Media Research. *See* ratings
Nieman Fellowship, 106
"Nightline," 43, 74, 101
Noble, J. Kendrick, Jr., 139
North, Oliver, 160
Northshield, Robert, 18
Norville, Deborah, 125
Novak, Robert, 75, 79–80

O'Connor, John J., 27
O'Neil, Roger, 223, 227–30
O'Neill, Thomas (Tip), 169
op-ed pages, newspapers, 96–97
organizational factors. *See also* management and managers
Overgaard, Cordell, 153
ownership of enterprise: business acquisitions and mergers, TV networks and, 3, 40; newspapers, 134–35, 253; wire services, 146

Palestine, 215–16
Paley, William S., 248
Palmer, Cruise, 134
Papers, Lewis, 248
Pauley, Jane, 125
Pentagon papers, 106
Persico, Joseph E., 248
personalities: documentaries and, 42; newspaper reporters as, 121–26; TV anchors as, 8, 15–26, 71, 124–25, 247; TV talk shows, participants on, 76–82
Philadelphia Inquirer, 78
Philo, Eric, 123–24
Picard, Robert C., 253
Pierce, Fred, 37
PLO, 39
political factors, 244–45: magazines and, 210; newspapers and, 127–28
politics, 249: Congress, use of TV by, 16; talk shows on, 73–82. *See also* elections
Poltrack, David, 48
Porter, Bruce, 198
Potomac News, 46
Presidential Debates: The Challenge of Creating an Informed Electorate, 250
Press, The, 250
Press and America: An Interpretive History, The, 253
Press and the Origins of the Cold War, 1944–1947, The, 252
Press Concentration and Monopoly: New Perspectives on Newspaper Ownership and Operation, 253
prime time: audience shares during, 9–10; CBS Gulf War specials during, 34

"Primetime Live," 20, 42
print journalism. *See* newspapers; magazines
profanity, 37, 39
professional associations: ANPA, 111, 117, 119, 179–83; ASNE, 6.
public opinion: disasters and, 224; local TV news, surveys by, 64; news sources, of public, 69–70. *See also* ratings
public relations, 121
public television: documentaries on, 43; talk shows, 74
Publishers Information Bureau, 195, 198
Pulitzer Prize, 133, 236
Pyne, Stephen, 229, 232

racial factors, 108. *See also* minorities
racism, 63
Rainbow Programming Enterprises, 30
Rangel, Charles B., 81
Rather, Dan, 5, 6, 19, 21–23, 26, 223
ratings, 8–11, 18–19, 27, 242; Arbitron, 15–16; CBS and, 23; documentaries, on ABC, 40–41; Gulf War and, 21, 28, 35; local TV and, 13, 15–16; networks, general, 21, 34, 48; networks, vs. local, 47–48; sweeps and, 4, 13
Reagan, Ronald, 60, 105, 249
Reagan administration, 17, 81–82, 101, 207–8, 224, 226, 254
regional trends: network affiliates, 13; newspapers, 127–36
regulation and deregulation, TV and, 17, 20
Reid, T. R., 235
Reinsch, Leonard, 249
religious influences: Christian, 60; Jewish, 39
research, 246–54: disasters, coverage of, 224–40; market, for newspapers, 113, 115–16; Super Tuesday, TV coverage of, 53–67
Reuters News Agency, 152, 155–56, 164, 171, 175–76, 182
Richter, Richard, 37
Ritchie, Joe, 180, 185
Rivera, Geraldo, 4

Roberts, Cokie, 121, 125
Robertson, Pat, 60
Robinson, John P., 246
Rock, Marcia, 246–47
Rooney, Brian, 228, 231
Roosevelt, Franklin D., 39, 40
Rose, Tom, 249
Rosenblatt, Roger, 138
Rosenfeld, Harry M., 177, 186
Rosenthal, Abe, 139–40
Rothermel, Richard, 232
Ruhe, Douglas, 153
Rusher, William A., 251
Russo, Joe, 154

Safer, Morley, 26
St. Louis Post-Dispatch, 133, 135
salaries. *See* wages and salaries
Salisbury, Harrison, 250–51
Sanders, Marlene, 246–47
San Francisco Chronicle, 252
San Francisco Examiner, 77
satellite technology, 241: Congress, use of TV by, 16; CNN, use by, 46; network to local TV stations, use of, 13, 45–47, 64–65; TV, general, 5, 12, 32, 45, 92, 241; wire services and, 150–51, 159, 175
Sauter, Van Gordon, 247
Sawyer, Diane, 8, 20, 42, 124
Sawyer, Forrest, 20
Scardino, Albert, 115
scheduling. *See* seasonal factors; time slots
Schieffer, Bob, 249
Schneider, Alfred, 37
Schoenbrun, David, 247–48
Schwarzlose, Richard, 171–72, 176, 251, 254
Scripps, E. W., 147
Scripps-Howard News Service, 179, 183–84
seasonal factors, TV news, scheduling of, 19, 48
Shales, Tom, 10, 42
Sheehan, William, 37
Shepard, Gary, 230
Siegal, Allan M., 138
Sigma Delta Chi, 133
Silverman, Fred, 26
Simon, Paul, 60

Simon, Todd, 132
Singer, Steve, 41
Siskel, Gene, 125
"60 Minutes," 23, 36, 42–43
Slater, Robert, 248
Small, Len R., 153
sound bites: disaster coverage, use of, 227–28, 232; political campaigns, use of, 57–58, 62–63, 249
South Africa, 41
Spanish-language newspapers, 131
specialists: newspapers, use of, 108, 115–16
specials. *See* documentaries
Sperber, Ann M., 248
sports and athletics: ESPN, 6; newspaper coverage of, 96
Squires, James D., 6
Standard Advertising Units, 89, 106
Standard Rates and Data, 195–96
stars. *See* personalities
Steinle, Paul, 154, 163
Stephen, Mitchell, 252
strikes, labor, 9, 123
Stringer, Howard, 23
suburban newspapers, 102, 118, 128
Sughrue, Karen, 75
Sullivan, Mike, 227
Sulzberger, Arthur, 139
Sulzberger, C. L., 213
Sunday newspapers, 87–88, 90, 92, 101, 111, 117, 134, 137, 210–11
Super Tuesday, 53–67
supplemental news services, 177–88
Supreme Court, coverage of, 158
sweeps, 4; network and affiliates, relationship, 13
Swerdlow, Joel, 249–50
syndicates: Fox TV, 4, 10, 14, 125; newspapers and, 77, 98–99, 112; TV network news programming vs., ratings of, 48. *See also* Fox Television

tabloid television, 4–5, 26–27; daytime slots and, 4–5
Talbot, Strobe, 76
talk shows, 73–82
TASS, 156
Tatarian, Roger, 163
technological innovations, 252: Congress, use of TV by, 16; newspapers and, 89, 102, 107, 124; TV and, 5, 31–32, 66, 162, 241; wire services and, 145–46, 148–52, 162, 168–69, 175–76. *See also* computers and computer science; satellite technology; videotapes
telephone services, newspapers and, 113, 117, 119
television, 1–82; books on, 246–50; content analysis of, 55–63; coverage of crime, 14, 15; coverage of disasters, 227–40; documentaries on, 34, 36–43, 247; entertainment TV, 2, 3–5, 16–28, 31, 34, 48; historical perspectives on, 5–8, 246–50; magazines and, 207–8; *Newsweek,* relations with, 8–9, 76, 79, 201–5, 210–11, 213–19; public broadcasting, 43, 74; regulation of, 17, 20; satellites, use by, 5, 32, 45, 241; technology and, general, 5, 31–32, 66, 162, 241; wire services, impact of, 18, 146–47, 149, 162, 174–75. *See also* affiliates; cable television; local TV stations; networks; time slots; *specific networks*
terrorism, 39, 217–18
Tewes, Bob, 229
"This Week with David Brinkley," 74
Thomason, Mims, 163
Time, 39, 133, 138, 191, 193–205, 209–10, 211, 216, 217–18, 252; disaster coverage by, 223
time factors: news, time spent on by recipients of, 199; newspapers, time spent reading, 100, 111; TV news, delivery rate, 70
time slots: daytime television, programming, 4–5; documentaries and, 41; local vs. network news, 48–49; outside prime time, 11; round-the-clock coverage, by television, 31, 97; prime time, 9–10, 34; seasonal factors, news scheduling and, 19, 48
Time Warner, 199–200
Tisch, Lawrence, 6, 17
Toronto Star, 117, 140–41
"Today Show," 74, 125

total market coverage, 113–14
Tower, John, 74, 79
trash television. *See* tabloid television
Tuchman, Gaye, 228, 231
Tumber, Howard, 253
Turner, Ed, 26, 28
TV Guide, 22
"20/20," 36, 43

Udell, Jon G., 253
unions.   *See*   labor-management
    relations
United Kingdom, 175, 218
United Press International (UPI),
    146, 147–65, 167, 171–76, 178,
    185
Urban, Christine, 119
USA Today, 4, 89–90, 96, 101, 108,
    112–13, 116, 201, 217, 227, 236,
    251
U.S. News and World Report, 76, 191,
    193–95, 198, 201–5, 210, 218

Vázquez Raña, Mario, 154
videotapes: amateurs, produced by,
    13–15; Fox Television, use of, 14;
    timeshifting via, 10
video vérité, 36
Vietnam War, 5, 31–32, 82, 214, 216,
    247
von Hoffman, Nicholas, 77

wages and salaries, 121–22; TV an-
    chors, 8, 16, 22, 124; TV political
    talk shows, participants of, 76
*Waiting for Prime Time: The Women of
    Television News,* 246–47
Wald, Richard, 108–9, 200
Wall Street Journal, 81, 90, 108, 139,
    158, 206, 242
Warman, Richard Saul, 199
Warner Communications, 199
Warren, Larry, 229
wars: Gulf War, 11–12, 21, 23, 26–28,
    30, 32, 34–35, 244; Falkland Is-
    lands, 218, 253; Six Day War,
    Middle East, 215–16; Vietnam
    War, 5, 31–32, 82, 214–16, 247;
    World War II, 104–5
Washingtonian, 77, 79
Washington Post, 42, 75, 78, 81, 90, 94,
    107–8, 123, 129, 139, 157, 158,
    174, 178–80, 227, 254

Washington Star, 174
"Washington Week in Review," 74, 76,
    79, 125
Watt, James, 224
Webster, James G., 13, 48
Westin, Av, 5–6, 216
Westmoreland, William, 247
White, William Allen, 127
Whitney, Helen, 37
Wilkins, Lee, 253
Will, George F., 80
Willis, Jim, 253
Wire Service Guild, 152–53
wire services, 140–88, 251: affiliates
    of, general, 148, 152, 155; broad-
    cast journalism and, general,
    146–47, 149, 162; computer use
    by, 148–51, 176, 179; content
    analysis of, 159–64, 173–74, 180–
    82; economics of, general, 146–
    57, 180; elections and, 145; his-
    torical perspectives on, 145–69,
    171–73, 177–80; local copy vs.,
    130–31, 156; management of,
    general, 152–53, 176; mid-
    western newspapers and, 129;
    satellites, use by, 150–51, 159,
    175; subscription fees of, 147,
    179–80; supplemental news ser-
    vices and, 177–88; technological
    innovations, general, 145–46,
    148–52, 162, 168–69, 175–76;
    TV, impact on, 146–47, 149, 162,
    174–75. *See also specific services*
Wolfson, Lewis W., 254
women: anchors, 63, 125, 246–47;
    newspapers and, 94, 108, 252
World Monitor, 19
"World News Tonight," 18–19, 21, 48
World News Wire, 154
World War II, 104–5
Wright, Jim, 75, 79

"Youth Terror—The View from Be-
    hind the Gun," 37, 40

Zahn, Paula, 20
Zuckerman, Mortimer B., 197